MW00474410

Selected Letters of A. M. A. Blanchet

Selected Letters of

A. M. A. BLANCHET

Bishop of Walla Walla & Nesqualy

1846–1879

——◆——

EDITED BY

Roberta Stringham Brown
and Patricia O'Connell Killen

TRANSLATED BY

Roberta Stringham Brown

UNIVERSITY *of* WASHINGTON PRESS

Seattle and London

© 2013 by the University of Washington Press
Printed and bound in the United States
Composed in Minion, a typeface designed by Robert Slimbach
Designed by Dustin Kilgore

17 16 15 14 13 12   5 4 3 2 1

All rights reserved. No part of this publication may be reproduced or transmitted in any form
or by any means, electronic or mechanical, including photocopy, recording, or any information
storage or retrieval system, without permission in writing from the publisher.

University of Washington Press
PO Box 50096, Seattle, WA 98145, USA

www.washington.edu/uwpress

Library of Congress Cataloging-in-Publication Data
Blanchet, Augustine Magloire Alexander, 1797–1887.
[Corresondence. English. Selections]
Selected Letters of A.M.A. Blanchet, Bishop of Walla Walla and Nesqualy (1846-1879) / edited
by Roberta Stringham Brown and Patricia O'Connell Killen ; translated by Roberta Stringham
Brown. — First edition
pages cm
ISBN 978-0-295-99263-1 (hardback)
1. Blanchet, Augustine Magloire Alexander, 1797–1887—Correspondence. 2. Catholic Church—
Bishops—Correspondence. 3. Catholic Church—Washington Territory—History. 4. Washington
Territory—Church history. I. Brown, Roberta Stringham. II. Killen, Patricia O'Connell. III. Title.
BX4705.B5525A4 2013   282.092—dc23   013008903

The paper used in this publication is acid-free and meets the minimum requirements of American
National Standard for Information Sciences—Permanence of Paper for Printed Library Materials,
ANSI Z39.48–1984.∞

FRONTISPIECE: Father A. M. A. Blanchet, ca. 1837–38. See figure 2, p. 90.

Contents

Preface

More than a decade ago, while doing research in the Archives of the Archdiocese of Seattle, we first encountered a set of five leather-bound letterbooks that had laid largely untouched for a century and a half. Penned in ornate nineteenth-century scrawl, mostly in French with occasional Latin or English, their 1,164 pages contain copies of outbound letters that tell of the struggles, setbacks, and successes of Washington's first Roman Catholic bishop, Augustin Magloire Alexandre (A. M. A.) Blanchet. From our initial perusal of the letterbooks, we sensed their value.

Unlike one of the many recipients of these letters, Governor Isaac Stevens, who resided in the region for less than four years, Bishop A. M. A. Blanchet spent over three decades, as the longest serving institutional leader in a single role from the end of the United States' and Great Britain's joint occupancy in 1846 through most of Washington's territorial period. Stevens saw his time in Washington as preparatory to roles on a national stage; Blanchet's appointment was for life. Stevens viewed his responsibilities through the lens of a Protestant nationalist narrative of the United States. As a pastoral leader in a transnational organization, Blanchet perceived his charge through the travails of indigenous residents and the tousle of ordinary newcomers, including himself, whose life journeys had brought them to this far reach of North America. The correspondence recorded on these pages reveals, in ways that other leaders' exchanges do not, the cosmopolitan reality of Washington Territory, where English was a minority-spoken language well into the latter half of the nineteenth century. We knew it was time for these letters to be made available to a wider audience.

And so began our work of collecting, translating, and researching the more than nine hundred letters recorded in these books, forty-five of which we have selected for this volume. Our differing backgrounds contributed to a fruitful collaboration. A seventeenth-century French literature specialist concentrating on women's spirituality and the history of New France, Roberta has turned to researching French Canadian presence in the Pacific Northwest. At the start of the project, she conducted research in archives in

Montreal, Quebec, Paris, and Lyons. She translated the corpus of Blanchet letters into English and subsequently wrote introductions and annotated a portion of the selected letters. Patricia is an American church historian whose research and publications have focused on the Pacific Northwest. In making the initial selection of letters for this volume, Patricia examined the translations as she scrutinized the ways the letters both chronicled and challenged common narratives. She conducted research in Canada and in regional archives and also wrote a portion of the introductions and annotations for this volume. Through the flow of exchanged drafts, we explored and debated the many ways the letters expand on and offer alternative narratives of Washington's territorial history.

Our hope for readers of this book: that they come away with a deeper appreciation for Washington's territorial history as, ultimately, a moving mosaic of peoples representing multiple ethnicities, cultures, and convictions. These peoples made their way in natural and social environments that were being drastically remodeled by events that were often beyond their control. Confronted by seemingly endless change and challenge, the individuals and communities who emerge in these letters drew on their particular cultural resources—including religious and spiritual traditions—inner resilience, intelligence, family and ethnic bonds, and basic instinct, to build their lives.

The goal of making those people and their lives accessible to readers shapes the structure of this volume. The introductions that precede each letter provide historical background and context and relate what happened between one letter and the next in the unfolding story of Blanchet's episcopacy. They illuminate the complexity of roles Blanchet played and the shifting perspectives from which he wrote to a widely dispersed group of recipients. To his friend Ignace Bourget, Blanchet was a fellow French Canadian Catholic often at odds with both British and American colonial interests. To U.S. government powers, he was a fellow Euro-American colonist. To the pope, he was an obedient and devoted bishop. Compressing the introductions to provide background, transition, and orientation to the topic within a few paragraphs meant hacking and chiseling the reams of information we gathered for each letter. The volume's chronology provides another structure for following the unfolding story of the bishop's life and episcopacy, placing it within a broader historical context.

Following each letter are extensive explanatory notes and references for the reader who wishes to pursue the topics further. In the interest of space, we have not defined terms that are readily available in printed and electronic standard references. An unnumbered source annotation at the end of each letter indicates the primary archival source we used for the text of the letter at hand; it is followed by sources of variants, copies, and summaries to which we referred. Full titles and archival locations of our main source for each, including depositories in the United States, Canada, and Europe, are listed in the bibliography.

In the interest of authenticity, the five selected letters written in English are reproduced word for word. The forty selected letters that were written in French have been translated into twenty-first-century English, but the translations preserve the bishop's register and tone, his sentence and paragraph order, and, when it doesn't interfere significantly with the fluency of reading, his punctuation, capitalization, and complimentary closes. The translations retain French phonetic spellings of geographical names that did not have a uniform spelling at the time the letters were written, such as *Wallamet* for *Willamette*, and they retain variant spellings that were generally uniform at the time: *Nesqualy* for the Catholic diocese of that name, but *Nisqually* for the Indians, the river along which they still live, and the fort, and *Yakima* for the river, the valley, and the city, but *Yakama* for the reservation and the Indian nation living in the area. Following contemporary U.S. practice, we have opted for uniform spellings for the names of individual Indians, and employ the ethnic term *Indian*. For historical accuracy, we have retained the French spellings of persons from French Canada and French-speaking Europe, with the exception of a few priests who are more widely known today by the English spelling of their names. The titles *Mr* (Master) and *Monsieur* (Sir), frequently used at the time for secular clergy (those not belonging to a religious order), are replaced by the modern term, *Father*. We have provided other occasional variants or needed explanations at appropriate places in the texts of the letters themselves in brackets. Any use of parentheses in the letters is by the bishop himself and appears in the original text.

Given the chronological span of the letters, their subjects, and the divergent motivations and actions of the people who emerge from them, it is not surprising that we confronted sensitive topics—topics that are the subject of lively debates among contemporary interpreters. Our approach to three in particular merits a few words: the use of ethnic labels; the rapprochement between missionaries and Indians; and the relation between our own perspectives and those expressed in the letters.

Francophone descendants of the colonizers of New France (1534–1760), including those living in the Northwest, have been known and have described themselves by four different labels, *Canadien, métis* (and *Métis*), *French Canadian*, and *Québécois*, over various historical periods and geographic regions. The Iroquois term, *Canadien*, is believed to have been first used by Jacques Cartier in 1535, to refer to the Iroquois living in the St. Lawrence Valley. During the eighty some years between Great Britain's division of the old French region of Canada into Upper Canada (the future Ontario) and Lower Canada (the future province of Quebec) in 1791 and the erection of the Dominion of Canada (uniting Quebec, Ontario, New Brunswick, and Nova Scotia) in 1867, the term *French Canadian* (*franco-canadien*) gradually began to be used by those with a growing sense of their ethnic distinctiveness (French speaking, Roman Catholic, often of Latin rather than Anglo descent). With the Quiet Revolution of the 1960s these people assumed the term *Québécois*. Throughout the majority of his letters, Blanchet refers to himself and his French-speaking compatriots as *Canadien*. It is clear from the context of the letters that in doing so, he is speaking of these and not of all peoples within the political borders of today's Canada. To make clear this historical ethnic distinction, we have retained, without italics or quotation marks, his use of *Canadien* in the translations and, as appropriate, in our annotations.

Another ethnic label that appears in the letters, *métis* (*métisse*), is the French generic term for persons of any mixed racial descent. Nineteenth-century francophone correspondents both north and south of the forty-ninth parallel employed this term, among others, for persons of indigenous (frequently Cree, Ojibwa, or Chippewa) and European heritage. Having arrived in the region well before the influx of United States emigrants, the métis helped found and maintain nineteenth-century Roman Catholic mission settlements in the Pacific Northwest. Later francophone immigrants from eastern Canada were drawn to locales such as Vancouver and Walla Walla where there were clusters of the older francophone residents. In referring to the inhabitants of these settlements, Blanchet and fellow clerics generally use the traditional and inclusive term of the time, *Canadien*. On the occasions when the clerics speak of both *Canadiens* and *métis* living in a particular settlement, we have retained these two terms as well, as it is not clear if they employ the terms in an overlapping sense or in reference to two groups of individuals. We also have retained the clerics' use of the lowercase "m," in *métis*, both for historical accuracy and to distinguish them (many of whom for various reasons did not overtly identify themselves as such) from Canada's later designation of *Métis*, with an initial capital, for the self-proclaimed and politically recognized mixed-heritage inhabitants of the initial province of Manitoba.

The second sensitive and contested topic, the interaction between Indians and missionaries, is central to the letters. Quite distinct Indian groups with their own cultures lived within the geographical area that is the subject of this book. Their responses to Christian evangelization were shaped by a variety of factors, including individual experiences mediated through their own indigenous traditions, understandings of spiritual power, material and political interests, and their assessment of missionaries and others with whom they interacted. Those missionaries we meet through the letters also were individuals. They were shaped by their cultural backgrounds, including religious traditions and personal spiritual experiences, and by the people and situations they encountered. It is impossible to know the missionaries' most deeply held convictions. A careful reading of the letters supports the conclusion that they were assailed by moments of doubt, that they sometimes were influenced by indigenous beliefs and the spiritual practices of those with whom they lived, and that their perspectives on Indians, and on their roles as missionaries, evolved over time.

Not only are the deepest beliefs of these individuals, be they Indians or Euro-Americans, elusive to the interpreter, the outward signs of religious devotion they chose to display often had multiple meanings as well. Christian doctrines, symbols, practices, and objects such as vestments or medals embossed with the images of saints were expressions of colonization, sometimes deliberately and sometimes unintentionally; yet they also, by their very nature, served as powerful means of subversion. They were equally as capable of inspiring resistance as they were compliance. Hence, while bearing a cross could be a sign of submission and assimilation to white, Christian domination, it also could signal political, if not necessarily, religious opposition.

And—to briefly introduce another important group that emerges in these letters—some of Washington's most influential pioneer women proudly wore their habits and wimples, not out of passive submission, but as communal signs of rugged strength and independence.

Given these considerations, we think it a serious error to assume that the missionaries and Indians in these letters held rigidly circumscribed and unchanging sets of beliefs and traditions. It is also an error to assume that the meanings of any of their beliefs and practices, or of their ornaments and clothing, were uniform and univocal. Hence, when treating their interactions, in both our introductions and annotations, we have attempted, to the extent possible, to let the persons in the letters speak for themselves from within their particular context in a specific moment. We also have refrained from making sustained general arguments about these encounters, knowing that a full and theoretically informed development of issues the letters raise would have required either many fewer letters or a much longer volume.

Finally, given the contested nature of the topics covered in the letters—cultural conflicts, Native American–missionary interaction, and religion—we have sought with particular care to avoid imposing our own personal presuppositions. To the extent possible, we have presented historical actors in their own terms, even when they expressed ideas and perspectives or acted in ways that grate on contemporary sensibilities. We recognized that, for most of these individuals, religious and spiritual forces were vitally important and real, so real, that they motivated actions and colored perspectives. Thus, our interpretations attempt to maintain a space of attentiveness to difference that recognizes the integrity of our subjects' experience. Our stance is best characterized as an embrace of the "in-between"—a space that honors the "discrepant moralities, ways of knowing, and religious impulses" of people different from ourselves—Indians, missionaries, soldiers, settlers.[1]

Such an approach has required a disciplined suspension of the impulse to bring closure to interpretations, however brief they may be, of issues these letters raise. It pays off, we think, in the potential of seeing more clearly into the searches, struggles, and story of the individuals and communities who come to life through the letters of A. M. A. Blanchet.

1. Robert Orsi, *Between Heaven and Earth: The Religious Worlds People Make and Scholars Who Study Them* (Princeton, N.J.: Princeton University Press, 2005), 198.

Acknowledgments

The many people who helped us along the way are as widely scattered as the destinations of the letters themselves. Historical documentarian Georges Aubin of L'Assomption, Quebec, spent much of 1985–86 transcribing the A. M. A. Blanchet letterbooks in their original French language, to which he added additional letters, some references, and a collection of related and incoming letters, including large numbers from depositories in Montreal, all of which he generously lent us for the project (see the Bibliography). He and his wife, Renée Blanchet, a great-grandniece of the bishop, welcomed us to their home, drove us to the locations of Blanchet's early assignments as priest, provided family images related to the bishop for our use, and extended their inspiring support and friendship throughout the years. Archivists in Quebec, aided our quest for original letters and background information as well. We are thankful to Marcel Gagné, S.J., of the Archives of the Archdiocese of Quebec, and his assistant, Pierre LaFontaine; Monique Montbriand, of Montreal's Archives of the Chancellery of the Diocese of Montreal; and Marie Claude Bélande, of Montreal's Providence Archives. In Paris, R. Sintes, archivist of the church of Notre-Dame des Victoires (Our Lady of Victories), happily led his American visitor up the winding staircase to a dusty collection of memorial brass lockets sent to the church during the nineteenth century—Blanchet's undoubtedly among them—and shared other helpful documents. In Lyons, Odile Lolom, archivist of today's Oeuvres Pontificales Missionnaires, made accessible the original annual reports that Bishop Blanchet sent to this important funding organization, four of which we have translated for this volume, and rich deposits of related materials. She also arranged housing at the original home of the association's foundress, Pauline Jaricot. In Belgium, John Steffan, of Louvain's American College of the Immaculate Conception, helped satisfy our curiosity about this seminary where a number of Northwest priests and eventual church leaders were trained during Blanchet's episcopacy.

Our quest for information and documents relied as well on archivists and librarians here in the Pacific Northwest. Christine Taylor, former archivist of the Archdiocese of Seattle, first made the letterbooks available to us, encouraged our work, and participated with us in early conference presentations on the letterbooks. Her assistants, Sarah Nau and Norman Dizon, unfailingly provided generous assistance. Current archivist Seth Dalby, assisted by Manny Keller-Scholz, continued to support the project with his astute insights and by sharing additional, recently cataloged documents and images. During our forays to Portland, Shawna Gandy of the Oregon Historical Society Research Library, as knowledgeable of local history as she is of the invaluable collections in this library, located other materials that have helped bring the letters to life. Our reconstruction of the essential role that Montreal's Sisters of Providence played in early Washington would not have been possible without the rich collections of Seattle's Providence Archives, generously made available to us by archivist Loretta Zwolak Greene, her associate Emily Hughes Dominick, and visual resource archivist Peter Schmid. David Kingma, archivist for the Oregon Province of the Society of Jesus, also welcomed us and provided resources related to Blanchet's interactions with Jesuits.

From the start, we benefited from fruitful conversations at scholarly conferences. In 1999, we presented papers at a joint session of the Canadian Society of Church History and the Canadian Catholic Historical Association. With their depth of knowledge and international perspectives, Mark McGowan, Terence Fay, S.J., Luca Codignola, Bruce Guenther, James Opp, Elizabeth Smyth, and others helped us conceptualize Blanchet's episcopacy on its own terms, and not primarily as a counterpoint to the dominant east-to-west, Protestant-inflected narrative of U.S. history. A National Endowment for the Humanities (NEH) summer institute on French travel writing from the Americas, held at the Newberry Library, enriched our interpretations of the letters. An Institute for Editing Historical Documents, sponsored by the National Historical Publications and Records Commission, refined technical aspects of producing these texts.

As our work progressed, our argument was strengthened by the constructive criticism, incisive questions, and insights other scholars shared in response to our presentations at other meetings in North America—the American Catholic Historical Association, the American Academy of Religion, the American Council for Quebec Studies, the American Society of Church History, the Pacific Northwest Historian's Guild, the Pacific Northwest History Conference, and the Western Society for French History—and at less formal gatherings with local associations and among colleagues. We are indebted to the many individuals who engaged us around the various dimensions of this project.

Others to whom we owe thanks for sharing their expertise on particular individuals, events, or locations include Jean Barman of the University of British Columbia; Monsignor Kevin Codd of the Diocese of Spokane and former rector of the American College of Louvain; Jean Fisher, librarian, Special Collections of Northwest Room, Tacoma Public Library; Theresa Langford, curator of Fort Vancouver National Historic Site; Michal McKenzie of Keuka College; and Sam Pambrum of Walla Walla. We are indebted as well to Rochelle Snee and Eric Nelson of Pacific Lutheran University, who assisted us with Latin phrases, and to the Reverend Jon Taylor of the University of Great Falls, who provided translations of all the Latin passages in letters included in this volume.

Pacific Lutheran University, where we taught and held administrative positions throughout most of this project, supported both our research and conference participation. Religion major Angela Steiert served as research assistant in the very early stages of the project. A Faculty Excellence Award helped subsidize travel to archives in Europe, and a Kelmer-Roe Fellowship for collaborative student-faculty research in the humanities allowed us to engage French major Asha Ajmani as research assistant. As well, the Social Sciences and Humanities Research Council of Canada supported in part our initial 1999 presentation to the joint session of the Canadian Catholic Historical Association and the Canadian Society of Church History.

As the manuscript emerged, many others provided assistance. Father Jim Harbaugh, S.J., parochial vicar at St. Leo Church of Tacoma, and Dr. Betsy Downey of the History Department at Gonzaga University, read the nearly final version in full and provided valuable response. At the University of Washington Press, Julidta Tarver, acquisitions editor, read and responded to drafts, always with warm encouragement. Marianne Keddington-Lang, with Tim Zimmerman, shepherded us through the final acquisitions process with grace and steadiness of hand. The volume is far stronger for the constructive, critical suggestions of our three anonymous reviewers. Managing editor Mary Ribesky patiently responded to questions and saw to the final production of the book.

Closer to home, we thank our husbands, Timothy Brown and David Killen, for their patience and support. Astute readers and thinkers, they gave fresh perspectives on our interpretations, endured vacations turned into archival visits, and willingly read the final manuscript. Lastly, we acknowledge the pleasure this gift of long-term collaborative work has brought us both. Through our engagement with each other and with the many individuals who have contributed to the completion of this volume, we have come to recognize ever more profoundly what it means to be part of a community of scholars.

Selected Letters of A. M. A. Blanchet

Introduction

On May 8, 1847, the Right Reverend Augustin Magloire Alexandre Blanchet, bishop of Walla Walla, gave the signal to pull out from Westport, Missouri. And so the bishop, his eight fellow missionaries, and eight others, along with their three wagons, two teams of oxen, one team of cows, and all their supplies, commenced their journey on the Oregon Trail. Five days later they joined a group of twelve wagons under the leadership of Captain Wiggins. Since departing from Montreal on March 23, Bishop Blanchet and most of his party had already traveled nearly two thousand miles by sleigh, stagecoach, train, and steamboat. They would traverse the remaining 1,670 miles by wagon, foot, and horseback. Five of the nine missionaries, recently arrived from France, had joined up with the others at St. Louis.[1]

Bishop Blanchet and his companions were among more than four thousand people with upward of 850 wagons who traversed the Oregon Trail in 1847, the largest crossing to date.[2] Like other emigrants over the trail, the Canadien Roman Catholic bishop and his companions were propelled by a vision of what was possible in the Oregon Country. Their fortunes, like those of others, would be influenced by multiple factors, many they could neither anticipate nor control. And, like all who emigrated, Blanchet and his companions would be forced to revise their aspirations as they wrestled with the actual material and social circumstances in making their way in the Oregon Country.

The initial days on the Oregon Trail were difficult. The party was plagued by bad weather, ignorance of how to drive oxen, broken axels, and a disappearing guide. But with the assistance of fellow overlanders, Blanchet's party developed the skills to manage the journey. On May 22 the bishop and his group left Captain Wiggins's train and struck out on their own. They could not accept the party's decision to shoot any Indian who would not withdraw from the path of the wagons. On May 26 they joined the train of Captain McGowan. Over the weeks that followed, they made themselves useful by comforting the sick, burying Catholics who died, and baptizing both emigrants and the children of Catholics they encountered in settlements along the initial length of the trail.[3]

On August 7, the train reached Fort Hall in the easterly reaches of the

Old Oregon Country, near today's city of Pocatello, Idaho. From there, on August 14, Blanchet, and fellow missionaries Father Pascal Ricard, Brother Georges Blanchet (no relation to the bishop), and Deacon Louis-Pierre Godefroi Rousseau set out by horseback as part of a Hudson's Bay Company (HBC) overland brigade. They rode ahead in order to determine sites for the anticipated Catholic missions before the wagons and supplies arrived. The brigade reached its destination, the HBC's Fort Walla Walla, located near the juncture of the Snake and Columbia Rivers, at three-thirty in the afternoon of Sunday, September 5, 1847. Three weeks later, word reached the fort that the remainder of the party, exhausted and hungry, had emerged from the Blue Mountains, gateway to the Walla Walla region.[4]

Reunited at Fort Walla Walla on October 3, 1847, A. M. A. Blanchet and his companions could not have anticipated the cultural and political upheaval about to take place in the immediate vicinity. Neither could they have imagined the adaptation, creativity, compromise, and resilience that would be required over the next three-plus decades to build and sustain a lasting Catholic presence in today's Washington State.

<hr>

A. M. A. Blanchet (1797–1887) was a strongly built man with a pleasant mien. He turned fifty while on the Oregon Trail. A portrait from his middle age shows his graying, receding hair and bushy eyebrows, a firmly set mouth, and clear, expressive eyes. Talented musically, he often sang the Mass, in the tradition of the time. Save for his dress, Blanchet might have been mistaken at first glance for a Canadien trader on the streets of St. Louis. In fact, he was a shy, socially awkward man, a moralist and a hound for rules, a worrier who was easily angered, at times prickly and crusty. He clung tenaciously to his identity as bishop, and to the authority it carried. Not everyone liked him, especially not his more socially adept vicar-general, J.B.A. Brouillet, who on two occasions tried to leave the diocese. Yet those whose ties with the bishop penetrated his official persona wrote of his tenderness and sensitivity, his "apostolic" humbleness.

In spite of—or perhaps on account of—his human flaws, A. M. A. Blanchet was fitted for a difficult task of long duration. Having been raised in a large, modest farming family near Quebec City, he faced the harsh winters along the Columbia River, or the mud-soaked roads of Puget Sound, with accustomed ease. Educated and trained for the priesthood in Quebec's Seminary for Foreign Missions—a branch of the prestigious seminary by that name in Paris—Blanchet was smart, widely read, and deeply curious; he harbored a fascination for politics as well as religious matters. He was good with numbers, and while intensely religious, he also was thoroughly pragmatic, a stickler for the bottom line.

Blanchet brought extensive pastoral experience to his missionary project. After ordination in 1821, at the age of twenty-three, he served at St.-Gervais, near Montreal, then as pastor to returning Acadians at Cheticamp, Nova Scotia, and the Magdalen Islands in the Gulf of St. Lawrence. From there he was recalled to take important posts as a parish priest in the Montreal region, serving at St.-Charles in St.-Charles-sur-Richelieu from 1830 to 1838. He later served trappers at the HBC post of Les Cèdres south of Montreal, followed by a post as titular canon of the Cathedral of St. James in Montreal. During the last post, he also held the position of chaplain to the newly formed Sisters of Charity of Providence.

Perhaps most significant, Blanchet had experienced, firsthand, the politics of keeping the Catholic religion afloat. His pastoral sensibility and political sympathies during the Patriote insurrection of Canadiens against their British occupiers in Lower Canada led him to aid his parishioners before they fought in the battle of Saint-Charles on November 25, 1837. British authorities interpreted his actions as support for the revolt. Arrested for high treason, Blanchet was imprisoned in Montreal on December 16, 1837. He was released on bail on March 31, 1838, after the bishops of Montreal and Quebec interceded with the government on his behalf. All of these experiences informed A. M. A. Blanchet as he negotiated the challenges that confronted him in his missionary diocese.

For the travel-weary party, on that day of October 3, Fort Walla Walla was strange in its newness. Yet as a social order where HBC officers, employees, and indigenous peoples interacted, it was familiar. Their hosts, HBC clerk William McBean and his French-speaking métis family, were devoted, practicing Catholics who welcomed them with food, shelter, and other creature comforts. McBean's immediate material support of the party represented the policies of the HBC at that time. In 1838, the company had approved the entry of Fathers François Norbert Blanchet (brother of A. M. A. Blanchet) and Modeste Demers into the Columbia District (the HBC's name for the territory that included the Oregon Country), allowing them to travel with the annual brigade from Montreal.[5] Subsequently, the HBC did not oppose the establishment of the Apostolic Vicariate of Oregon in 1843 or its elevation to an ecclesiastical province in 1846.[6] HBC authorities considered the influence of Catholic missionaries on the Indians with whom and among whom the company operated, and on its employees, as a pragmatic economic good.

Two other pieces of the order familiar to the newcomers also were in place in the vicinity of Fort Walla Walla. Scattered up the Walla Walla River valley were some fifty families who, like the McBeans, were of mixed Euro-American and Indian heritage. The men, most retired from HBC employ, had served as boatmen, guides, interpreters, and trappers, and many were Catholic by ethnic and familial heritage. Similar settlements were found close to other HBC forts strung throughout Bishop Blanchet's vast diocese.[7]

Additionally, communities of friendly Indians, some intermarried with the settlers, some having been fur-trade employees themselves, were, for varying reasons, willing to host the evangelizing priests on their lands. For these indigenous peoples, still numerous in spite of epidemics, Christianity was not new; it had already disrupted, undermined, shifted, and been incorporated into their native ways. Christian evangelization had begun with Catholic Iroquois and métis employed in the fur trade and intensified with the arrival of Protestant missionaries in 1834 and Catholic priests in 1838.

Underlying this HBC-influenced social order lay a culture that was predominantly rural and multicultural, with porous boundaries among groups. Perhaps imagining the Diocese of Walla Walla in terms similar to HBC-run Canadian lands to the north, Blanchet anticipated Indians remaining on their lands, living in significant ways as they had for centuries, with a group of them practicing Catholicism within their own social and economic niches. He imagined rural farms and settlements and seminomadic Indian populations coexisting.

Though they arrived anticipating a missionary project within the contours of this old order, the Catholic missionary party was, in fact, only a few short weeks away from a clash that would mark the territory for a dozen years and lead to the familiar order's unraveling. In the process, those who continued to identify with it would become losers in a contest of political, economic, and cultural power.

It began with the killings of the Protestant missionaries Dr. Marcus Whitman and his wife, Narcissa Prentiss Whitman, and twelve others at their Waiilatpu mission not far from Fort Walla Walla on November 29, 1847 (see letter 2). It drew to a close with the U.S. Senate's ratification of Indian treaties and the establishment of reservations in 1859. This period saw successively larger waves of American emigrants coming on the heels of gold rushes and silver strikes, Indians' defense of their lands through a series of "wars," and continuous violence. By the end of these twelve years, the HBC had removed to Fort Victoria on Vancouver Island. Indians who had survived the period's violent conflicts and epidemics had left the territory, moved onto reservations, or were sustaining themselves off-reservation.

Though the Catholic Church was identified with the previous social world and faced multiple threats to its existence in the Pacific Northwest during this period, it survived. Three potent factors, all initiated by a resilient, forward-thinking bishop, contributed to its survival and strength. The first was financial stability. Among his money raising activities, A. M. A. Blanchet undertook two lengthy voyages to Mexico (1851–52) and Europe (1855–56), during which he gathered substantial and urgently needed funds for the missionary diocese. The second factor was the support he received from missionary sisters. While in his homeland at the end of the second voyage, he negotiated the transplanting of a venturesome, talented group of Sisters of Providence, led by Mother Joseph, to Columbia City (Vancouver). These exceptionally capable women from Montreal were harbingers of what would become a network of social and health services under their direction and care. Finally, while in Europe, Blanchet laid the groundwork for the eventual arrival of highly educated, multilingual, and committed priests from the American College of the Immaculate Conception in Louvain, Belgium, who would become the second generation of pastoral leaders and administrators for his diocese. Additionally, the service of an outgoing and tireless vicar-general, J. B. A. Brouillet, kept the diocese afloat during the bishop's travels and the heat of the Yakima Wars (1855–58).

As a result of these initiatives, the project of building the Catholic Church in what is today's Washington State endured. The Church emerged from the tumultuous twelve years having evolved in ways different from what the original group that trekked over the Oregon Trail had anticipated.

The achievements during A. M. A. Blanchet's remaining twenty-one years of leadership depended upon continued resilience, initiative, and imagination, exercised within a context in which he had no choice but to cooperate with elements of a new social order, an ascendant Euro-American Protestant world. His model for this collaboration was Montreal, where the Catholic

Church had successfully negotiated a working relationship with political authorities who were explicitly Protestant.[8]

Taken altogether, Bishop Blanchet's thirty-three-year episcopacy spanned two social, political, and cultural orders that each left profound marks on the Pacific Northwest. The HBC constituted the older, British colonization movement in western North America. The company provided the dominant and only form of nonindigenous political and economic power in Old Oregon from 1821 until United States settlers in the Willamette Valley erected a provisional government in 1843.[9] Though the HBC lost political control of Oregon south of the forty-ninth parallel through the 1846 treaty ending joint occupancy of the Oregon Country, it remained a real, though gradually declining, power in the region through 1860.[10]

The newer colonization movement, based in the United States, was a Euro-American empire in the making that rested on individual entrepreneurship and nationalistic sentiment. The Americans involved in the effort to settle Oregon framed the project culturally in terms of democratic freedom and, for most, Protestant Christianity. For most farmers, ranchers, and businessmen, "settling Oregon" stood for conquest. For missionaries, such as the Methodist Jason Lee, religious, nationalistic, and economic ambitions quickly converged. Lee's 1834 missionary venture to convert Indians in Oregon became overshadowed by his project of building an American colony in the Willamette Valley. Those who shared Lee's view would play a major role in the organization of the provisional government in Oregon in 1843. Subsequently, various parties, often clashing over conflicts of interest, were involved in this second, U.S.-Protestant colonization movement. Despite their conflicts, which often arose from differences in personal ambitions, regions of origin, and national politics, especially around the issue of slavery, they shared a sense that the land was rightfully theirs as a result of treaty and, for some, divine destiny.[11]

By 1860, Old Oregon was divided into Oregon State (1859) and the Washington Territory (established in 1853, with boundaries adjusted in 1859 and again in 1863). The Cayuse (1848–50), Yakima (1855–58), and Coeur d'Alene /Palouse (1858) Indian wars had ended. The Indian reservation system had been established. Vancouver, Walla Walla, Olympia, and Steilacoom had become towns. Bishop Blanchet with his priests, sisters, and interested lay Catholics had nurtured Catholic liturgical life and social services to basic levels of stability. The Church no longer depended on the HBC.

Blanchet's three-plus decades of correspondence does more than reveal the bishop's resilience and determination. It tells of circumstances that led to sometimes forced and sometimes unacknowledged compromises. And, it reveals the challenges involved in building stable institutions in the fluid and often conflicted environment of Washington's territorial period. Letters addressing the situation of Canadien and Indian Catholics disclose populations that left little written record and that, over these decades, were increasingly eclipsed by political and economic developments. His letters to public officials provide the perspective of a cosmopolitan institutional leader on regional and national political dynamics. The letters also display the degree to which international events influenced the fortunes of the Catholic Church and life more broadly in Washington Territory.

In our time, saturated as it is with myriad modes of communication, Blanchet's letters are valuable artifacts of another age. Letter writing then was a powerful mode of communication. Blanchet's missionary project, establishing Catholic structures in a frontier land, depended upon his communicating with persons both near and far, of wide political and cultural orientations, of varying social strata, and of differing degrees of political, economic, and ecclesial power in relation to his own. Given the expanse and isolation of the diocese, the written word was the only tool at Blanchet's disposal, the primary means for him to exercise his authority over those he saw as subordinate and to express his desires and concerns to those in positions of power above him. Letters wove together the diocesan Catholic project and tied that project to a global Catholic Church. They not only served to influence, request, and command but also were a way to maintain spiritual friendships. Of a laconic disposition, a person who thought and often stewed before he wrote, Blanchet chose words carefully.

The letters in this volume, most translated into English and published for the first time, expand our understanding of missionary history in the Pacific Northwest. They supplement a story framed until now primarily in terms of Protestants and Jesuits. They provide a fuller perspective on the Catholic Church in Washington and its contributions to the emergence of the Pacific Northwest. They also invite more global interpretations of the region's history.

The letters do more. They bring to life individuals and communities whose existence is not prominent in the historical record. What emerges from the letters is a cosmopolitan frontier, where indigenous languages, Euro-American tongues, and all ranges of mixes, as well as Chinese, were spoken; where French was the lingua franca of educated Euro-Americans; and where many people could communicate in at least two or three of these languages. This population existed in a setting of often unstable systems of power, rapid change, personal triumphs, and heartbreaks, a setting in which religion was never just about religion.

1. The bishop's three missionary collaborators from Canada were Father Jean-Baptiste Abraham Brouillet, his vicar-general; Louis-Pierre Godefroi Rousseau, a deacon; and, Guillaume Leclaire, a subdeacon. Also part of his party were Ferdinand Labrie, his servant; Joseph and Gilbert Malo, two brothers who were hired as carpenters; and three others "traveling at their own expense." The bishop's two nieces, Louise Henrietta Peltier and Soulanges Peltier, also accompanied him. His party was expanded in St. Louis by the arrival of five Oblate of Mary Immaculate missionaries from France: Father Pascal Ricard, superior; deacons Eugène-Casimir Chirouse and Jean-Charles Félix Pandosy; Brother Georges Blanchet (not related to the bishop); and Célestin Verney, a lay brother. A. M. A. Blanchet, *Journal of a Catholic Bishop on the Oregon Trail: The Overland Crossing of the Rt. Rev. A. M. A. Blanchet, Bishop of Walla Walla, from Montreal to Oregon Territory, March 23, 1847 to January 23, 1851*, trans. and ed. Edward J. Kowrach (Fairfield, Wash.: Ye Galleon Press, 1978), 21–22, 30, 36–50, 68; Georges Aubin, "Les quatre soeurs Peltier nièces de Monseigneur en Orégon," *Mémoires de la société généalogique canadienne-française* 39, no. 2 (Summer 1988): 91–93; Ronald Wayne Young, O.M.I., "The Mission of the Missionary Oblates of Mary Immaculate to the Oregon Territory (1847–1860)" (Ph.D. diss., Pontificia Universitas Gregoriana, 2000), 60–61.

2. Julie R. Jeffrey, *Converting the West: A Biography of Narcissa Whitman* (Norman: University of Oklahoma Press, 1991), 213; Blanchet, *Journal of a Catholic Bishop*, 15, 62.

3. Blanchet, *Journal of a Catholic Bishop*, 36–50.

4. Ibid., 61–67.

5. Wilfred P. Schoenberg, S.J., *A History of the Catholic Church in the Pacific Northwest, 1743–1983* (Washington, D.C.: Pastoral Press, 1987), 26–40.

6. The ecclesiastical province comprised the area from the Rocky Mountains to the east, the Mexico and later United States–California border to the south, the Pacific Ocean to the west, and the Arctic Pole to the north. With its establishment in 1846, F. N. Blanchet was appointed archbishop of Oregon City. His fellow missionary, Modeste Demers, was assigned the Diocese of Vancouver Island, and A. M. A. Blanchet, the Diocese of Walla Walla. Five other districts, potential dioceses, were identified and attached to the three dioceses for which bishops and archbishop were provided: Nesqualy, Fort Hall, Colville, Princess Charlotte, and New Caledonia. All this was for an area that, by F. N. Blanchet's own reckoning in 1846, included only six thousand Catholics, nearly all Native Americans. The bishop of Quebec, Joseph Signay, and the archbishop of Baltimore, Samuel Eccleston, S.S., in 1843 jointly requested that the Oregon mis-

sion be made an apostolic vicariate. Signay earlier had considered turning the territory over to the Apostolic Vicariate of Oceania. See Schoenberg, *Catholic Church in the Pacific Northwest*, 77–97; and Edwin Vincent O'Hara, *A Pioneer Catholic History of Oregon* (Portland, Ore.: Glass and Prudhomme Company, 1911), 84, 97–100.

7. A. M. A. Blanchet was responsible for the Diocese of Walla Walla as well as the districts of Colville and Fort Hall. This made him responsible for all of Washington east of the Cascades, eastern Oregon, Idaho, and portions of western Montana and western Wyoming.

8. Terence J. Fay, *A History of Canadian Catholics: Gallicanism, Romanism, and Canadianism* (Montreal: McGill-Queens University Press, 2002), 29–47; Terrence Murphy, ed., and Roberto Perin, associate ed., *A Concise History of Christianity in Canada* (New York: Oxford University Press, 1996), 55–107.

9. Richard Somerset Mackie, *Trading beyond the Mountains: The British Fur Trade on the Pacific, 1793–1843* (Vancouver: University of British Columbia Press, 1997), 31–33.

10. Great Britain and the United States agreed to jointly occupy the Oregon Country for a ten-year period, beginning in 1818 with the Anglo-American Treaty. The joint occupancy agreement was renewed in 1827. The issue of possession came to a head again in 1843 and eventually was resolved by treaty, with the boundary set at the forty-ninth parallel in 1846.

11. For many involved in the Oregon provisional government, "divine destiny" favored white Protestants from the United States. The democratization of religious authority that emerged from the Second Great Awakening and nationalist sentiment reinforced their view. The federal government's opening of the Oregon Country to settlement before Indian title to lands was extinguished by treaty further confirmed these beliefs. See Nathan O. Hatch, *The Democratization of American Christianity* (New Haven, Conn.: Yale University Press, 1991); Ernest Lee Tuveson, *Redeemer Nation: The Idea of America's Millennial Role* (Chicago: University of Chicago Press, 1968); and Francis Paul Prucha, *The Great Father: The United States Government and the American Indians* (Lincoln: University of Nebraska Press, 1984), 1:392–409.

To Charles Dufriche-Desgenettes,
Pastor of Notre-Dame des Victoires, Paris,
February 25, 1847[1]

An engraved metal locket in the shape of a heart contained a folded piece of paper with the names of Bishop A. M. A. Blanchet and his missionaries. Shortly before his departure from Montreal for his journey west, Blanchet wrote to Paris to arrange for this devotional object to be placed at an altar dedicated to the Holy and Immaculate Heart of Mary. The ritual act, simple in itself, was laden with meaning. Recalling a vassal's oath of fealty to his lord, it represented a vow on the part of Blanchet and his clerics to serve Mary through prayer and imitation of her virtues, in exchange for her protection and support. In the understanding of the missionaries, the ritual assured the presence of this supernatural support in their new diocese even before they arrived. Blanchet also wrote to request that individuals in Montreal, Paris, and elsewhere, in sharing this special devotion to Mary through member-ship in an archconfraternity, pray for and remember his missionaries and the people with whom they would work, thus uniting Blanchet's missionary venture more intimately with the Church worldwide.

Montreal, February 25th 1847

Father,

The Holy Apostolic See is sending me to Oregon, there to work for the conversion of Infidels and to govern a diocese, this in spite of my weakness. Before departing, I feel an urgent need to ask that you recommend me to the prayers of the associates of the Archconfraternity of the most Holy and Immaculate Heart of Mary.[2] Before my consecration I had the joy of living in a diocese deeply devoted to the Heart of Mary. There it was my fortune to witness the great marvels that came about through Her whom the Church so rightly calls the Refuge of Sinners, the Consoler of the Afflicted, and the Gate to Heaven. In seeking all the help I will need to accomplish the work entrusted to my weak hands, I could do no better than present myself to her pure and unstained heart. I must proclaim aloud that she has already secured significant favors for me. In order that she might continue to protect me, I wish to consecrate myself once again, along with my diocese and all my collaborators, to her tender and compassionate heart. To that effect, I wish to deposit a heart containing the names of the first Bishop of Walla Walla and of the Ecclesiastics who will accompany him, in the favored Church of N.-D. des Victoires, where you are the honorable Pastor. Monsignor of Montreal very much wanted to make this little offering for me upon his return from the Holy City.[3]

You will receive this heart as a memorial that will continually tell Mary that she has in Oregon, as in Canada and Europe, children devoted to her service, propagators of her religion, and that she will have here, I am confident, followers of her virtues. In becoming Christian, the Indians will be children of Mary.[4] They will sing her praises. They will offer themselves to the Heart of Mary so that she might guide them to the Sacred Heart of Jesus, unending source of all that is good. The Mother's direction can but lead to the Son.

From you, Father, who have no need, being in the care of Mary, I ask that you remember me when you do your Holy Sacrifice of the Mass.

Accept the esteem with which I am, Father,
your most humble and obedient servant
A. M. Blanchet, Bp. of Walla Walla

ARCHIVES OF THE BASILICA OF NOTRE-DAME DES VICTOIRES, PARIS; ARCHIVES OF THE ARCH-DIOCESE OF SEATTLE (HEREAFTER CITED AS AAS), A2: 24.

———•———

1. Ordained in 1807, Charles Dufriche-Desgenettes (1778–1860) was among the large group of clerics and laypeople known as "ultramontanes" for their loyalty to the authority of Rome and opposition to France's nationalization of the Church following the Revolution of 1778. From 1819 to 1830, during the time of Bourbon political restoration in France, he served as pastor of the parish of Foreign Missions (St. Francis-Xavier), a center of Restoration Catholic piety and missionary endeavors situated in the sixth arrondissement of Paris. Following six years of political exile after the fall of the Bourbons in 1830, he served from 1836 to 1860 as pastor of

Notre-Dame des Victoires (Our Lady of Victories), a parish church. "Charles Desgenettes: Une vie sanctifiée par Marie, 1778–1860," http://www.notredamedesvictoires.com/desgenettes.htm (accessed April 18, 2012).

2. "Infidels" was a standard term at the time for people who were not Christian. Founded by Father Dufriche-Desgenettes in 1836 and recognized by Pope Gregory XVI in 1838, the Archconfraternity of the Holy and Immaculate Heart of Mary quickly spread throughout Europe and missionary lands, including British North America and the United States. Notre-Dame des Victoires subsequently served as a sanctuary and pilgrimage center for Marian devotion, eventually housing some thirty-seven thousand ex-votive offerings to Mary, many of them devotional hearts. The archconfraternity continues today as the Universal Association of Marian Devotion and is still housed at the Basilica of Notre-Dame des Victoires. "La Basilique à travers les ages," http://www.notredamedesvictoires.com/lesages.com (accessed April 18, 2012).

3. Most devotional hearts of the mid-nineteenth century, like those deposited at this church, were made of bronze or copper and engraved with ornamental designs featuring the letter M, for Mary. Two sculpted lilies, representing Mary's purity, emerged from the top, as if growing out of the heart. Words of a favor requested or already received were written on the paper within. In a related letter to Bishop Bourget, Blanchet wrote: "The names of the secular clergy who need to be placed in the heart at N.-D. des Victoires are: Messieurs J. Bte. Brouillet, priest, Louis Godefroy Rousseau, deacon & Guillaume Leclerc, subdeacon. The Regulars, Obl M. will be Father Pascal Ricard, and Georges Blanchet who is not a priest, and two others, who will not come until next year, it appears, are: Eugène-Casimir Chirouze that I name Kérouse, and J. Ch. Pandosi. As for the Jesuits, I don't think that they are yet in the Diocese of Walla Walla properly speaking, although several whose names I do not know, are under my jurisdiction. Your Excellency could perhaps find out their names in Paris" (Blanchet to Bourget [in Paris], February 27, 1847, Archives of the Chancellery of the Archdiocese of Montreal [hereafter cited as ACAM], file 195.133, 847–3; AAS, A2: 29–31). This and subsequent citations from the French have been translated by the editors. Blanchet is referring here to Bishop Ignace Bourget (1799–1855). Native of Montreal and classmate of A. M. A. Blanchet at the Seminary of Quebec, Bourget was ordained to the priesthood in 1822, appointed coadjutor to the bishop of Montreal with right of succession in 1837, and appointed second bishop of Montreal in 1840. As bishop, he led a popular revival of Catholic institutions and piety, and worked to elevate the Diocese of Quebec to the status of an independent ecclesiastical province in 1844. Instrumental as well in the elevation of the Apostolic Vicariate of Oregon to an ecclesiastical province, Bourget consecrated A. M. A. Blanchet to the episcopacy in the cathedral of Montreal. In 1841, he established the Archconfraternity of the Holy and Immaculate Heart of Mary at his cathedral; the devotion spreading quickly, he affiliated all parishes in his diocese and was known to preside at the Paris church during visits. See Léon Pouliot, *Monseigneur Bourget et son temps*, vol. 2, *L'Evêque de Montréal* (Montreal: Editions Beauchemin, 1955–56); *Dictionary of Canadian Biography*, s.v. "Bourget, Ignace."

4. In Catholicism, Mary, as Mother of Christ, is believed to welcome all persons regardless of status or spiritual condition as her children in faith. The term "children of Mary" was used commonly for all pious Catholics, referencing Mary's power as mediatrix between the faithful and Jesus. It extends the allusion from the passage in John's gospel where Jesus, from the cross,

pronounces the disciple Mary's son (John 19:25). All biblical references are from the New American Bible, new Catholic translation (Nashville: Thomas Nelson Publishers, 1983).

To François Norbert Blanchet, Archbishop of Oregon City, December 12, 1847[1]

Ten months, a voyage of over three thousand miles across the continent, and the killing of Marcus and Narcissa Whitman and twelve other Americans by young Cayuses stand between this letter and the first. Indian resistance to a religious conversion that required them to become farmers, the Whitmans' hospitality to swelling numbers of American emigrants, and Cayuse traditions of avenging themselves on healers who failed to save their dying patients, all had led to repeated threats made against the lives of the missionaries at Waiilatpu over several years.[2] With events moving rapidly toward armed conflict between the entire Cayuse nation and a volunteer force of settlers from the Willamette Valley, this letter details events from Blanchet's point of view: his contacts and those of his clergy with Dr. Whitman and Cayuse leaders before the killings, the deaths of Cayuses from dysentery and measles, threats to the lives of his priests, fear of an all-out war, and gratitude for being spared.

Addressed to his brother, the letter is personal in tone. It betrays deep concerns. Previous experience gave Blanchet reason to worry. Caught in the conflict between Canadiens and British during the first Patriote insurrection, he was accused of treason and imprisoned in 1837; he had supported the Patriotes in his parish before a decisive battle in which they were defeated. Now Blanchet once again faced the challenge of defending those he was charged to serve—in this case Native Americans and Canadiens—without offending a more powerful political force in doing so. By a twist of irony, influential anti-Catholic settlers would identify Blanchet and fellow clerics with the British, who had imprisoned him in 1837.

Though the dispute over political sovereignty in the Oregon Country was settled in 1846, its population remained a mix of multiple ethnicities and nationalities. In the process of seeking Oregon's adoption as a U.S. territory, some settlers reinforced their American identity by casting other groups as foreign, such as HBC employees, Catholics, people of mixed descent, and even Indians, though most had resided much longer on U.S. lands, if not within states or territories, than the more recently arrived American settlers. The proximity of Blanchet's new missions and the Walla Walla HBC post to the scene of the killings at Waiilatpu, an American gateway to Oregon, provided a tool the settlers could use to construct a set of dangerous "others," thereby further solidifying their identity. Blanchet's previous experience in Canada and his travels across the United States and frontier lands sensitized him to the effects that this dynamic of differentiation could have upon his nascent mission.

Nehiaoui (Umatilla) December 12th 1847

My dear *Seigneur* & beloved brother,

Since my last, events have taken place here that may have very grave consequences, both civil and religious; I hasten to apprise you of them.[3] In order to explain their full import, I must back up and give a brief overview of all that has ensued with respect to our missions since I first arrived in my diocese.

It was on September 23rd, at Fort Walla Walla, that I first saw Dr. Whitman. He was returning from The Dalles.[4] He showed much displeasure at my arrival to these reaches. He spoke of religion, repeated the normal accusations against Catholics, reproached them for the alleged persecutions that the Protestants had endured at their hands & claimed that one need not be baptized to be a Christian; finally, that he knew why I had come: that Tawatoé had requested me, or rather that it was due to his influence that I had been elected Bishop of Walla Walla!![5] that he was going to oppose me with all his power; that he didn't like Catholics; and for this reason, would come to our aid with food only if we were starving.[6]

He set to work right away, heading for the lodge of Peopeomoxmox, Chief of the Walla Wallas, where he spoke most harshly of the Black Robes, if I can believe the report of an Indian who was there.[7] He asked the same chief to accompany him to the Cayuses & to The Dalles, but his wish was not granted.[8] It was readily apparent that this excursion had no purpose other than to dissuade the Indians from welcoming the missionaries. However, the doctor felt pressed to take yet a further stand. So, what does he do? Along with Reverend Spalding,[9] he goes to the site where the emigrants, emerging from the Blue Mountains, reach the Nehiaou River, a few miles above Young Chief's house; & why? to acquaint the Americans with his views of the missionaries, & bring them over to his side, if this were possible;[10] also to convince the Cayuses that the Black Robes are of no use. Dr. Crosby[11] along with an Irish man reported the substance of their speeches to Father Brouillet,[12] adding that Dr. Whitman had said aloud that *the priests' lives were in danger.*

Subsequently I saw the doctor on a number of occasions, somewhat more self-controlled, with the exception of when he appeared at the Fort with Tawatoé. After I had spoken with him for some time without making any progress, and explained the ladder as well, he was so beside himself that he told me, should he ever become a Catholic it would be only out of malice.[13]

A few days before I left the Fort, during the final week after Pentecost, I saw Reverends Spalding & Rodgers, who appeared to be gentlemen, not bearing the prejudices or fanaticism of the doctor.[14] On Saturday, November 27th, the day of our arrival, the doctor and Reverend Spalding had shown up as well. Dr. Whitman had paid me a visit that Sunday afternoon. I invited him to stay for our midday meal, but he declined the offer, fearing the delay and wanting to get home the same evening. I have since been told that he had been warned by a Cayuse that his life was in danger, in his very home. The next day Reverend Spalding had supper with us; gratified by the welcome I gave him, he was clearly ready to provide Father Brouillet with information about the Sahaptin language (Nez Percé).[15] In an earlier discussion, he had admitted ingenuously that in the last eleven years he had baptized twenty-two adults. He did not leave without inviting Father Brouillet to pay him a visit at his home.

It was Father Brouillet's plan first to visit the nearby Cayuses, then to call on those living close to the doctor, having heard that a great number of them were sick, & many dying.[16] On Tuesday, November 30th, he set out, but being waylaid by other Indians nearby who were ill, he did not arrive until evening. Alas, upon alighting from his horse, what mournful news!! He was told that the doctor, his wife & eight or nine Americans including Reverend Rodgers had been massacred the day before in the house, or outside, & that the bodies were still lying where they had fallen.[17] How painful the night must have been, obliged as he was to stay in the very lodge of an individual who was most embroiled in this wretched affair! Wednesday, he rushed on to shroud and bury the dead, & to visit the widows, children, and the orphans, numbering 45. He demanded that they be spared and cared for, then headed back in the direction of the mission, accompanied by the interpreter and Tilocate's son. He hadn't gone four miles when he met Reverend Spalding; this man begged for mercy through the interpreter; but Tilocate's son responded that he could not take it upon himself to spare him, that he needed to consult with the others, and he thereupon returned to the camp. Meanwhile, the Reverend managed to flee, placing his horses in the interpreter's care. Some Indians say they saw him on the Feast of the Immaculate Conception.[18]

On Thursday I summoned Tawatoé and his brother, Achekaia.[19] I expressed my contempt for this butchery, and told them I trusted they would do no harm to the women, children, and orphans, and would give them enough to eat, should they not be willing to let them go. Their response was *that they pitied them, would do them no harm, and that their lives would not change.*

What could have motivated this massacre? When I had met with the chiefs at Fort Walla Walla, Camaspelo (*Gros Ventre*) had said that as far as he was concerned, he would not force the doctor to leave. I told him I didn't ask that he do so, that the doctor could very well remain where he was, but that if he should leave, I would willingly buy his property. Very well, it was from this same chief that the order to kill everyone had come.[20]

I do not know the motive for this change of heart, but here is what the Cayuses say: Since the doctor has been with us, almost all of our chiefs' children and a great many others have gone to their graves. They counted thirty and some deaths in the same few months that measles and dysentery had entered their camp. The camp in question is in the vicinity of the doctor, so they accuse him of having poisoned the sick in his care. They also say that a few days earlier, in a discussion about the Indians, Reverends Wilbur & Spalding had ended up saying that very soon there would be no more Indians in Oregon, that these words were overheard by an Indian who understood English & who had given his report to the chiefs.[21] This is how they justify the massacre.

Their action seems to be a declaration of war against the Americans.

There is even talk of a coalition. Just how far will this go? I cannot say. I hope that a prudent governor will find the means for appeasing them without resorting to arms. Perhaps he will find the wisdom to investigate whether or not there is any truth to what appears to have motivated the butchery.

We must offer our many thanks to God for not having provided us the opportunity to live next to the doctor over the winter. We would have had the pain of witnessing the tragic scene, and some may have tried to blame us.

The Indians themselves realize that the missionaries could suffer from their act. They sense that we cannot live in a house stained with human blood; this explains why they resolved to burn it. I believe this was the best thing to do.

We will hasten to instill in them the principles of religion as a means of calming their temperament.[22] There is no other way to do this. Some are showing zeal to attend Father Brouillet's instructions. They very much like the chanting of the Canticles.[23] We will draw them increasingly in this way. McKay, the very person who did not think it wise to let me in Tawatoé's house before he returned, was one of the first to hearken and to learn the prayers, with all his family. He has a child in heaven who is praying for him. A few days before I arrived, Mr. Rousseau,[24] who was preparing the house, had been called to baptize the child. Recognizing he was sick, this child of about seven years of age had said to his father: "You see I am sick, don't let me die without having the Black Robes come to baptize me."[25] A few days later he was in heaven, where he is interceding for his nearby relatives and for the entire nation. There are a number of others, Cayuses as well as Walla Wallas, who have died after receiving baptism and who are going to assist us with their prayers. Father Brouillet has given himself entirely to studying the language. He has already translated the Lord's Prayer, the Hail Mary, the Creed and the beginning of the catechism.[26] Although he finds the language difficult, I have reason to believe that in a few months he will be handling it very well.

I am most affectionately, My dear *seigneur,*
Your devoted brother
Aug. M. Alex. Bp. of Walla Walla

AAS, A2: 45–48.

1. François Norbert Blanchet (1795–1883) arrived in the Oregon Country as one of the first two permanent Roman Catholic missionaries, on November 24, 1838. Upon receiving news from Rome that the Columbia District had been raised to an apostolic vicariate and that he had been named its bishop, he departed for the British Province of Canada and for Europe on December 5, 1844, and returned August 13, 1847, two weeks before his brother arrived at Fort Walla Walla. During this voyage, he helped secure the advancement of the Apostolic Vicariate of Oregon to an ecclesiastical province (which allowed for suffragan bishops to assist him), was named its archbishop, raised funds, and recruited sisters and priests. Confidants despite their differences in personality and skills, the two brothers communicated regularly. By the time this letter was written, the archbishop already had met Deacon Rousseau and Brother Blanchet (two clerics who had traveled with A. M. A. Blanchet to Oregon) during their trip downriver to gather supplies, and he had sent former trapper Louis Moukemine upriver to work as interpreter for his brother (Blanchet, *Journal of a Catholic Bishop*, 69, 71).

2. Marcus Whitman (1802–1847), a missionary physician sponsored by the Protestant American Board of Commissioners of Foreign Missions (ABCFM), established his mission at Waiilatpu in 1836, in the hope of helping convert Cayuses and Nez Percés to Christianity and transform them to a sedentary agricultural way of life. Stephen Dow Beckham, ed., *Oregon Indians: Voices from Two Centuries* (Corvallis: Oregon State University Press, 2006), 60; Jeffrey, *Converting the West*, 208–15; Jennifer Karson, ed., *Wiyáxayxt / Wiyáakaáawn / As Days Go By: Our History, Our Land, and Our People—the Cayuse, Umatilla, and Walla Walla* (Pendleton, Ore.: Tamástslikt Cultural Institute; Portland: Oregon Historical Society Press; Seattle: University of Washington Press, 2006), 64.

3. Consequences, including attempts to implicate the Catholic missionaries in the Whitman killings and restrictions on their missionary work, unfold in subsequent letters of this volume. See in particular letters 9 and 23.

4. "Very narrow passages of a river from which water escapes with a great force are called *dalles*. A number are found on the Columbia, the sides of which are mostly columns of basalt." "Mission de la Colombie," *Notice sur les Missions du Diocèse de Québec, qui sont secourues par l'Association de la Propagation de la Foi* (Notices on the Missions of the Diocese of Quebec, which are assisted by the Association of the Propagation of the Faith), no. 2 (1840): 18. One of the oldest inhabited locations in North America, The Dalles, on the Columbia River just east of the Cascade Mountains, was a center for Native American trade for at least ten thousand years; it was also an important point on the Oregon Trail. Whitman had become an eager advocate of establishing another station at The Dalles site, a surprising step "in light of the spiritual impasse at Waiilatpu" (Jeffrey, *Converting the West*, 209). During this trip to the site, he purchased a former Methodist mission on behalf of the ABCFM and left his nephew in charge.

5. Tawatoé (Young Chief) was among the chiefs of a Cayuse band living on the Umatilla River. He provided a house on his lands for Blanchet and his diocesan clerics, who moved in on November 27. Other Cayuse chiefs, Tilocate and Tamsucky, had lands at Waiilatpu, close to the Whitman Mission.

6. "He [Whitman] refused to sell wheat or anything else, though he had plenty. He told us

that, being Catholic priests, he would use every means to oppose us, but being men, if he found us reduced to starvation, he would prevent us from dying." Deacon Godefroi Rousseau quoted in Jacques Rousseau, M.S.R.C., "Caravane vers l'Orégon," *Les cahiers des dix* (Montreal), no. 30 (1965): 227. This article excerpts selections from letters that Rousseau sent to family members between January 10, 1846, and March 22, 1849. It provides a valuable second perspective on the Blanchet correspondence.

7. Peopeomoxmox was hereditary chief of the Sahaptin-speaking Walla Wallas who lived along the Columbia in the area of its confluence with the Walla Walla River, site of Fort Walla Walla, and east along the Walla Walla to its junction with the Touchet River. Early Catholic missionary Father Modeste Demers visited the chief and his people during the summers of 1838 and 1840, as did Methodists Henry Perkins and Daniel Lee. Peopeomoxmox groomed his son Elijah Hedding for succession as chief and sent him to the Willamette Mission school, where in 1843 he very likely made contact with John Sutter. A year later Elijah was murdered by a white man at Sutter's California fort while hunting and trading furs for cattle and wild horses with other plateau Indians, at Sutter's invitation. Upon return, in May, Peopeomoxmox presided over an inquiry that twenty to thirty chiefs held of Whitman, Spalding, and other mission personnel to consider whether Whitman was worthy of death, the outcome of which was a warning that though they would do no harm to the missionaries, their young men might. Robert Boyd, *People of The Dalles: The Indians of Wascopam Mission* (Lincoln: University of Nebraska Press, 1996), 336–39; Robert Ruby and John A. Brown, *The Cayuse Indians: Imperial Tribesmen of Old Oregon* (Norman: University of Oklahoma Press, 1972), 100. During the Yakima War of 1855, white volunteer troops killed Peopeomoxmox and mutilated his body (see letter 36). First used by Iroquois in New France to refer to Jesuit missionaries, the term "Blackrobes" (*Robes noires*) became generalized to refer to all Catholic priests. Catholic Iroquois from Montreal settled among the Flathead (Salish) beginning in the late eighteenth century. In one version of Pacific Northwest history, in 1831 the Iroquois Ignace La Mousse led a delegation of Flathead and Nez Percé to St. Louis seeking priests.

8. Called "Cailloux" (people of the stones/rocks) by French-speaking traders, the Cayuses were a strong, imperial tribe numbering some five hundred in 1780. They measured wealth primarily in horses. Their migration from areas farther south during the early nineteenth century extended their tribal lands across the upper reaches of the Walla Walla, Umatilla, and Grande Ronde Rivers of present-day Oregon and Washington; they controlled trade routes up the Snake River and participated in the HBC's trapping brigades. Disease contributed to their reduction to possibly as few as two hundred by 1841, and emigrant trails on their lands disrupted patterns of aboriginal trade and land use. Speakers originally of Waiilatpuan, they adopted the Sahaptin spoken by their more numerous neighbors, the Nez Percés, with whom they maintained close kinship and economic ties. Ruby and Brown, *The Cayuse Indians*, 3–20.

9. A missionary sponsored by the ABCFM, Henry Spalding (1803–1874) emigrated with the Whitmans to the Northwest, arriving in 1836. He established the Lapwai mission for the Nez Percés, on a site near present-day Lewiston, Idaho. According to the signed testimony of J. P. Poujade, Spalding met Poujade's arriving wagon train at Willow Spring at the foot of the Blue Mountains to warn him that "the Indians are getting very bad" and "[are] threatening to turn them out of the mission," for which he faulted the Catholic priests who had "put the Indians up

to kill all the American Protestants on the road to Oregon," and he advised the group to wait for a larger company, to assure its safety. J. B. A. Brouillet, *The Authentic Account of the Murder of Dr. Whitman and other missionaries, by the Cayuse Indians of Oregon in 1847 and the causes which led to the horrible catastrophe*, 2nd ed. (Portland, Ore.: S. J. McCormick, 1869), 89–90. Parts of this sectarian-inspired testimony are cited as well in Hubert Howe Bancroft, *History of Oregon*, vol. 1, *1834–1848* (San Francisco: History Company, 1886), 643.

10. Dr. Whitman frequently met and assisted emigrant parties, constructed a new "shorter & better" wagon road from the Umatilla to The Dalles, and in 1845 prevented hostile Walla Wallas and possibly Cayuses from attacking a large party of emigrants (Jeffrey, *Converting the West*, 212). In this instance Whitman may have warned emigrants of Catholic clerical presence. In light of ensuing events, Blanchet presented a single intent, overlooking other possible motivations on Whitman's part, such as highlighting the need for alertness given Indian hostility toward earlier caravans in the summer of 1847.

11. A physician traveling as part of an emigrant wagon train that reached Oregon on November 30, 1847, Dr. John Crosby (1794–1866) settled in Multnomah County and practiced medicine in Portland for the remainder of his life.

12. Jean-Baptiste Abraham Brouillet (1813–1884) was born and raised in the village of St.-Jean-Baptiste, now a suburb of Montreal. He attended the Upper and Lower Seminaries of St.-Hyacinthe and was ordained by Ignace Bourget in 1837. He taught philosophy at the Collège de Chambly, served as vicar in the parish of St.-Joseph-de-Chambly from 1837 to 1841, and helped edit the diocesan journal, *Mélanges religieux, scientifiques, politiques, et littéraires* (which published numerous articles on the Oregon missions). He was curé at St.-Georges-de-Henryville from 1842 to 1846 and of Ste.-Marguerite-de-l'Acadie from 1846 until his departure with A. M. A. Blanchet for Oregon, where he was serving as vicar-general of the Diocese of Walla Walla and missionary of St. Anne at the time this letter was written.

13. A pictorial means for presenting "salvation history"—the history of Christianity told from a theological perspective—the ladder, in its original form known as a Shale Stick (meaning "stick from heaven" in the Chinook jargon), was used to evangelize Indians by the first Catholic missionaries in the Oregon Territory, Fathers F. N. Blanchet and Modeste Demers. The term *ladder* derives from the successive marks moving from the bottom up, representing the 40 centuries before Jesus, the 33 years of his life, and (followed by a cross) more recent Christian history, depicted by 18 marks and 39 points. Demers gave a ladder to Peopeomoxmox during his visits in the summers of 1838 and 1840. For additional information, see Philip M. Hanley, "The Catholic Ladder and Missionary Activity in the Pacific Northwest" (master's thesis, University of Ottawa, 1965); and Kris A. White and Janice St. Laurent, "Mysterious Journey: The Catholic Ladder of 1840," *Oregon Historical Quarterly* 97, no. 1 (1996): 70–88.

14. Blanchet is referring here to the final week of Pentecost, the longest season of the Catholic liturgical year (worship cycle), starting with the Feast of Pentecost (celebration of the gift of the Holy Spirit to Jesus of Nazareth's disciples) fifty days after Easter (celebration of the resurrection of Jesus) and concluding with the beginning of Advent, the season before Christmas that begins each liturgical year.

15. The largest of the Sahaptin-speaking tribes, the Nez Percés lived in villages on the Clearwater River and its branches, in today's state of Idaho.

16. A hunting party to Fort Sutter in central California, led by Peopeomoxmox, is believed to have brought back measles in late July, from which the Plateau Indians were suffering; it appears unlikely that Oregon Trail emigrants carried the disease to the Plateau Indians. Robert Boyd, *The Coming of the Spirit of Pestilence: Introduced and Infectious Diseases and Population Decline among Northwest Coast Indians, 1774–1874* (Vancouver: University of British Columbia Press; Seattle: University of Washington Press, 1999), 146–48.

17. Andrew Rodgers, of Missouri, taught American immigrants at the mission. He was killed at the same time as Narcissa Whitman, with whom he had a close friendship. Blanchet does not seem to be aware that he was not a minister.

18. Tilocate was headman of a band of Cayuses neighboring the Whitman Mission. He was implicated in the Whitman killings by the territorial government, though there was no proof of his involvement, and was one of five executed for the killings (Karson, *As Days Go By*, 64). See letter 3. Catholics commemorate the conception of Mary, mother of Jesus, on December 8. Increasing emphasis on the "immaculate" nature of her conception strengthened the importance of this feast. See letter 11.

19. "In the early 1840s Chief Five Crows (Achekaia) was reputed to be the richest man in the country, possessing upwards of a thousand horses, cattle, many slaves, and five wives." According to reports, at one point he dismissed his wives in order to seek the hand of the daughter of one of the HBC officers and was rebuffed (Ruby and Brown, *The Cayuse Indians*, 59). In 1852, Five Crows would assist with the restoration of Catholic missions among Cayuses at St. Anne and would donate lands for the establishment of St. Rose of Lima and funds for pews.

20. In a marginal note of this letter, Blanchet wrote, "I have since learned that Gros Ventre had given neither order nor consent. A. M. Bl., Bp. W.W." Camaspelo (Gros Ventre), brother-in-law of Tilocate and chief of another Cayuse Umatilla camp, warned Whitman of the plot to kill him when Whitman came to assist his sick child. George W. Fuller, *History of the Pacific Northwest* (New York: Alfred A. Knopf, 1947), 146.

21. James Harvey Wilbur (1811–1887), a Methodist minister, appointed missionary to Oregon in 1846, worked as missionary and educator in the Portland and Umpqua regions until he assumed the post of superintendent of education for the Yakama Reservation (Fort Simcoe) in 1860 and then agent there in 1862. Known for his commitment to eradicating Catholicism from the territory and from among the Indians in the name of Methodism, Wilbur served in various capacities at Simcoe almost continuously from 1860 to 1880. Robert E. Ficken, *Washington Territory* (Pullman: Washington State University Press, 2002), 65–66. See also letters 24 and 28.

22. By principles of religion, Blanchet is alluding here to traditional Christian teachings of compassion for sinners, repentance, and forgiveness, as replacement for vengeance.

23. The Canticles are prayers based on Scripture and were traditionally chanted as part of the "hours" of the Divine Office (daily prayer cycle) of the Roman Catholic Church. Priests generally translated them into local indigenous dialects.

24. Louis-Pierre Godefroi Rousseau (1823–1852), born in St.-Henri-de-Lauzon, across the St. Lawrence from Quebec City, was one of eleven children in a family of very modest means; three of the children became priests; three, nuns; and two, doctors. He attended schools in Nicolet and Ste.-Anne-de-la-Pocatière and was studying at the Seminary of Montreal, where he was ordained deacon, before he departed with A. M. A. Blanchet for Oregon.

25. Blanchet reports the baptism of the McKay child in his *Journal* entry dated November 28, 1847. He speaks there of a daughter. The baptism of the father, Ignace Stocouli, surname McKay, second chief of the Cayuses, is recorded February 13, 1848, in the baptismal registry of St. Anne. Blanchet, *Journal of a Catholic Bishop*, 78, 131; "Missions of St. Ann and St. Rose of the Cayouse (1847–1888)," in *Catholic Church Records of the Pacific Northwest*, vol. 7, edited by Harriet D. Munnick and Adrian R. Munnick (Portland, Ore.: Binford and Mort Publishing, ca. 1989), 10–11–12. This pagination in the volume replicates the pagination of the original church registry.

26. The catechism comprises Catholic prayers and compilations of questions with answers that summarize basic Catholic Christian doctrine. The catechism was translated so that those being evangelized could be taught in their own language.

LETTER 3

To Célestin Gauvreau, Vicar-General, Superior, College of Ste.-Anne-de-la-Pocatière, [January] 1848[1]

On January 2, three weeks after writing his brother and in the company of the HBC personnel who had come to rescue the Waiilatpu hostages, Bishop Blanchet with Deacon Rousseau and Father Ricard, O.M.I., accompanied the survivors, mostly widows and children, to Fort Vancouver and Oregon City. In an attempt to avert war, Blanchet delivered letters from the Cayuses to George Abernethy, Oregon provisional governor, requesting peace in exchange for surrender of the guilty, but the first armed volunteers had departed for the upper country before he reached Oregon City. The three clerics then proceeded south to St. Paul on the Willamette, where the archbishop, François Blanchet, resided, arriving on January 15.

There, while waiting for hostilities to end, Blanchet wrote a series of nineteen letters to a friend who was grand vicar of the Archdiocese of Quebec, telling of his overland journey and arrival in Oregon. This is the eighteenth of that series of letters. Later, Blanchet revised and compressed the series into six, which were published in Quebec in 1851.[2] Given the departure of many Canadiens at this time to search for gold in western regions of North America, the story of his overland journey and first weeks after arrival would have generated considerable interest.

Drawing on the timeline and text of his journal to relate the first weeks in the Oregon Country, this letter reveals the optimism of the newly arrived Catholic clerics before the Whitman killings. Noteworthy are Blanchet's perceptions of the hospitality of HBC employees and of the Columbia Plateau Indians' desire to have Catholic priests as well as the relative ease with which he located the first mission sites for the new diocese. Already familiar with the geography and the indigenous people from the correspondence of his brother and of Father Demers, Blanchet had a sense of belonging in what he had envisioned as his place of ministry.

St. Paul on the Wallamet, [January] 1848

Ad Majorem Dei Gloriam[3]

Father,

On September 5th, the very day of my arrival, Peopeomoxmox, the Great Chief of the Walla Wallas, paid me a visit. The Canadiens[4] call him *Serpent Jaune* [Yellow Snake], even though the name translates as Yellow Bird. The chief told me that the true name of his nation is Wallôlla. I seized this opportunity to talk with him about a mission for his nation. He had recently lost his wife & a child. He told me that his heart was sick. I offered him some words of consolation & encouragement, & finally told him that I intended to establish missions among nations that wanted them, & that I would be pleased to begin with the nation that was the namesake of my diocese.

He came back the next day, appearing less hesitant to accept my offer than the day before. Sorry to see that I was considering residence among the Cayuses, he seemed to want me to settle on his land, but did not tell me where I might find a suitable location.

SEPTEMBER 6TH

It had been three weeks since I last observed the Holy Sacrifice of the Mass.[5] On September 6th I had the pleasure of celebrating it for the first time in my diocese. The altar was set up in the dining room of the Fort. Mr. McBean, his family, and all the Catholics attended with much reverence.[6] How might

I relate the experience of saying Mass for the first time in my own diocese after a trek of five and a half months! How might I witness before God all the gratitude we owe Him for the many favors He granted us during our voyage! Faith must be livened, recalling the untainted Lamb who sacrificed Himself on the cross, and who at each Mass renews the offering He made to the Holy Father on Calvary, by which He fully and superabundantly atoned for us all through Him.

SEPTEMBER 11TH

Reverend Father Ricard was anxious to know where he might settle with his brothers.[7] On the eleventh he left with Great Chief's brother and the Fort interpreter to visit the Yakamas and see about settling on the Yakima River.[8] As he came to a spot a few miles from the mouth of the river, he found several lodges of Walla Wallas. These Indians invited him to settle among them and promised to bring logs for buildings down by way of Priest's Rapids. (Priest's Rapids is named for a local Indian who was known for preaching to passers-by, undoubtedly in order to obtain a few pinches of tobacco or the like.) On this same day several Indians said they intended to go in search of the logs. They so urged him not to look farther that he felt compelled to say he would remain. He returned to the Fort, his heart overcome with joy and consolation. A few days later Yellow Bird gave him a fair expanse of land forming a peninsula several miles in length between the Columbia and the Tchamnappen River (known as the Yakima).

SEPTEMBER 13TH

When I first arrived at the Fort, Mr. McBean told me that on August 31st, Reverend Father Joset[9] had planted a cross along the shore of the Youmatallam River on the land belonging to Tawatoé (Young Chief), with the intent of building a chapel there.[10] He also informed me that the chief had been requesting priests for a number of years. I was already aware that he intended to offer his house to the missionaries. Although I knew that Young Chief was still on a hunting expedition in the mountains, I was impatient to see what the house was like & if it would be suitable for occupancy once the wagons arrived.

Mr. McBean insisted on accompanying me, along with his interpreter.

It was a forty-mile trip. After riding for six and a half hours, we came to the cross that Reverend Father Joset had planted. It was leaning over considerably. I asked the Indians how this had happened. Their answer was that some Americans had tried to knock it down.

Young Chief's house was built seven years ago by Mr. Pambrun, who had charge of Fort Walla Walla at the time.[11] Measuring twenty by thirty feet, it was built of squared timbers. The roof and walls had been plastered with mud, but little remained, so the timbers were all exposed. I decided to stay there anyway & that evening I called upon the Indians who claimed to be guardians of their chief's property. What then was my surprise when they objected to my staying there before the return of their chief! Their reasons seemed nothing but pretexts. Mr. McBean, who was fully aware of the arrangements Tawatoé had made, could not get over his surprise; just before leaving, Tawatoé had informed him through a Walla Walla named Patakwi that, should the priests arrive before he returned, they could take his house and all the land they wanted.[12] We returned to the Fort the next day, taking our midday meal near sunset.

I was disappointed, but quickly consoled myself, thinking that God must want me to be elsewhere, or at least to postpone my settling. As it happened, God inspired me with the idea of uniting all the Cayuses together into a single mission; and meanwhile, to assemble the chiefs in order to discuss this idea & to locate the mission wherever they wanted.

Young Chief showed up at the Fort on October 26th, a few days after he had returned from hunting. He assured me that he would welcome the priests on his lands and give them his house. I then conferred with him about my idea of a single mission. It appealed to him right away, and he even suggested that we settle near Dr. Whitman where most of the Cayuses were located, saying that he would go there himself with his followers; he added that he had a right to Tilocate's land through his wife, and that if this chief consented, he was prepared to donate some of it. I thereupon sent for Camaspelo and Tilocate.

NOV. 4TH

They arrived at the Fort on November 4th, accompanied by some of their followers. The palaver went on for quite some time. Tilocate, who was Dr. Whitman's right-hand man and taken for a Protestant, put a great many questions before me: "If it was the pope who had sent me; if he had told me to ask for land; how priests made a living in my country, that is to say, who provides for their keep; if the priests would give presents to the Indians; if they would make them plow their land; if they would help them build houses; if they would feed & clothe the poor, &c." He listened very attentively to all I had to say in response. He said that his followers would comply with whatever he decided, & concluded that he would not go against the word of Tawatoé (Young Chief), and would give some land for the mission.

A few days later, Father Brouillet visited the land that had been offered, with the intent of selecting a site for the mission & chapel. He found Tilocate & his followers very hospitable. The latter appeared even more anxious to have priests, but said they were trying to get Dr. Whitman to leave. They proposed that Father Brouillet build a little house for the winter wherever he liked, and that come spring, he could have the doctor's house and all his property in time to plant crops. Unwilling to accept such a plan, Father Brouillet lost no time notifying Young Chief that we would take his house.

On November 11th, Mr. Rousseau left with some men to see to repairing, or rather, to rebuilding it. Returning on the 26th, he reported that it was ready for occupancy though much remained to be done.

Father Brouillet, Mr. Leclaire[13] and I parted on the 27th, and by four o'clock that afternoon, we had covered the forty miles & I was in my provisional palace.

The house had been plastered with mud inside and out, the windows as well, the floor repaired, doors made, roof installed, chimneys raised to just above the roof, . . . some mats here and there. We were sheltered from the weather; this was almost a home, we were happy. Mr. Rousseau, who had remained at the Fort to arrange for transporting the luggage, arrived at St. Anne on December 1st toward three in the afternoon. By evening, everything was in place.[14]

This letter is long enough, & perhaps too long, but I wanted to finish telling about my new residence.

I am &c.
Aug. M. Alex. Bp. of Walla Walla

AAS, A3: 55–57.

1. Seminary classmate of A. M. A. Blanchet, Célestin Gauvreau (1799–1862) was ordained in 1824, after pastoral work in Quebec and New Brunswick. He became professor of theology at the Seminary of Quebec in 1836 and then vicar-general of the diocese in 1843.

2. *Rapport sur Les Missions du Diocèse de Québec et autres qui ont ci-devant fait partie* (Report on the Missions of the Diocese of Quebec and others that have hitherto been a part), no. 9 (1851): 1–28. The *Rapport* was a publication of the Quebec archdiocese's branch of the Society for the Propagation of the Faith. Copies of letters written by A. M. A. Blanchet and J. B. A. Brouillet relative to the killings at the Whitman Mission and their aftermath (see letter 9) also were published in issue 8 of the same journal in 1849 and in *Mélanges religieux*, August 8, 1848.

3. Translated from the Latin as "To the Greater Glory of God," this phrase was a common heading in clerical letters and was often abbreviated as *A.M.D.G.*

4. An early French explorers' term for indigenous peoples of the St. Lawrence Valley, *Canadiens* came to designate peoples of French descent born in British North America, and eventually took on connotations of resistance to British domination. Many Canadiens in the Oregon Country were métis, descendents of French-speaking fur trade employees and Indian women.

5. The Mass is a central Catholic liturgical ritual that, at the time, was conceived primarily as an unbloody reenactment of the death of Jesus of Nazareth. During the Mass the priest says prayers over bread and wine, which, within Catholic ritual and theological understanding, become, in essence, the body and blood of Christ.

6. William McBean (1790–1872) served as chief trader of Fort Walla Walla from 1846 to 1851. Likely born at the Lake Superior post of Folle Avoine of a mother of mixed Cree descent and a father of mixed Scotch and Canadien descent, he was briefly educated in Montreal before serving as interpreter and then as clerk at various HBC posts in New Caledonia (British Columbia), where in 1834 he married Jeanne Boucher, also of mixed descent. Bruce McIntyre Watson, *Lives Lived West of the Divide: A Bibliographical Dictionary of Fur Traders Working West of the Rockies, 1793–1858*, 3 vols. (Kelowna: Centre for Social, Spatial, and Economic Justice, University of British Columbia, Okanagan, 2010), 2:634–35.

7. Pascal Ricard, O.M.I. (1805–1862), was superior of the five Oblates of Mary Immaculate who left Marseilles on February 1, 1847, and joined Bishop A. M. A. Blanchet in St. Louis, shortly before they began their trek over the Oregon Trail. See letter 15, note 2, regarding their work among the Yakamas and subsequently with other Indians.

8. The Yakamas were one of the most numerous of the Sahaptin-speaking people. Their traditional lands included the watershed of the Yakima River, a primary watercourse in central and south-central Washington. The difference in spelling between the names of the tribe and the river is still maintained.

9. Born in Berne, Switzerland, Joseph Joset (1810–1900) entered the Jesuit Order in 1830 and was ordained in Fribourg in 1840. He arrived in St. Louis, Missouri, in 1843 and the following year was sent to the Mission of the Rocky Mountains, where he served as superior general from 1846 to 1849, succeeding Peter De Smet, S.J. His first station was at St. Paul Mission near Colville and, after 1857, at Sacred Heart Mission, where he was known as "the apostle of the Coeur d'Alenes." Catholic missionaries erected crosses to indicate areas they had evangelized and claimed for Christ and the Church.

10. This is Blanchet's phonetic rendition of the English pronunciation of the name Umatilla, for the river located in northeastern Oregon. There was no uniform spelling at the time.

11. Born in Vaudreuil, near Quebec, Pierre Pambrun (1792–1841) entered the employ of the HBC in 1815 and arrived at Fort Vancouver in 1826. Appointed chief clerk of Fort Walla Walla in 1832, he advanced to chief trader in 1833. A Roman Catholic noted for his skilled management of affairs, hospitality, Catholic instruction of Indians, and friendship with the Whitmans and Spaldings, he was killed in an accident with a horse, May 5, 1841.

12. According to Deacon Rousseau's correspondence, Young Chief had been promised priests for several years, and had stayed behind from the annual buffalo hunt the year before in order to greet them upon arrival, but no longer trusting the promises, he had decided to join the hunt in 1847, leaving orders with his young men to welcome any priests and provide the house should they arrive. Rousseau further understood that, since then, it was Dr. Whitman himself who dissuaded the young men from providing the house and who gave the order to overturn the cross that Reverend Father Joset had planted next to it. Rousseau, "Caravane," 227.

13. A native of Montreal, Guillaume Leclaire (1821–1893) accompanied Blanchet to Walla Walla as a seminarian. He remained with Father Brouillet at the Umatilla mission of St. Anne after the Waiilatpu killings, until the mission had to be suspended because of the Cayuse War. He was ordained a priest on October 21, 1849.

14. The name St. Anne, for the mother of Mary, was given to this first mission in the Diocese of Walla Walla.

LETTER 4

To Members of the Councils of the Society for the Propagation of the Faith, Lyons and Paris, [March] 1848[1]

Blanchet was not idle during his time at St. Paul on the Willamette. In addition to assisting with pastoral duties and writing letters, he continued to discharge his responsibilities as bishop by seeking resources and planning for a return to his diocese of Walla Walla, after the conflict between settlers and Cayuses slackened.

This communication, written less than three months after his arrival in St. Paul, is one of many letters of solicitation, in addition to annual reports, that Bishop Blanchet sent throughout his tenure to the principal funding association for Catholic missions in the United States and throughout other parts of the world. The letter calls attention to a possible oversight on the part of the society, describes his helplessness in a new diocese without its support, and explains why this is an opportune moment for the society to contribute generously to travel expenses for bringing additional missionaries. It omits any mention of the ongoing strife between settlers and Indians in his diocese.

Recorded notes from the society's meetings reveal that the letter's arguments led to a recommendation for an increase from 8,000 francs finally allocated for the years 1847 and 1848 to 15,000 francs (roughly $3,000 then and $85,500 today), out of a total of 634,087 francs allocated to all missions throughout the Americas for 1849.[2]

St. Paul, [March] 1848

A.M.D.G.

Gentlemen,

I had been dismayed to read in your response to the letter I sent from Montreal on October 20th 1846 that you would be unable to draw from your reserve funds on my behalf. I had consoled myself, however, in reading that you would likely come to my aid in the spring of 1847.

Since I left Canada, I have been waiting for news of your decisions. Having still heard nothing, I am deeply concerned.

What would happen if I were left to my own resources? As you know, everything in my diocese remains to be done. There is neither chapel nor house for the missionaries. Provisions must be transported at great expense over a distance of more than three hundred miles. Visits and other necessary travel also require funds. Add the expense of building chapels, of devotional objects, of lodging the missionaries. You are aware of all this, I need not describe the details. I rely on your wisdom, fully aware that you are committed to providing for new missions.

I am consoled to report that since my arrival, several Indian nations have emerged from the state of torpor in which they were living. The Walla Wallas, the Cayuses, the Yakamas, the people of The Dalles & the Nez Percés have all requested *Black Robes*. The harvest appears to be ripe but I lack workers to gather it in.[3] Generous donations from the society would put me in a position to give the bread of the Word to all those who earnestly seek it.[4] This is a most opportune moment, because the Presbyterian Ministers along with others have fallen into disfavor among the Indians. I would like to benefit from this moment, to thwart any desire they may have once again to mislead yet more of these poor children of nature. A few additional missionaries will give me that capability. The glory shall be yours.

I am, respectfully &c.
[A. M. A. Blanchet, Bp. of Walla Walla]

AAS, A2: 71–72.

———•———

1. A marginal note in the letterbook records that this letter was sent to both Antoine (le baron) de Jessé, President, Central Council of Lyons, and Alphonse de la Bouillerie, President, Central Council of Paris. The Oeuvre de la Propagation de la Foi (The Society for the Propagation of the Faith) was formally established when, at an instigation of Monsignor Louis Guillaume Valentin Dubourg, bishop of New Orleans, and his vicar-general, a group of industrialists of Lyons voted in 1822 to assume Pauline Jaricot's "Réparatrices du Sacré Coeur de Jésus." Pauline Jaricot, daughter of an industrialist, had begun her Réparatrices in 1818 to support missions in non-Catholic countries and the spiritual welfare of postrevolutionary workers during a period of rapid industrialization. Miss Jaricot's Réparatrices du Sacré Coeur de Jésus consisted of networks of groups of ten persons each that met weekly for prayer, to read missionary letters, and to donate the sou (penny) expected of each member. The Society for the Propagation of the Faith was consecrated by Pius VII in 1823 and quickly reached beyond the borders of France; its publication of missionary letters in the *Annales* offered geographical, spiritual, and anthropological information on foreign lands. In 1922 the society and three others were placed under the international umbrella organization of the Oeuvres Pontificales Missionnaires, and they are still active today.

2. "Procès verbaux," Conseil Central de Lyon, 1849, 69, Archives des Oeuvres Pontificales Missionnaires, Lyons, France (hereafter cited as OPM). The currency conversion is based on the consumer price index and is for the year 2010. MeasuringWorth.com, http://www.measuring-worth.com/uscompare.

3. This phrase refers to Matthew 9:37–38: "The harvest is good but laborers are scarce. Beg the harvest master to send out laborers to gather the harvest."

4. "Bread of the word" refers to the gospel or message about Jesus as life-giving food.

List of Items the Bishop of Walla Walla Requested of Bishop Demers, [March 1848][1]

St. Paul, the temporary home of Blanchet and other missionary personnel during unrest east of the Cascades, was located amid well-established French Canadian and métis farmlands along the banks of the Willamette River. It was these earliest settlers, mostly retirees from the HBC, who initially had requested priests in 1834. The Catholic church in St. Paul was one of only three brick buildings in the entire region. Close by, resident Jesuits ran a school for boys, and the Sisters of Notre Dame de Namur maintained a girls' convent school. Since the archbishop's return from Europe in August 1847, with additional clergy and sisters, the community had witnessed one celebration after another, including on November 30 the solemn consecration of Father Modest Demers as bishop of Vancouver Island. On March 12, Bishop Demers joined the spring fur express (brigade) en route to Quebec. After raising funds in Quebec he departed for Europe to seek more funds and missionaries for his diocese. A. M. A. Blanchet's request for ecclesial vestments and objects, to be purchased in Paris, was one of many documents and letters packed in the bags of the newly consecrated bishop.

Though it may seem contradictory for someone who has just complained of insufficient funds to be ordering vestments and ornaments, for Blanchet and his missionaries these items were essential to Catholic life. In rural settlements and villages, the regular peal of church bells and the sharing of uniform sacramental rituals linked the everyday drudgery of survival to the eternal and supernatural and served as reminders of devotional commitments. Used in ritual practices and celebrations in Rome, Quebec, Paris, Baltimore, and St. Paul, these items bound the faithful and their missionaries to the church universal, at once a supernatural and a global, cosmopolitan entity. In requesting these supplies, Blanchet is anticipating within his own diocese a cathedral church in a populous settler community such as St. Paul, as well as missionary chapels.

1. Three or four pieces of black fabric for summer cassocks.[2]

2. Two pieces of black woolen fabric for winter cassocks.

3. One piece of purple fabric for summer cassock.

4. Purple woolen fabric for two winter cassocks.

5. Six pieces of linen for surplices, albs, &c.[3]

6. Purple ribbon for two or three cinctures.

7. White, red, purple, and black narrow ribbon, for various uses.

8. Three pieces of printed calico, for curtains.

9. A few pieces of tapestry for the altar, &c.

10. Durable black woolen cinctures for the ecclesiastics.[4]

11. *St. Liguori Compendium* by Neyraguet.[5]

12. Six reams of good letter paper.

13. Three bells for churches, one weighing 450 lb., two weighing 200 lb.

14. Six small bells for churches, one font, one violin.[6]

15. Red velvet, three rods. One instrument of peace.[7]

16. Four corpora for processional crosses.[8]

17. Six small copper candelabra for a chapel, 15 to 18 inches in height.

18. Two small wood stoves 2 feet in height, sheet metal for pipes. Two monstrances, twelve to eighteen inches in height.[9]

18. Phials for holy oils similar to those of His Lordship the Archbishop.[10]

19. Medals of the Sacred Hearts of Jesus and Mary: 6 gross.[11]

20. Abbé Pascal's *Liturgical Dictionary.*[12]

AAS, A2: 72.

---

1. Modeste Demers (1809–1871), a priest from the Diocese of Quebec, served the Red River mission of St. Boniface in today's Manitoba and came to the Oregon Country with Father François Norbert Blanchet in 1838. He was consecrated bishop of Vancouver Island on November 30, 1847.

2. A cassock is an ankle-length garment with a fitted waist and fuller skirt worn by clergy.

3. A surplice is a knee-length vestment worn over the cassock during a liturgical service; an alb, an ankle-length, white garment with narrow sleeves, is also worn by clerics at liturgical services.

4. Ecclesiastics include all men ordained to serve the church—deacons, priests, and bishops.

5. The *St. Liguori Compendium* is a summary of the writings of Saint Alphonsus Liguori

(1696–1787; beatified in 1816) of Naples. Missionary, theologian, and founder in 1732 of the Congregation of the Most Holy Redeemer (Redemptorists) for work among the poor, he emphasized a forgiving, personal Christ of the Passion in reaction both to Enlightenment deism and to rigorist or "Jansenist" emphasis on a distant Christ of judgment and punishment. Espoused by Rome and ultramontane circles in France, including Eugène de Mazenod, founder of the Oblates of Mary Immaculate, and Frederick Ozaman, founder of the Society of St. Vincent de Paul, Liguori's work encouraged the practice of confession and frequent Communion as aids to regeneration and criticized the "Gaulist," more rigorist orientation officially endorsed by the Church in France and elsewhere. Ordering this work signaled Blanchet's desire to consult Liguori on questions of absolution, as well as his own ultramontane stance, which aligned him with the majority of clergy of the United States and Canada, including his mentor, Bishop Bourget.

6. A. M. A. Blanchet liked music, played the violin, and wanted instrumentally accompanied singing at services. He also sang Gregorian chant.

7. The instrument of peace was a small, oblong metal plaque about the width of a hand, bearing the image of the Crucified Jesus or of Mary with Child in relief. The priest presiding at a mass wore the instrument by sliding a band attached to its back over the third, fourth, and fifth fingers—the three that were not needed to hold the host. After consecrating the bread, the priest presented the instrument to the offerer, saying, "Pax tecum" (Peace be with you). This custom has long since been abandoned. *Le Grand heritage: L'Eglise catholique et les arts au Québec* (Quebec: Musée du Québec, 1984), 351; Jean Simard, *Les Arts sacrés au Québec* (Quebec: Editions de Montague, 1989), 168.

8. The corpus, a rendition of the crucified body of Jesus of Nazareth, usually was made of a precious metal, such as silver or bronze, and was attached to a wooden cross, in this case one made locally. At the start of Mass the celebrant's assistant carried the cross while proceeding up the center aisle, then placed it near the altar where it was visible to all participants. This practice continued throughout the nineteenth century. L'abbé R. Aigrain, *Liturgia: Encyclopédie populaire des connaissances liturgiques* (Paris: Bloud and Gay, 1931), 201–4.

9. The number 18 repeats in the original. A monstrance is a mounted receptacle used to display the consecrated host for adoration. The portion touching the host, called the lunule, is constructed of gold or silver; the visible sides are often of glass. The monstrance is topped with a small cross. It is distinguished from the ciborium, a bowl-shaped container with a domed cover, used to store consecrated hosts for the celebration of Mass (Aigrain, *Liturgia*, 308–9).

10. Receptacles are used to preserve and carry three different oils: the first, known as chrism, for the sacraments of baptism, confirmation, and ordination; the second, for anointing catechumens; and the third, for anointing the sick. The phials, often in the form of simple drinking flasks, were traditionally made of silver or pewter and had close-fitting lids. In requesting receptacles like those of the archbishop, Blanchet may be indicating a desire not to receive the mass-produced, plated vessels that some manufacturers in France had begun to make during the Industrial Revolution (Aigrain, *Liturgia*, 309).

11. Medals with religious images, such as the Sacred Heart of Jesus and the Immaculate Heart of Mary, are distributed as reminders and aids to devotion, prayer, or other forms of private, nonliturgical worship. They are worn on a chain or cord around the neck, pinned to clothing, or carried in pockets.

12. Liturgy refers to the complex of public rites, ceremonies, prayers, and sacraments of the church, in contrast to private devotions. Uniform adherence to Roman liturgy was an important component of nineteenth-century ultramontanism. The book Blanchet appears to be requesting was first published in 1844 and enjoyed numerous editions thereafter: *Origines et raison de la liturgie catholique en forme de dictionnaire, ou notions historiques et descriptives sur les rites et le cérémonial de l'office divin, les sacrements, les fêtes, la hiérarchie, les édifices*, trans. Jean Baptiste Etienne Pascal (Paris: chez l'édituer, 1844). The translation was from an earlier Italian edition by Gabriel Avédikian.

LETTER 6

To James Buchanan, Secretary of State, March 31, 1848[1]

The list of liturgical items that Blanchet requested in letter 5 evoked visions of a settled diocese that belied local political reality. Rumors circulated in the Willamette Valley of a federal law that prohibited settlement among Indians by whites without executive authorization. Given the anti-Catholic bias of some leaders in the provisional government and their attempts to implicate Blanchet and his clerics in the Waiilatpu killings, it was not unreasonable to fear that, should the Oregon Country become a federal territory, they might use such a law to prevent Catholics from establishing Indian missions. In that case, work in the Diocese of Walla Walla and districts of Fort Hall and Colville—the mission of St. Anne among the Cayuses, the Jesuit missions in the Rocky Mountains, and the new Oblate missions among the Yakamas— would be brought to a halt.

Although President James Polk did not sign the bill to designate the Oregon Country as a federal territory until August 14, 1848, by March, when Blanchet wrote this letter, most persons assumed Oregon would be made a territory. Congress had been hotly debating the issue since 1844, and Oregon settlers had sent numerous memorials requesting adoption, but the slow process of settling the border issue with Great Britain, and Southern opposition to the stipulation making Oregon a free soil territory, held up legislation. Another memorial and reactions to the Whitman killings finally prompted approval.[2]

Blanchet wrote this letter with the assumption that adoption was imminent, making federal law the law of the new Oregon Territory, and consequently the need for government authorization to carry on Indian missions likely. The significance of the issues addressed in the letter called on Blanchet's experience with how the French Canadian bishops exercised political leadership under British rule in his homeland.

Blanchet had already written to Buchanan from Pittsburgh on his voyage west, to request a copy of U.S. laws, and he had received a response in St. Louis.[3] Now, in this second letter to Buchanan, Blanchet introduces himself as an adopted American, having while in Pittsburgh, along with the other clerics who accompanied him, declared his intention to become a citizen.[4] Ostensibly, this letter is an argument, on the part of fellow overland immigrants, for federal adoption of Oregon, a position strongly favored by Buchanan. It also provides the secretary of state firsthand accounts related to the Waiilatpu killings, intended to forestall attempts by others in Washington, D.C., to implicate Blanchet's clergy in them. The desire to receive executive authority for missions ("liberty to proceed")—a means, Blanchet explains, for avoiding another Waiilatpu misfortune—is not alluded to until the final sentence. Blanchet forwarded this letter to the Right Reverend Peter Richard Kenrick, bishop of St. Louis, requesting that he have "a priest who resides near the Executive, and that you know is able to represent the interests of the religion, present it."[5] Kenrick, who had lodged Blanchet for twelve days during his trip west, at this time had jurisdiction over lands that extended west and north abutting territory for which Blanchet was responsible. Blanchet assumed that Kenrick shared his concerns about Native Americans and knew that he had appropriate contacts in Washington, D.C. Blanchet also sent another, briefer letter directly to Buchanan that explicitly requested official authorization for Indian missions.[6]

We have found no record of a response, but indirect evidence that Blanchet's correspondence reached the capital is found in the bishop's letter of July 14, 1849 (letter 10), in which he recounts newly appointed Territorial Governor Joseph Lane's warm support for the Catholic missions.

St. Paul on the Wallamet, March 31st 1848

Honorable Sir,

I am eager to seize this first opportunity to write to you & through you, to inform the President of the Union of my voyage to Oregon, of details concerning my residency here, and of the deplorable events that have taken place since.

I departed from Westport on May 12th, along with Missionaries from Canada & France. We traveled alongside emigrants from the States, and our wagons did not reach Fort Walla Walla until October 6th. It is difficult to imagine the misery, weariness, disgust, tedium, and discouragement of most of the families that we saw along the way, occasioned by the length of the trip, sickness, extreme heat, dust, the exhaustion of the animals & the death of many.[7] Will the benefits of the Oregon Territory compensate for all this suffering? That is for the emigrants to say. But what I can say for certain is that in return for their suffering and losses, the emigrants should certainly be entitled to the paternal protection of the Union government. This they cannot be denied.

At Fort Hall, three missionaries and I joined the Hudson's Bay Company brigade so as to locate suitable mission sites before the wagons arrived.[8] We reached Walla Walla on September 5th, after twenty days of travel. After a preliminary survey, I decided that one group of missionaries would settle north of the Columbia on or near the Yakima River; & that the others would start a mission among the Cayuses near the camp of Tawatoé (or Young Chief), who had been requesting priests for many years. This chief is head of the entire nation, and he had set aside a house for the missionaries. He was hunting when we arrived, so I was obliged to wait until he returned. Assuring me upon his return that he held the priests in high esteem, he made the house available to me. The friendly inclinations of nearly all the Cayuses prompted me to have it repaired right away. It was not until November 27th, however, that a few missionaries and I were finally able to move in. The house was neither a royal castle nor a manor, but thanks to the dry mud that served as shingles, plaster, and mortar for the chimneys, I found myself sheltered from the weather. What more could I have asked for? I rejoiced with my priests that we could begin our work of bringing redemption and civilization to the Indians.

Alas! Just two days later, the dreadful scene of Waiilatpu took place, inspired by the enemy of the human race, this in spite of his many losses (thanks to the preaching of the Gospel of Jesus Christ our Savior) in this empire where he had once held reign.

The detailed report that my vicar general, Father Brouillet, addressed to Colonel Gilliam & that I attach, will fully inform you of this catastrophe.[9] To say anything more positive would be a lie. The captives' rescue at the end of December by the Hudson's Bay Company, my own efforts & earlier measures to spare the captives' lives, and the chiefs' present inclinations and desire to negotiate peace, were all documented mid-January in the *Oregon Spectator* so I am not describing them here.[10]

Though the Cayuse chiefs all convened to make proposals for Governor Abernethy, their cooperation does not imply that they all participated in the murders.[11] Tawatoé and Camaspelo most definitely were not involved, nor were their followers, whose lodges were some twenty-five miles from Waiilatpu, close to the house where I was living. The followers of Tilocate who lived next to Doctor Whitman were the only ones involved, and not all of them, since some helped spare the lives of Americans.

If the followers of the innocent chiefs took up arms to resist the volunteers, they clearly did so only because they feared that the volunteers intended to take their entire nation; when they heard that this was not so, they dissociated themselves from the murderers & have stopped fighting Colonel Gilliam's army, according to the reports that have been circulating the last few days, and that I trust.

If peace is made, which cannot be delayed, if the murderers alone are pursued, it is my belief that we will never again lament a misfortune like Waiilatpu. There is no doubt that once the Indians comprehend the gravity of homicide, they will make a greater effort to avoid it. Once they come to know God, to fear and to serve Him, the frightful crimes they now commit so thoughtlessly, and even lightheartedly, will fill them with remorse. This, then, defines our task as missionaries, & with the help and grace of our Lord, we hope to succeed. All we desire from the government is complete liberty to proceed.

Accept my sentiments of respect &c.
[A. M. A. Blanchet, Bishop of Walla Walla]

AAS, A2: 74–77.

1. As secretary of state from 1845 through 1849, James Buchanan (1791–1868) knew well the politics of Oregon, having negotiated the 1846 Oregon Treaty with British envoy Richard Pakenham. Subsequently, he advocated strongly for Oregon's adoption as a territory. He would later serve as president of the United States (1857–61).

2. The provisional legislature sent a memorial to Washington, D.C., on October 19, 1847, by way of Panama. Governor Abernethy sent J. Quinn Thornton, as his private agent, along on the same ship, to present the memorial in person and to represent land and political interests of the minority missionary (Methodist) party. Following the Waiilatpu killings, the legislature designated Marshal Joseph Meek, former mountain man of the American Fur Company, to report on the incident and to present the same memorial in person to President Polk, urging the U.S. government to take control of Oregon and handle the Indian "troubles." Meek represented the provisional legislature and majority "American Party" of Oregon, which upheld U.S. Enlightenment principles of freedom, including religion (Bancroft, *History of Oregon*, 1:617–21, 755–59).

3. In this first letter to Buchanan, Blanchet wrote, "As it is very likely that a great number of colonists will settle near the establishment I will be starting, I see it as very important for me to know all the laws that govern this part of the Union," and he requested that two copies be sent to him in St. Louis (Blanchet to Buchanan, April 5, 1847, AAS, A2: 34). In the form of a response, Buchanan sent him copies of a letter addressed to Mr. Shively, who was named postmaster at Astoria (Blanchet, *Journal of a Catholic Bishop*, 32).

4. Blanchet, *Journal of a Catholic Bishop*, 26–27.

5. Blanchet to Kenrick, March 30, 1848, AAS, A2: 74.

6. This additional letter states: ". . . knowing now the clauses of this law, I am anxious to comply with it and request that you obtain authorization, that is, the liberty to place my missionaries with the nations that express the desire to have them . . ." (Blanchet to Buchanan, April 1, 1848, AAS, A5: 62).

7. News that the boundary question had been settled, and in anticipation of a federal donation land claim law, between four and five thousand people, mostly of comfortable means, arrived with the 1847 emigration. Insufficient rangeland to support the number of stock added to the normal hardships of the journey that year. Most emigrants were enterprising, self-reliant frontier people from the western border states. They were culturally distinct from many Protestant missionaries and speculators of New York and New England, who generally arrived by ship, not all intending to take up permanent residency. Blanchet identified himself with the majority "American" group of overland, border-state settlers with whom he had traveled, and also shared some political and cultural views with them. Bancroft, *History of Oregon*, 1:623.

8. Located at the junction of the Snake and Portneuf Rivers in today's eastern Idaho, Fort Hall was an important way station on the Oregon Trail, where "the traveler made his preparation for the last stage of the journey to the mouth of the Columbia. Oftentimes wagons were left here and packhorses substituted, but as the road became better known, wagons were taken clear through." Hiram M. Chittenden, *The American Fur Trade of the Far West* (New York: Press of the Pioneers, 1935; repr., Lincoln: University of Nebraska Press, 1986), 1:478 (page citation is to the 1986 edition). Built in 1834 by American Fur Company trader Nathaniel Wyeth, the fort

was sold to the HBC following the demise of the American Fur Company in 1837. Voyageurs in the employ of the HBC made scheduled overland journeys by boat, foot, and horse, transporting furs, supplies, mail, and passengers between headquarters in Montreal and the network of company posts across North America.

9. In this long report, Father Brouillet narrated events between the November 27 settlement of the missionaries at Mission St. Anne through the arrival of Peter Skene Ogden to rescue the hostages: his burial of the victims, his rescue of Reverend Spalding, and the assembly of chiefs at St. Anne to agree upon and sign their request for peace (which Blanchet delivered to Governor Abernethy in Oregon City). The full text of the letter, dated March 2, 1848, from Fort Walla Walla was published in *Mélanges religieux*, August 8, 1848, and in *Rapport sur Les Missions du Diocèse de Québec*, no. 8 (1849): 8–16. Edward J. Kowrach translated and published the letter in *Blackrobe Buries Whitmans*, by Jean-Baptiste Abraham Brouillet (Fairfield, Wash.: Ye Galleon Press, 1978), 154–59. Former sheriff in Missouri, Cornelius Gilliam (1798–1848) served in the Black Hawk and Seminole wars and in 1844 led an emigrant company to Oregon, where he organized and was minister of the Freewill Baptist Church in Polk County. Appointed colonel of the regiment of five hundred Willamette Valley volunteers in the Cayuse conflict, he was killed in a gun accident during the campaign.

10. The *Oregon Spectator* (the first newspaper in the Oregon Territory) published a series of letters related to the Waiilatpu killings in its January 20, 1849, issue. These included, among others, an account by James Douglas of Chief Factor Ogden's ransom and rescue of the hostages, an English translation of Bishop Blanchet's report to Governor Abernethy that described the council he held with the Cayuse chiefs, the resulting agreement signed by the chiefs to release the hostages unharmed if a peace commission of "two or three great men" was sent, and a request from the chiefs that the Americans no longer travel through their country. Unfortunately, that report did not reach Governor Abernethy until January 10, the day the regiment of volunteer troops departed from Vancouver, under the command of Colonel Gilliam, with the governor's initial instructions to punish the Cayuses.

11. George Abernethy (1807–1877), of Scot ancestry and living in New York City, departed for Oregon in 1840 on the *Lausanne*, one of fifty-two people who responded to Reverend Jason Lee's plan to colonize Oregon with Methodists following the missionary's failure to convert dying Indians (Bancroft, *History of Oregon*, 1:170). Abernethy ran the Methodist warehouse in Oregon City and participated in schemes to jump the private land claim of John McLoughlin, former chief factor of the HBC. He was narrowly elected governor under the Oregon provisional government, serving from June 3, 1845, through March 3, 1849. Though Abernethy initially called for volunteers to attack the Cayuses, he later recommended negotiations and capture of only the murderers. Abernethy wrote directly to President Polk six days after the above letter, telling the president of his appointment of peace commissioners, and efforts to separate the murderers from others, and requesting that "whether Congress passes a bill extending the jurisdiction of the United States over us or not, that at least one Regiment of Dragoons will [be] sent into Oregon to protect us from the Indians, and protect immigrants." Abernethy to Polk, April 5, 1848, [letterpress copy], MS 929, box 1, folder 13, George Abernethy Papers, Oregon Historical Society Research Library, Portland.

To James Buchanan,
Secretary of State,
April 1, 1848

The bishop followed up his first letter to the secretary of state with the following piece of evidence, possibly in order to counter claims of Catholic missionary involvement in the killings at Waiilatpu.

[St. Paul on the Wallamet], April 1st 1848

Sir,

I have just read a letter written by a man of trust, and believe it my duty to pass the following facts it mentions along to you.

It appears that for several years the Cayuses had threatened Dr. Whitman & told him to leave their lands. Americans staying at Waiilatpu in March found letters written to the doctor in 1844, which note that even then the Indians were talking about getting the doctor to leave.[1] One of the bourgeois of the Company, who had been stationed in Walla Walla for five years & who left three years ago, told me himself and several others as well that while he was at the Fort, he had on a number of occasions warned the doctor that it would be better for him to leave; that the Indians were unfavorably disposed toward him, & that he would meet misfortune if he persisted in staying there.[2] On several occasions his friends on the Wallamet had repeated the same warnings. In spite of all this advice, when measles and dysentery ravaged all the tribes of our lands last autumn, the doctor remained determined to continue his mission and seemed to scorn the threats of the Indians and the fears of his friends. The Cayuses lost well over thirty people within a few weeks, even though the doctor distributed an abundant supply of medications to them.

Given their prejudices against the doctor, the hatred that certain ones entertained for him, they were easily convinced that the doctor was giving them bad medicine and causing them to die. A métis by the name of Joseph Lewis was only too successful at this.[3] He told the Indians that he was their friend, that he knew the Americans & the doctor, and he warned them that if they didn't hasten to kill the doctor, they would all be dead by spring. Distraught at the sight of so many kin dying, persuaded that there was a desire to see them die as well, and pressured by the advice of the métis, the Indians were led to commit the deplorable excesses of November 29th, which have thrown this entire country into a labyrinth of problems, the end of which is difficult to anticipate . . .

Once again, most respectfully, &c.
[A. M. A. Blanchet, Bishop of Walla Walla]

AAS, A2: 77–78.

———•———

1. Blanchet is referring to letters found by volunteer troops who were constructing Fort Waters, named after the colonel who replaced Gilliam, from adobes of the demolished Whitman Mission at Waiilatpu. When the peace commissioners and others left for the Willamette Valley on March 20, they presumably carried such letters with them.

2. The title "bourgeois" was commonly used for superintendents and managers of HBC forts. Blanchet is referring to Archibald McKinley, chief factor of Fort Walla Walla, a Scotch Presbyterian and close friend of Whitman, who, during Whitman's 1843 absence on the east coast, brought his wife to the post for protection after she reported an attempted attack on her, and some Cayuses burned the mission mill. Fuller, *History of the Pacific Northwest*, 134; Jeffrey, *Converting the West*, 175–78.

3. A person of mixed descent, possibly part Delaware, Joseph Lewis arrived at Waiilatpu in the fall of 1847 and remained after receiving assistance from the Whitmans. In the earliest accounts of the Waiilatpu killings, he was accused of spreading rumors among the Cayuses that the Whitmans were trying to poison them in order to take possession of their lands for themselves and other countrymen, a rumor the deaths from the measles epidemic reinforced (Bancroft, *History of Oregon*, 1:652). Sources show that he warned other U.S. immigrants who stopped by the mission in the fall of 1847 that they would do well not to winter there, given the unrest of the Cayuses. Lewis and others knowledgeable about the connection between the arrival of missionaries and eventual displacement of Indians by settlers shared this information with Cayuses (Jeffrey, *Converting the West*, 211, 215–18).

To George Abernethy, Governor,
Provisional Government of Oregon,
April 29, 1848[1]

The adoption of a federal law against whites settling among Indians was not the only threat to Catholic missions in the Diocese of Walla Walla. Hostilities between volunteer troops and Plateau Indians presented an immediate obstacle. Father Brouillet and Deacon Leclaire had evacuated Mission St. Anne on February 19. Before they left, Tawatoé and other Cayuses were received into the Church. The Oblates had evacuated their mission starts as well—St. Rose among the Walla Wallas and Immaculate Conception among the Yakamas. By April 1, all the missionaries had joined Bishop Blanchet and Oblate Superior Ricard, who were temporarily residing in St. Paul. While there, they received a circular from one of the war commissioners, forbidding them to continue missions with the Cayuses and Walla Wallas.[2]

By April, hostilities were abating. Along with his fellow clerics, Blanchet was anxious to resume work. He also was eager to establish the new mission of St. Peter at The Dalles, where he had decided to relocate the see of the Diocese of Walla Walla. On behalf of himself and his missionaries who were equally anxious to resume work they had begun east of the Cascades, he wrote to Governor Abernethy to request that the interdict be lifted.

In this letter, Blanchet assumes that Abernethy, a Methodist, is a religious person who therefore cares for the welfare of Indians. He explains his duty as bishop in language congenial to Protestants; for example, he emphasizes teaching the "Word," so that Indians will obey divine law. It is interesting to note how different Blanchet's presentation to the Methodist Abernethy is from his presentations to fellow Catholics.

Sir,

On coming to this country which was to be my adoptive land, I foresaw that I had two important duties to discharge; the one towards God, whose unworthy minister and ambassador I am, the other towards this country and society. You are aware, that these two duties being so intimately connected together, an attempt to separate them would be a culpable prevarication. I trust, Sir, that the time I spent in my Diocess [sic] has not been misspent, and I can safely say the same for my fellowlabourers [sic] in the holy ministry. For why have we been sent forth by the head of the Church? Was it not to christianize our poor infidel Indians, and to make them servants of God? But, to christianize these unbelievers is nothing else than first to teach them the duties which they owe to God and to mankind, that is to say, to teach them to love God with their whole hearts, and their neighbors as themselves; and then to confer Baptism. Why are these Indians so miserable, unless because either they have no knowledge of this law of the Creator, or do not sufficiently comprehend it?

Let us teach them, that He who has created them demands perfect submission to his holy will, and the practise of the commandments which He has revealed to man. Let us teach them how, according to the words of our Saviour, all the commandments are contained in these two, namely, the love of God and the love of our neighbour. As soon as they shall be well acquainted with this, they will be no longer addicted to revenge, murder and numerous other crimes, which habit has rendered almost natural to them. Who then is to teach them these duties? The minister of the Lord, no doubt. Yes, Sir, you will know that such is our bounden duty. The obligation is truly great, yet it is not above our strength, if God assists our labours, which I trust He will do. It is on this account that I am anxious to continue the work which we have so successfully commenced. Yes, I am desirous that circumstances permit us to return among these Indians, who wish to know God, as we do, in order to adore him and to love him with all their heart, and it is my intention to do so as soon as possible.

The two letters (copies of which I have the honour to forward to you herein enclosed, the one from Teies, the other from Tawatoé (the young chief), requesting their Missionaries to return to them immediately), show how desirous they are of being instructed.[3] Who would not rejoice in beholding how God inspires them with such excellent sentiments? And we, who are aware of the good to be done, how can we refuse to fly to their succour? For I am well persuaded that the wholesome admonitions of the Priests, whilst the Indians repose confidence in them, shall be of great avail in confining them within the limits of their duty. You may perceive among the Yakamas, how they receive and obey the admonitions of their Missionaries, who by gaining over to God adorers in spirit and in truth, rejoice in labouring for the welfare of the country and for the happiness of society. This is all the glory which a Minister of the Gospel of Jesus Christ can desire.

Please accept the assurance of high esteem and respect with which I remain, Sir, your very humble & obedient Servant
Aug. Magl. Alex. Blanchet, Bishop of Walla Walla &c.

BLANCHET TO ABERNETHY, APRIL 29, 1848, MS 929, BOX 1, FOLDER 9, GEORGE ABERNETHY PAPERS, WRITTEN IN ENGLISH; AAS, A3: 89–91, AND AAS, A2: 79–81, FRENCH VERSIONS.

———•———

1. An attitude that some settlers by this time seem to have had toward Abernethy's capacities to govern is reflected in a letter that missionary Rousseau wrote on February 23, 1848, to his family in Canada: ". . . the provisional government is pitiful, and our governor is as capable of governing as I would be of doing needlework" (Rousseau, "Caravane," 231).

2. Tawatoé was baptized by Father Brouillet on February 13, 1848, under the name François Xavier (Munnick and Munnick, "Missions of St. Ann and St. Rose of the Cayouse," in *Catholic Church Records of the Pacific Northwest*, vol. 7, 10–11–12). Oblate activities prior to evacuation are recounted in Young, "Mission of the Missionary Oblates," 76–77; Pierre Ricard, O.M.I., "Les origines de nos missions de Orégon, d'après un mémoire de P. Ricard," *Missions de la Congréga- tion de Marie Immaculée*, no. 197 (March 1912): 74–83. A translation by Anne Bounds of the same is published in *Kittitas Frontiersmen*, ed. Earl T. Glauert and Merle H. Kunz (Ellensburg, Wash.: Ellensburg Public Library, 1976), 78.

3. Yakama chief Teies and his brother Owhi both held lands in the Kittitas Valley where they had welcomed Oblate missionaries. On the page following a Blanchet registry copy of the above letter to Abernethy is a brief letter addressed to Father Brouillet from Fort Walla Walla's factor, William McBean, dated April 6, 1848, and signed by an interpreter, a witness, and Young Chief's mark, stating: "I am requested by Young Chief today to inform you that the spot of land that he gave you is yours and his young men request you to come as soon as possible and convenient to establish your mission and continue to instruct them" (AAS, A2: 81). It can be assumed that this

is one of the two letters to which Blanchet is referring. The letter would have been written after the March 13 departure of the last missionaries, Brouillet and Leclaire, from Fort Walla Walla. The letter can be interpreted as an apology, some Cayuses having "showed their displeasure by burning his house," that is, the priests' residence at St. Anne, which Brouillet and Leclaire had left on February 19, after some of the Indians took up arms against the volunteers. Denys Nelson, "Yakima Days," *Washington Historical Quarterly* 19, no. 2 (April 1928): 119.

LETTER 9

To Jean-Charles Prince, Bishop of Martyropolis, Coadjutor of the Diocese of Montreal, January 27, 1849[1]

The immigration of 1847, the Cayuse War, the transition of Oregon into a U.S. federal territory, and the California gold rush signaled the end of "Old Oregon"—a region comprised of Indian villages with complex social ties, fur trappers, and sparse Euro-American settlements coexisting in an economy dominated by the fur trade. Blanchet and his fellow missionaries had envisioned continuation of that older Oregon before their departure from Montreal. Despite rapid changes and the difficulties they caused, Blanchet and his collaborators remained committed to their continuing mission.

Receiving no objection from Governor Abernethy to his request (see letter 8), the bishop and his missionaries returned to their diocese, where Father Rousseau and he began Mission St. Peter at The Dalles, according to plan. Written during what was an exceptionally cold winter there, this letter links the immediate aftermath of the Whitman killings, presented in letter 2, to the bishop's current situation. It describes glimmers of success and stirrings of support from lay Catholic settlers amid multiple sectarian-related trials. The letter's more personal passages reveal Blanchet's need to feel connected to his fellow clerics in Montreal through shared ritual and mutual remembrance, as well as the consolation he received from imagining such bonds. Though he had settled in what was now a territory of the United States, Blanchet's Canadien roots sustained him.

St. Peter of Waskopam, January 27th 1849

A.M.D.G.

Monsignor,

Last February I wrote to Your Excellency and the gentlemen canons, hastily reporting some of the trials the Lord had apportioned us.[2] Alas! Our good, amiable, & virtuous senior confrere had departed from this place of pilgrimage six and a half months earlier, but I did not know until June, when I received your letter of August 9th, written upon his death bed![3] At the moment of our leaving, he had been so very distressed that he could not hold back his tears; was he aware then that we would not see one another again here below? As it was charity that drove him to his tomb, may heaven be his reward. *Ibunt justi in vitam aet* [*ernam*] ["The just shall find eternal life"].

Since my last, God has deigned once again to put us to the test. May his holy name be blessed! The ill will & sectarian spirit of certain ministers, including—who would have believed this?—the very person who owed his life to Father Brouillet, have nourished and intensified the strong prejudice some citizens hold against the bishop and his clergy. In listening to them, one would think that the missionaries themselves were the very authors of the massacre. In fact, Colonel Gilliam reported that in passing through Fort Vancouver, he had overheard some volunteers say that the priests would be the first to be slain. To what extent did the colonel share the sentiments of his soldiers? That I cannot say.[4] Whatever the case may be, Father Delevaud, missionary at the fort, apparently succeeded in convincing him that any rumors circulating against the missionaries were false, for the colonel eventually admitted that he could not understand why the reverend, their author, was behaving in such a way.[5] One of the clerks there was taken utterly by surprise. Due to this and other such news, I feared for the missionaries residing at St. Anne, where the army was to pass. Yet I relied on the goodness of He who probes the depths of human hearts and who knew of our innocence, and on the saints, protectors of my diocese, whom I invoked with confidence and perseverance, & finally, on the prudence of the Vicar General, knowing that with the first news of hostilities, he would abandon his station and its dangers. In a word,

I was convinced that no harm would come to the missionaries.

In spite of this, I wrote to Colonel Gilliam, so as to mitigate any prejudice that he might still be harboring (see letter No. I).[6]

I was relieved when Father Brouillet arrived at St. Paul & informed me that the army's opinion of the missionaries had changed for the better.[7]

During the months of February and March, prejudice among those with common sense seemed to have lessened, but was still pronounced among others. Due to a few relentless rumors, there was even concern that fanatics might take action against the religious settlements in the Wallamet Valley. But the métis, sons of Canadiens, had acted zealously in boosting the size of the army and in doing so, had made a good impression.[8] Public prayers were not halted. From time to time we received news of a siege, of skirmishes; & as you can well [*imagine*], the truth was not always told, nor all the truth.[9]

Come April, I thought the war was drawing to an end. What led me to believe this was that those Indians who were innocent, having finally understood that the Americans merely wanted to punish the guilty, and not to exterminate them all, had disassociated themselves from the guilty & had made peace. Abandoned to their resources, the guilty had been unable to resist for long. In addition, initial zeal to provision the troops had all but vanished, to such an extent that the volunteers [*claimed*] that while sacrificing themselves for their country, they were being left to starve.

However pleasant I found my stay in St. Paul, I was impatient to return to my diocese & was prepared to do so with the first opportunity. Anxious to know the government's views, I sent a letter to his Excellency, Governor G. Abernethy (see letter No. II) & attached copies of the letters that Tawatoé (Young Chief), great chief of the Cayuses, & Teies, one of the Yakama chiefs, had sent to their missionaries, requesting their return (see No. VIII).

Convinced that an appeal to the chiefs of the various Indian nations in my diocese would be useful, I sent each a copy of a circular I had written in a style as close to theirs as I could muster (see No. III).[10]

A few days later, having still received no response from the governor, I took his Excellency's silence as a sign of approval, and sent Father Rousseau to The Dalles to see if the Indians, known as the Waskos, were favorably disposed toward prayer.[11] He returned on May 22nd, exhausted and bearing the good news that the Waskos as well as Indians he met on a branch of the Des Chutes River very much desired priests.[12] Everything seemed to favor my return. So, on May 26th, I bid farewell to monsignor the archbishop & his clergy & along with my two priests, set out for The Dalles (Waskopam), the territory of the Waskos.

At Fort Vancouver, we rented a barge to transport a full year of provisions. This happened to be the least favorable season, when the waters are at their highest. We nevertheless made the voyage without any serious accident. The precious and aurifrigiata miters, along with a few items of little importance, were soaked.[13] I had set out in a tchinouk [Chinook] canoe, but after the wind all but capsized us, I abandoned it for the barge. On June 9th, we portaged the Falls, a little more than midway from Fort Vancouver; & on June 10th, after walking for some twelve hours, we reached Waskopam at about two in the morning.

The next day, Pentecost, I celebrated Mass in the Indian camp, at their request. I noticed that the women did not participate.

An American had taken the piece of land I intended to build on. After some looking around, we found another. It is contiguous with the Methodist and Presbyterian Mission site, about a mile southwest of the river.

On June 14th, we began having wood hauled for a provisional cabin. All was going well. Glad to be in my diocese & soon to be sheltered from the sun's heat, I was anticipating no further obstacles when Father Rousseau received a letter from Mr. Lee, 2nd Colonel of the army & Superintendent of the Department of Indian Affairs (see letter No. IV). It seems that the prince of shadows had not been resting & that he wanted to halt our instruction of the Indians at any price. As we were not banned, however, from residing and building there, we continued to prepare the timber.[14]

Since most of the army had left Waiilatpu for the Valley, I thought that Father Brouillet might be of use to the Cayuses, even without settling among them. He could stay instead at Fort Walla Walla. Upon his arrival there, however, a new trial awaited. He was carrying a letter from Peter Ogden, Esq., bourgeois of Fort Vancouver, which forbade him from residing at the fort for more than a few days. Father Brouillet assumed thereupon that he had no choice but to leave immediately and camp some distance away, & he would have done so were it not that Mr. McBean, clerk and guardian of the fort, begged him not to leave. This kind gentleman, already feeling in peril, feared that a refusal to lodge Father Brouillet might infuriate the Indians & lead them to destroy the fort & perhaps to massacre those who were there. For this reason, Father Brouillet thought it best to ignore the order & to act instead in the interest of those very persons who had insulted him. A more disinterested decision could not have been made. Mr. Douglas and Mr. Ogden had welcomed us openly during our first visit at Fort Vancouver; in fact, having noticed that I was not taking meals at the fort, the first had repeated on several occasions that *I should not consider myself a stranger and should not feel uncomfortable dining there.*[15] What could have occasioned this change of heart? It was said that they did not approve of the missionaries returning to their stations. This was probably the case, but politics must have been involved as well.[16]

While this scene was taking place in Walla Walla, another was readying itself at Waskopam. After the missionaries had left for Walla Walla, I spent time every day with the Indians, & used my little knowledge of tchinouk to talk with them of prayer & to explain some parts of the Catholic Ladder. Doctor Saffarans, Mr. Lee's Indian agent, was informed that I was continuing to instruct the Indians in spite of the superintendent's ban. Faithful to his duty, he thereupon wrote to me that I must discontinue my teaching (see letter Nos. V, VI, and VII).

The outcome of this last scene was more fortunate than I had anticipated; in a sense I am glad to have provoked it, as it soon became clear that we could begin instruction, provided we be prudent.[17]

But if some individuals were trying to impede us & to halt the effects of our zeal to the east of the Cascade Mountains, others to the west were no less determined. The press that Reverend Griffin ran in the Twalaty Plain served marvelously to soothe Reverend Spalding's itch to write against us.[18] At every possible moment, this good & reverend gentleman poured out the venom of hatred he nursed for Catholicism—like a torrent that, having been held back for some time, spills out, threatening to overturn everything it encounters, with this difference, however, that the reverend gentleman attacked *the very rock that all of hell itself is unable to shake.* The darkest imputations & the most false accusations flowed from his pen on every possible occasion; even the visible head of the church was not spared his whip, but he escaped injury. (See numbers four and five of the first issues of the *Oregon American*.) And the reverend did all of this with impunity, because we had no press at our disposal to deny the imputations & prove the falsehood of the accusations. Our only choice was to suffer patiently & leave our defense in the hands of He who sees & knows all.[19]

Finally P. H. Burnett, Esquire, a widely known lawyer who had entered the bosom of the church a few years earlier, obtained permission to print a series of responses that would have discredited those written against the Catholics. Such an unveiling of his lies would have given Reverend Spalding the retaliation he was due. But hardly had a few letters been printed when the *Oregon American* disappeared from the scene, thanks to *yellow fever* (thirst for California gold).[20]

As you see, Monsignor, since we first arrived in this land of liberty, we have endured many battles. I can say though, that we have never lost faith that sooner or later victory would be ours. Ah yes, let it be known, feeling so very well supported by the prayers of the [members] of the Propagation of the Faith, we always believed that these trials would ultimately be of benefit to Religion. And this we still believe.

During and after these malicious attempts on the part of Lucifer, the last of the volunteers abandoned their war headquarters. The ministers serving the Kettles, who live among the Spokanes, came down the river, escorted by about fifty volunteers; those at The Dalles had already left in the fall, a few days after the massacre.[21] As a result, there is no longer a single Protestant minister in the entire territory under my jurisdiction; & I do not believe that any wish to come here.

Mr. Lee has resigned his commission as superintendent and is heading for California in search of gold, which he thinks will be more profitable. People in the valley are no longer thinking of anything but gold.

So this, Monsignor, is the state of affairs since the end of September. We have begun instructing the Indians who have come to winter by us, and feel no threat whatsoever. Father Rousseau, who is in charge of this mission, translated the Christian prayers into Walla Walla; & his knowledge of the tchinouk jargon has served him well. Most of the des Chutes know the Our Father, the Hail Mary, the Ten Commandments; soon they will be able to recite the "Apostles Creed" &c.[22] Father Rousseau is not in the best of health. I fear he may succumb.[23]

The Waskos, on whose lands we are settled, have not yet come for instruction. We do not know why, though Homeus, their chief, said that Governor Abernethy had threatened him, saying that when the newly appointed governor arrives, any Indians who had come to listen to us would be chased from their lands, & us along with them. Although the governor was formerly attached to the Methodist mission & is still known to be a zealous member of the sect, his position at the time would seemingly have disallowed such language. For this reason, I cannot fully trust the chief's word.[24]

It consoles me, nevertheless, to inform you that the Waskos have shown a desire to start instruction once the snows melt. Their language is entirely different from Walla Walla, so this will mean still more work for Father Rousseau, who will need to translate the prayers into Wasko as well.[25] I forgot to tell you that the Indians of the area had all acquired some knowledge of the religion of the Methodist ministers who lived here, & that they have had considerable communication with the whites, for which they are no better off. Several say that the ministers baptized them.

The entire summer and autumn were spent in building. You must think that we are well lodged! This is hardly the case. For two months we had two workmen, but one left. Progress was slow. From time to time we had a métis or an Indian to help saw the boards &c. But even our one skilled worker was simply an apprentice carpenter, roofer, & woodworker. You can see why our house is not yet finished. The little cabin that has served as our refectory, dormitory & chapel is fifteen by twelve feet in size. It sheltered us from the heat of the sun, but not from the snow & the autumn rains. I would have liked to abandon it sooner.

At long last, on October 29th, twenty Sundays after Pentecost, the bishop's palace was covered with shingles, window frames were set in place, the joints were sealed with a thick mortar of clay; mats partitioned the chapel, & the missionaries had prepared a table to serve as the altar; a dais, a pyx, nothing was lacking![26] On this day, forever in my memory, Jesus Christ sought to take dominion of the palace. The sacred host was placed in the pyx. Oh! How grand this day was for the missionaries! What a consolation for them to be so close to the holy sacrament & able to visit it daily.

Every day, Monsignor, between four-thirty and five in the evening, you will find me telling my needs & those of all my friends and benefactors to my God. It is around eight o'clock then for you, and you are at evening prayer or vespers. We are praying for one another at the same time. What a pleasant thought! And in the morning, when I say mass at six-thirty, it is about nine-thirty for you: what might keep you, in the midst of your daily occupations, from making an elevation to God on my behalf? Perhaps it will ascend toward the throne of the Eternal at the same time as my memento to you.

In spite of the consolation of the holy sacrament, I still wanted to move out of my little cabin where the roof was leaking everywhere. On December 2nd—with the chimney completed, timbers sawed and laid to support the floor, mats hung for the partition & the floor in place—I took up lodging next to the chapel. Father Rousseau had thought he could spend the winter in the cabin, but was obliged to abandon it on account of the cold.

The interior of my chapel is twenty-four by eleven feet; my room is of the same dimensions, & there is a passage between the two, seven to eight feet in width.

I have not yet officiated as bishop. I will do so once the chapel also has a floor.

Please accept these minute details with indulgence, as well as the rest of this letter. And after you have read it, be so kind as to hand it on to Monsignor Turgeon so that he might extract whatever he believes would be of interest to the readers of the Reports of the Propagation of the Faith of Quebec.[27]

[A. M. A. Blanchet, Bishop of Walla Walla]

AAS, A3: 71–76.

1. Jean-Charles Prince (1804–1860) was ordained in 1826; he directed the Upper Seminary of St. Jacques in Montreal (1826–30) and the Seminary of St.-Hyacinthe (1830–40), where J. B. A. Brouillet was a student for seven of the same years. In Montreal (1840–52), he served as chaplain to the Sisters of Providence and was fellow canon with A. M. A. Blanchet at the cathedral. As coadjutor (assistant) to Bishop Bourget, he was in a position to help Blanchet secure personnel and financial support from the diocese. His title follows the ecclesiastical practice of using the names of dioceses no longer in existence for names of coadjutor bishops.

2. The term *canon* refers to clergymen in residence at a large cathedral and living in community, as members of a chapter. Between February 22 and February 26, 1848, while in St. Paul, Blanchet wrote four lengthy letters to former fellow chapter members of the Cathedral of Montreal (Father Prince and Fathers Hyacinthe Hudon, Alexis-Frédéric Truteau, and Joseph-Octave Paré), telling of his voyage and of the killings at Waiilatpu and the aftermath (copies of the letters are located in AAS, A3: 35–46). Written almost a year later, this fifth and final letter in that series picks up at the end of the fourth, in which he told of his trip downriver with the hostages, of his observation of troops on their way upriver, and of leaving Fathers Brouillet and Leclaire at Mission St. Anne. Blanchet likely would have learned of the subsequent events he

recounts in this letter from his priests and others who arrived in St. Paul from the upper country on March 25, 1848.

3. Abbé Hyacinthe Hudon (1792–1847), vicar-general of the Montreal diocese since 1842, honorary canon of the Cathedral of Chartres in France, died of typhus, which he contracted while ministering to victims of the 1847 epidemic that erupted among the influx of immigrants to Montreal that year.

4. It is likely that Colonel Gilliam shared these initial sentiments with his troops. He was angry at the HBC as well, following recent news that under the Oregon Treaty the company would retain a legal right to its lands south of the forty-ninth parallel, and indignant that the company, preferring negotiation to war, had refused a loan of $100,000 to supply the troops. Gilliam spoke of taking the fort by force of arms in order to supply his troops, tendering a draft on the United States Treasury in payment. Fortunately, "the impending wrath of the irrepressible Gilliam was averted" (Bancroft, *History of Oregon*, 1:681–82).

5. Father Bartholomew Delevaud, from Savoy, was one of the twenty-one clerics and sisters who responded to Archbishop F. N. Blanchet's call for missionaries during his voyage to Europe, and he arrived with the archbishop on August 25, 1847.

6. Letters identified by roman numeral are listed as such in the original; Blanchet is referring to copies of correspondence he enclosed with this letter. The bishop's letter to Colonel Gilliam refutes two accusations made by Spalding and some former hostages, namely, that Father Brouillet baptized the murderers and that Catholic missionaries were building at Whitman's place at the time of the killings (Blanchet to Gilliam, AAS, A2: 51–53).

7. A draft version of this letter states: "In March, Father Brouillet, Mr. Leclaire and the Oblates arrived at St. Paul on the Wallamet, and told me that once the volunteers were better informed about what had taken place, their opinion of the missionaries improved & that the colonel in particular was entirely in their favor and belatedly took their defense against their disparagers. The letter I sent him at the end of January may have contributed to his appeasement and turn-about with regard to us" (AAS, A3: 67).

8. According to the recollections of an 1847 immigrant: ". . . when our own Cayuse War broke out, we held a meeting on French Prairie, we were very anxious to know how the French people were going because we considered they held the balance of power. At the general meeting old Tom McKay delivered an address to the people and particularly to the halfbreeds . . .; in the course of an hour he had about sixty in the ranks. Any difficulty that would arise amongst the Indians that required fighting, Captain McKay was sent forward. . . . When the Captain took the stand he did for Dr. Whitman and the American settlers, we down here were very much relieved" ("Emigrant Anecdotes by John W. Grim, Salem, Oregon, 1878," MS P-A 38, Bancroft Library, University of California, Berkeley). Thomas McKay was the son of Dr. John McLoughlin's wife, Marguerite Waden (Cree and Swiss), by her former marriage to Alexander McKay. Intimately associated with much of early Oregon history, Thomas McKay helped select the site of Fort Vancouver, accompanied Peter Skene Ogden's trapping brigades into the Snake Country, built Fort Boise, and married Chinook chief Comcomly's daughter, by whom he had four children; subsequently, he married a Cayuse woman with whom he had two children, before wedding Isabelle Montou, daughter of an HBC employee. Feared and loved, he was known for his daring and animosity. His father (a Canadian partner of John Jacob Astor) lost his life at the hands of

Coastal Indians on the ill-fated ship *Tonquin* (1811) (Boyd, *People of The Dalles*, 319–21). McKay was confirmed and took first Communion as a Catholic at the Walla Walla post on Sunday, November 7, 1847 (Blanchet, *Journal of a Catholic Bishop*, 76).

9. The draft version adds that "victory was given, sometimes to one side, sometimes to the other, and the truth or all the truth was not always told." AAS, A3: 67.

10. In this circular, dated May 13, 1848, addressed to "the Great Chiefs of the Walla Wallas, Cayuses, Yakamas, Nez Percés, Palouse, and to the people of the Dalles and the Des Chutes," Blanchet speaks of the priests' opposition to war of any kind (". . . the priests do not wage war. They do not like war, even when it is just, because it results in bloodshed") and of his desire to see peace between the Indians and Americans; he advises the Indians not to number themselves among the "malicious" but to take pity on the guilty instead. AAS, A2: 81–83.

11. Blanchet's original letter and an English translation of it (letter 8) are in the archival files of the Abernethy letters. The archive does not contain Abernethy's response. In a letterpress copy, however, Abernethy wrote that "the Catholics have [*gone*] up as far as The Dalles," indicating his awareness of their return (Abernethy to Lee, June 5, 1848, MS 929, box 1, file 18, George Abernethy Papers).

12. Deacon Rousseau, who had accompanied his bishop downriver with the hostages, completed his preparation for ordination during a retreat at the Jesuit house of St. Paul, and was ordained on February 20, 1848. In letters home, he related details of his overland mountain trip to and from The Dalles. On this trip Rousseau and his guide, Baptiste, met up with Tom McKay, who, returning with his troops, assisted them with directions; Baptiste, who begged on several occasions to turn back due to the trip's difficulty, served as interpreter among the Deschutes, who tried to persuade Rousseau to start a mission with them and whose children he baptized; the Waskos gathered with their chief, Thomas, who expressed his contentment with having priests and told Father Rousseau to choose any of their lands that he pleased; at Fort Waskopam Rousseau received a cold reception from officers who were prejudiced against Catholics and appeared not to want them to have an establishment at The Dalles (Rousseau, "Caravane," 234–37).

13. A miter is a tall collapsible cap consisting of two similar sides facing front and back, sewn together and rising to a peak, and is worn by bishops, cardinals, and abbots in the Catholic Church. There were three types of miters, worn for different, prescribed ceremonies and times: the "precious," traditionally decorated with precious stones; the "aurifrigiata," made of gold cloth or white silk and decorated with embroidered threads; and the "simple," made of undecorated white linen or silk. Catholic emphasis on ornament, vestment, and ritual was in keeping with Indian religious practices, making them an important means for the missionary to communicate with those he was evangelizing.

14. ". . . it is desirable no further missionary effort should be made with the Indians East of the Cascade Mountains until the presence of . . . troops . . . shall render such effort safe and judicious" (Lee to Blanchet and company, June 15, 1848, AAS, A2: 90). An emigrant of 1843, Henry A. G. Lee (1818–1851) spent his first winter teaching at Lapwai mission and studying the Nez Percé language, before serving as interpreter for a quasi-official Indian agent, Elijah White. Member of the provisional legislature, Lee served briefly as editor of the *Oregon Spectator*. Appointed one of the three peace commissioners to meet with the Columbia Plateau Indians, he led the first regiment of volunteers to The Dalles. He was promoted to second colonel following the death of

Colonel Gilliam and succeeded Commissioner Joel Palmer as superintendent of Indian Affairs in the spring of 1848. Terence O'Donnell, *An Arrow in the Earth: General Joel Palmer and the Indians of Oregon* (Portland: Oregon Historical Society Press, 1991), 80.

15. Sir James Douglas (1803-1877), born in British Guiana of Scot and Creole descent became Fort Vancouver's accountant in 1830 and was advanced to chief trader in 1839. From 1845 to 1851 he served as Board of Management partner for the Columbia District. He was named governor of the colony of Vancouver Island in 1851, and of the colony of British Columbia in 1859. *Dictionary of Canadian Biography Online*, s.v. "Douglas, Sir James," http://www.biography.ca/009004-119.01-e.php?&id_nbr=4955 (accessed May 15, 2012). Peter Skene Ogden (c.1790-1854), born of loyalist Tory parents in Quebec City, led HBC Snake River Expeditions from 1824 to 1830, and was given command of the HBC New Caledonia District in 1835. Appointed Board of Management partner for the Columbia District in 1845 he remained at Fort Vancouver until his death. *Dictionary of Canadian Biography Online*, s.v. "Peter Skene Ogden," http://www.biography.ca/009004-119.01-e.php?&id_nbr=4109 (accessed May 15, 2012).

16. Settlers' suspicions of HBC-Catholic collusion with Indians east of the Cascades were inflamed by Lieutenant A. T. Rogers's July 1848 interception at The Dalles of a shipment of a two-year supply of arms destined for the Jesuit missions of the interior. Father Joset, superior of the Jesuits' Rocky Mountain Mission, had pleaded with the governor to lift the ban established during the Cayuse War on distribution of arms and powder to the Indians of the interior, arguing that the Indians could not live without hunting and needed to protect themselves from the predations of the ever-present Blackfeet. He ordered the shipment through the HBC in order to have it available when the ban was lifted. Under these circumstances, Brouillet's residency at the HBC's Fort Walla Walla and his drawing of Indians there for missionary purposes could have aroused further suspicions among nativist settlers in the Willamette Valley. *Oregon American and Evangelical Unionist*, May 25, 1849; Robert Ignatius Burns, S.J., *The Jesuits and the Indian Wars of the Northwest* (Moscow: University of Idaho Press, 1966), 65–66; Blanchet to Bourget, January 31, 1849 (ACAM, file 195.133, 849–1).

17. A copy of this letter, addressed to Henry Saffarans, Esq., Indian agent for Waskopam, dated July 19, 1848, is located in AAS, A2: 98–99. In response to that letter, Saffarans states: "As to the matter of explaining and instructing the Indians upon the common precepts of the Bible, there can be no objection, because I do sincerely consider it a most righteous and magnanimous act. . . . without distinction as to the church or mode of administration during the present crisis of affairs with them." Saffarans to Blanchet, July 20, 1848, AAS, A2: 99–100.

18. Pastor John Smith Griffin (1807–1899) organized the first Congregational Church in Oregon, known as the First Church of Tualatin Plains, in 1842. Griffin published the *Oregon American and Evangelical Unionist* intermittently in 1848–49 (the *Spectator* being by its bylaws prohibited from sectarianism) in an effort to counter Catholic influence in Oregon and to support a close cooperation between American Protestant Christianity and Oregon's provisional and later territorial governments.

19. Vicar-General Brouillet eventually refuted Spalding's charges in a pamphlet published in the *Freeman's Journal* in 1853, republished as *U.S. Congress Executive Document No. 38* in 1859, and again by the Archdiocese of Oregon City's *Catholic Sentinel* in 1869. In 1869, Spalding presented a new pamphlet that repeated most of his original claims and was signed by seven

Protestant groups of Oregon and three in the eastern United States, to the Oregon superintendent of Indian Affairs, who passed it on to Columbus Delano, secretary of the Interior, who then presented the document to the U.S. Senate in 1871, as *Executive Document No. 37*. Brouillet replied in a pamphlet published by the *Catholic Sentinel* in July 1872. For an overview of this exchange of pamphlets from a Catholic perspective, see F. N. Blanchet, *Historical Sketches of the Catholic Church in Oregon by Most Rev. Francis Norbert Blanchet*, ed. and introduced by Edward J. Kowrach (Fairfield Washington, Ye Galleon Press, 1983), 136–38. See also Clarence B. Bagley, ed., *Early Catholic Missions in Old Oregon* (Seattle: Lowman and Hanford, 1932), 1:137–41. The choice of terms and strong accusations in Spalding's documents, and the initial credibility they enjoyed, reveals the intense anti-Catholic prejudice that existed among some U.S. settlers and Indian agents.

20. Lawyer and 1843 emigrant from the border state of Missouri, Peter Burnett (1807–1895) took a lead in the legislative assembly of 1844 that, among other items, contested the constitutionality of the provisional government's statutes (the Organic Laws), including the size of missionary land claims. He converted to Catholicism in 1846 after extensive study of doctrine and apologetics; it was to Burnett that Brouillet wrote asking for clarification of the missionaries' rights the day after Lee's letter was received in The Dalles (AAS, A2: 86–87). Leader of the first wagon train leaving for California (guided by Tom McKay), he was again influential in the formation of state government there and served as first governor. For Burnett's published reply to Spalding's accusations, see "Stricture of Peter H. Burnett, Esq. upon Reverend H. H. Spalding's History of the Wahlatpu Massacre," *Oregon American and Evangelical Unionist*, August 16, 1848. The seven-page article concludes with a call for the end of sectarianism: "Among the overwhelming majority of our fellow citizens, the most liberal and enlightened state of feeling exists. This is not the age of bitterness and persecution."

21. Reverend Elkanah Walker (1805–1877) and his wife, Mary Richardson Walker (1811–1897), were Congregationalist missionaries who worked among the Spokanes. Reverend Cushing Eels (1810–1893) and his wife, Myra Fairbanks Eels (1805–1878), were working with them at the time of the Waiilatpu killings. This evacuation proceeded in compliance with Colonel James Waters's decision to urge all white inhabitants to remove from the Indian country, a decision that Bancroft suggests was aimed at Catholics (Bancroft, *History of Oregon*, 1:740–41).

22. The Deschutes Indians resided along the Columbia near Celilo Falls, today's Bonneville Dam area, and at the head of the Deschutes River. The French means "of the falls."

23. Weakened from malaria that he contracted in September 1847 during his first of many overland supply trips to the Willamette Valley, exhausted from his missionary circuit, and discouraged by the effect of alcohol on Indians at The Dalles, Rousseau received his *exeat* (approved release) to return home to Canada in April 1851. He contracted cholera on board the steamer *Empire City* and died from it on July 24, 1852, the day before the ship arrived in New York City. He received a Catholic burial at sea, shrouded in an American flag. One of his sisters, upon entry into the community of Sisters of Providence in Montreal in 1854 received the name Sister Marie-Godefroi in honor of her deceased brother (Rousseau, "Caravane," 252–53, 256).

24. Following Colonel Lee's resignation as superintendent of Indian Affairs, Abernethy assumed the responsibility himself. Correspondence indicates that he was at The Dalles at this time and so may have visited the Indians of the area.

25. Missionaries commonly referred to the dialects of Sahaptin, spoken by the Walla Wallas, Yakamas, Nez Percés, and other groups as Walla Walla. The second language to which Blanchet is referring is Upper Chinookan (or Kiksht, according to its speakers), dialects of which were spoken by the Wasco-Wishrams, Cascades, Clackamas, and "Multnomahs" or "Wapatos." The presence of these two ethnolinguistic groups reflects the significance of the Waskopam area as a "shatter zone" between Coastal and Plateau peoples. Boyd, *People of The Dalles*, 5, 33–35.

26. A pyx is a container used to hold the reserved, consecrated bread and to carry it to the sick. It was placed on a dais, or platform.

27. Pierre Flavien Turgeon (1787–1867) served as vicar-general of the Diocese of Quebec (1833–34), coadjutor of the diocese under the title Bishop of Sidyme (1834–50), and archbishop of the province of Quebec (1850–67). A note at the end of the second version of this letter reads: "In 1848, copies of this account were sent to Lyons, to Vienna, and in 1849 to Monsignor Turgeon in Quebec."

LETTER 10

To Members of the Councils of the Society for the Propagation of the Faith, Lyons and Paris, July 14, 1849

Cascading political and economic events in the six months between this letter and the last prompted Bishop Blanchet to make a number of trips from his see at The Dalles to Oregon City. From there, he wrote this letter. Addressed to the same major funding source as letter 4, this letter is again intentional in structure: positive missionary news accompanied by evidence for why, without additional funding, he would be unable to build on that success and proceed with his mission. The positive news of this letter's first half is the overcoming of sectarian obstacles that had threatened the diocese in letter 9. The negative news that follows is the increase in prices and wages occasioned by the California gold rush. Blanchet says nothing of the potential wealth to be found there, nor does he mention that in April, Ferdinand Labrie, a handyman and personal servant who accompanied him from Montreal, left for California, to spend three months searching for gold.[1]

This letter shows a bishop accommodating to, and increasingly engaged in, shifting local politics. It also reveals a bishop who is aware of the international scope of his religious responsibilities, as well as the seriousness and closeness with which his readers, be they in Canada, France, or St. Louis, are following the progress of his enterprise.

Dear President,

My former letters described the many difficulties I have faced since my arrival in Oregon. Today I am consoled to inform you that the problems brought on by the former government are behind us. On August 14th 1848, Congress voted to establish the Oregon Territory. The governor and other officials arrived early in March; thereupon the Constitutional Act was proclaimed, and the laws of the Republic became the laws of the Territory.[2] Since that moment, everything has taken a turn for the better. Instead of a provisional government with its inherent weaknesses, we have a strong, well-established government, capable of protecting the weak as well as the innocent. President J. K. Polk's appointment of General Joseph Lane as governor of this new territory assures us that the new government will be led with impartiality.[3] In fact, Governor Lane has demonstrated from the very start that he understands his mission perfectly. He has made it clear that his duty is to render justice to all, Indians as well as whites, and that he has the will and the power to do so.[4] As of now, no one has any doubt of this.

Religious persecution has ceased. Last year's restriction on our establishing Indian missions quickly vanished; and on several occasions, the governor expressed chagrin in learning that there were persons so very narrow-minded and imbued with prejudice that they had forbidden us to bring the light of civilization to the poor Indians. And what made even less sense to him, was that the Waskos had been told last fall that if they came to our instruction, the new governor would not fail to drive them from their lands, along with the priests who taught them. He hastened to reach The Dalles, to inform the credulous Indians that they had been misled; that they had nothing to fear from the government; that they could and should take advantage of the instruction offered them; that this in fact was the desire of the government.[5]

Though entirely within reason, his actions would not please everyone, especially not certain officials of the ex-government & those ministers who had influenced them the most. These *pious* and *charitable* ministers, who, for over a year, in their religious meetings and their newspaper, the *Oregon American*, had not let up publishing the darkest slander and most absurd imputations against us, believed at first that they would be able to influence Governor Lane as they had Governor Abernethy. They in fact rushed to pay him a visit, to share their views, and to urge him to follow in the steps of his predecessor. Fully confident, they provided him copies to read of all they had published and written against us & against Catholics in general. But they soon discovered that they were not dealing with a sectarian, i.e., a Methodist. "If you knew the Constitution of your country," he told them, "you would know that the government cannot nurture animosity or hatred of any religious denomination for another, that it must treat everyone equally and with impartiality."

This defeat, certainly unexpected, must have exasperated our ministers. How might they get compensation, revenge? On whom was their anger to fall? The *Oregon American*, having died for lack of support, was called back to life, not to express repentance, but rather to prove that it had died of impenitence. It was resuscitated solely to nourish the editor & his adherents' blind hatred of Catholicism; to pour out every condemnation imaginable. Then once again, it disappeared. You might think this would have been our deathblow, that we would have been done in. Quite the contrary. The ministers fell into the very ditch that they had been digging for us; they did themselves in. Unanimously, every person of common sense condemned them. Wherever we go, people tell us that it is not worth responding to these diatribes, that their cause has already been judged. The following two events confirm this view.

First, following this last sally, the reverend editor ran as *representative* for Congress, but he received only three votes in his county, including his own, & perhaps five in all the others.[6] The second event concerns the Sisters of the Congregation of Notre Dame, who in the last week of May had suffered their own share of insults and dreadful slander. But since then, they have taken in a good number of pupils, all Protestants. As a result, although they started their Oregon City foundation only a few months ago, they now have over fifty pupils, and three-quarters are Protestant or non-Catholic.[7]

I must tell you of the Constitutional Act, which allots 640 acres of land to all Indian missions that were established before the transfer of power (August 14th 1848).[8] Although this donation is intended for all religious denominations, it is in fact to the benefit of Catholics, for, after the massacre at Waiilatpu, the ministers abandoned the missions they had begun, with no intent of returning, or of establishing new ones. These good folks most certainly suffer from an undue fear of martyrdom![9]

If the truth were to be told, several public officials do not hesitate to say that Catholics alone know how to work successfully with Indians, that experience has shown this to be so. I need not tell you that these officials are not Catholic.

I was pleased to be recognized by the government, gladdened at long last to be able to evangelize the Indians of my diocese without fear of further harassment. But once again my joy was not to last. No sooner was I made aware of the government's liberal views than I received news that the Councils of the Society for the Propagation of the Faith had discontinued all funding to the missions; and to add to this misfortune, that my agent in Paris had found himself forced to protest my notes.[10] The consequence of this? Far from starting any new projects, for good or for bad, I had to hold back on the earlier ones, not knowing when aid might arrive. The Reverend Father Oblates of Mary Immaculate were also forced, at least for now, to abandon their mission among the Yakamas north of the Columbia.

Another cause of distress for the missionaries was the dramatic rise last spring in the cost of goods. The discovery of gold mining in California has only worsened the fate of our missions. As of now, a woodworker or carpenter cannot be hired for less than eight to ten piastres a day; nor a day worker for less than three to four piastres.[11] Moreover, it is impossible to come by servants. How are houses to be built for missionaries? As for chapels, one cannot even dream of building them. I will not be able to finish so much as the thirty by twenty-four foot house that we started last summer, which remains without floors and walls, & yet that served last winter as my cathedral and palace. To be correct, some mats were hung to separate the chapel from my living quarters.

In short, the ex-government's opposition has been followed by yet another hardship, by straits that are halting us in our tracks and preventing us from making any progress, or carrying out our plans.

What shall I do? Abandon myself to discouragement? Far be that from me! On the contrary, I have no doubt that God will provide us the means to accomplish his work, and I await the moment He has chosen in His infinite Wisdom, whatever the source of these means may be.

I understand that some members of the Council of Paris have criticized me, saying that I should not have sent any bills of exchange before knowing if my agent had funds at his disposal. I will not defend myself, for I assume that these gentlemen are aware of the hardships and troubles I have experienced, and the reasons for the increase in expenses. They will have realized that with such limited funding, I could not so much as meet the minimal needs, even with greatest restraint. They will have concluded from this that my only other choice would have been to deprive my missionaries of the barest necessities.

Knowing now that you apportion funds according to need, provided you are aware of them, I will describe in all candor those of my diocese. According to the Report, you always pay the expenses incurred for the transportation of religious orders (missionaries) to their missions. I already reported to you, I believe, that in 1847, Monsignor of Marseilles sent me five Religious from the Congregation of the Oblates of Mary Immaculate. Another arrived last year.[12] The voyage of the first five, from New York to Walla Walla, cost me a good 600 piastres; the second, from Montreal to Oregon, 200. Above all else, I am asking you to pay this expense of 800 piastres. These Religious also need an assistant if they are to continue their two missions among the Yakamas, funds for which you could place either at my disposal or directly into their hands.

As for me, as I mentioned, I began an establishment at Waskopam (The Dalles), the Mission of St. Peter. It is hardly off the ground. In addition, the Mission of St. Anne, among the Cayuses, is without a single building, for the house that I saw to repairing when we first arrived was reduced to cinders during the war. This mission, however, is the most promising. To abandon it would be a real loss.

In summary, Gentlemen Presidents, the Councils need to provide for three missions in addition to the one where I plan to settle. As yet, my diocese is without a chapel. Should they provide me the means for building one in The Dalles, whatever its dimensions, it will serve as my Cathedral—unless it should please the Holy See to place me elsewhere. I know that the Councils are not lacking the will. I pray that the Lord provide them the inspiration to meet my needs.[13]

I am respectfully &c.

A. M. Al. Bp. of Walla Walla

AAS, A2: 112–17; AAS, A3: 80–83.

———•———

1. Journal entry of April 19, 1849: "Ferdinand (Labrie) leaves for California with three Indians under his command. He ought to stay there for three months and then come back at the first opportunity. He has nine horses of ours, besides other items for trading. He travels with 12 or 15 Americans, who like him, go to look for gold, which is found in such great abundance that the men collect several ounces of it per day." A journal entry of January 7, 1850, states that Labrie returned to The Dalles that day. There is no mention of his bringing back gold. Blanchet, *Journal of a Catholic Bishop*, 107, 113.

2. On August 20, six days after passage of the territorial bill, Joseph Meek, newly appointed U.S. marshal, set out from the capital for the home of General Lane in Newburg, Indiana; Lane immediately accepted his commission as governor and traveled with Meek to St. Louis and Leavenworth, where they were joined by a company of fifty-five men, including an escort of twenty-five riflemen. After a grueling trek over the Santa Fe Trail (to avoid the snows in the north), they traveled by steamer from California to Astoria, in the company of Oregonians returning from the goldfields, and arrived in Oregon City on March 2. Frances Fuller Victor, *The River of the West* (Hartford, Conn.: R. W. Bliss and Company, 1870), 469–81. Governor Lane pronounced the brief constitutional act, or proclamation, on March 3, which states: ". . . I have this day entered upon the discharge of the duties of my office, and by virtue thereof do declare the laws of the United States extended over, and declared to be in force in said Territory, so far as the same, or any portion thereof, may be applicable." "Proclamation," box 1, file 7, Joseph Lane Papers, Oregon Historical Society Research Library, Portland.

3. James K. Polk (1795–1849) served as president of the United States from 1845 to 1849. Elected in 1844 on a U.S. expansionist platform, Polk, a Democrat, presided over completing the annexation of Texas (1845), of New Mexico and California as a result of the Treaty of Guadalupe Hidalgo ending the Mexican War (February 1848), and of Oregon. Lane's proclamation, rendering the Oregon territorial government a fact, took place on the final day of Polk's term. Joseph Lane (1801–1881) served in the state legislature of Indiana from 1822 to 1846. He was appointed colonel in the Mexican War, participated in General Zachary Taylor's defeat of Mexican general Antonio López de Santa Anna, and was brevetted as major general. He was territorial governor from 1848 to 1851, Oregon delegate to Congress from 1851 to 1857, and U.S. senator from 1859 to 1861. Lane retired from public service to a ranch near Roseburg, Oregon. He was baptized a Catholic in 1867.

4. Blanchet uses the term "Indian" in the French original (*Indien*), rather than the standard, non-prejudicial French term, *Sauvage*, and uses it henceforth in all letters in English and nearly all letters in French.

5. Since the resignation of H. A. G. Lee as superintendent of Indian Affairs, Governor Ab-

ernethy had taken affairs into his own hands, passing them on to Territorial Governor Lane. It was in this capacity that Lane visited the region of The Dalles, according to Hubert Howe Bancroft, to deal with the Klikitats who were perpetrating minor offenses against settlers. Hubert Howe Bancroft, *History of Oregon*, vol. 2, *1848–1888* (San Francisco: History Company, 1888), 66–67. Blanchet reports in his journal that Lane had dinner with him at his cabin and that he in turn dined in the governor's tent the following evening; Father Rousseau then joined Lane at subsequent meetings in The Dalles, at the governor's invitation (Blanchet, *Journal of a Catholic Bishop*, 108).

6. In this final issue, J. S. Griffin established his candidacy as a delegate to the U.S. Congress on a platform of uprooting Catholicism in the Oregon Territory. Among his statements are the following: "As an upright citizen seeing immense evils hanging over my country, I offer to remove them. . . . My opposition to the papists is to their papacy. Let them abandon the Roman Hierarchy, and form themselves into a Free Catholic church . . . ; but the hosts of Jesuits banished from Europe and even Italy itself for their treason against all civil governments, who are pouring into Oregon for the entire destruction of all our liberties, I will oppose in every righteous way, to the best of my ability" (*Oregon American and Evangelical Unionist*, August 16, 1848). Griffin and Meek both received forty-six votes, the fewest of the five candidates; Samuel R. Thurston of the Methodist missionary group, who won on an anti-HBC platform, received 470 votes, "in the absence of a large number of voters of the territory, notably of the Canadians, and the young and independent western men" (Bancroft, *History of Oregon*, 2:114). As delegate, Thurston saw to undermining John McLoughlin's personal land claim in Oregon City.

7. During his 1844 voyage in Europe, Peter De Smet, superior of the Jesuits of the Rocky Mountains, engaged six Sisters of the Congregation of Notre Dame, from Namur, Belgium, for the Oregon mission. Seven additional sisters arrived in 1847. The sisters founded a first convent school in St. Paul and a second in Oregon City, in September 1848. For lack of funds, they closed the St. Paul school in 1852 and the Oregon City school in 1853, McLoughlin having lost the land upon which it was located. Schoenberg, *Catholic Church in the Pacific Northwest*, 82, 99, 137.

8. Although the Oregon Territorial Act of 1848 voided the land laws of the provisional government for individuals, the first section granted 640 acres with the improvements thereon to missionary stations then occupied (Bancroft, *History of Oregon*, 2:261). Under this act, Father Pandosy filed a claim for the 640 acres surrounding the Immaculate Conception Mission on Manastash Creek in the Yakima Valley, on November 20, 1848. Young, "Mission of the Missionary Oblates," 86–87. The Oregon Territorial Act would be superseded on September 27, 1850, by the Donation Land Claim Act, which revived the provisional government's provision for private land claims of 320 acres for a single, nonindigenous man and up to 640 acres for a married couple who had become resident before December 1850.

9. A variation in a second version of the letter (found in AAS, A3: 80–83) adds: "But let us leave the ministers and their fanaticism here, and turn to more important matters. Providence is watching over these missions, there is no doubt."

10. The society temporarily suspended allocations to the entire province of Oregon until the Council of Paris had the opportunity to discuss the finances of these missions with their agent, Abbé Joseph Voisin, there being considerable concern over debts contracted to the HBC for building in the archdiocese during the absence of F. N. Blanchet ("Procès verbaux," Conseil de

Lyon, meeting of September 13, 1848, 47–50, OPM). France's Revolution of 1848 also delayed disbursement of allocations.

11. "Piastre" in French Canada referred to the silver coin valued then at approximately one dollar; it continued to be used as a popular term for the dollar in species, as opposed to paper. A variation in a second version of the letter (found in AAS, A3: 80–83) adds: "The abundance of gold has increased the price of workers, day laborers, and others by tenfold. As a consequence, the missionaries were forced to take on jobs beyond their call, so as to provide for their very sustenance."

12. He is very likely referring to Father H.-T. Lempfrit, O.M.I. (1803–1862), originally from France, who traveled overland from Longueuil, Lower Canada; arrived in October 1848 and spent the winter at St. Joseph's in Olympia; and served as the only priest in the Diocese of Vancouver Island during the absence of Bishop Demers in Europe.

13. At a meeting on October 2, 1848, it was announced that Mr. Charles Choiselat-Gallien, treasurer for the Council of Paris, gave Abbé Voisin 16,000 francs for the account of the dioceses of Walla Walla and Vancouver Island, to be split evenly, having allocated the same the previous year, indicating as well that the suspension was lifted ("Procès verbaux," 54).

LETTER 11

To Pope Pius IX,
November 1, 1849[1]

Blanchet wrote to Pope Pius IX from The Dalles a month after returning from a trip to Oregon City (see letter 10) and while recovering from malarial attacks. While he was downriver in July 1849, the *Morning Star*, a ship owned by the flourishing Catholic French company the Society of Oceana, brought a load of goods from France, mail, and news from Europe and the Pacific Islands.[2] Blanchet heard further reports on the revolutionary political upheavals in Rome, including the pope's flight to exile in Gaeta in November 1848 and of the abolition of the temporal powers of the pope by the Italian revolutionaries in February 1849.

The pope's sufferings during this crisis are one subject of the letter; Blanchet writes about them in sympathetic and quite personal terms. To Blanchet there was a direct connection between the attacks on the papacy in the *Oregon American and Evangelical Unionist* and the occupation of the Papal States by revolutionaries in Rome. But the formal occasion of the letter is a response to Pius IX's encyclical, *Ubi Primum*, issued on February 2, 1849. In it the pope made this request: "We eagerly desire, furthermore, that, as soon as possible, you apprise Us concerning the devotion which animates your clergy and your people regarding the Immaculate Conception of the Blessed Virgin and how ardently glows the desire that this doctrine be defined by the Apostolic See. And especially, Venerable Brethren, We wish to know what you yourselves, in your wise judgment, think and desire on this matter."[3]

It might seem odd from a contemporary perspective that Pius IX, given his deteriorating position as a political prince in Europe, would be writing to his bishops about doctrine. But it was not peculiar from either the pope's or Blanchet's perspective. Both believed that supernatural, timeless realities mattered more than political upheavals. The pope's concern with the Immaculate Conception can be interpreted both as an act of symbolic resistance to the assault on papal powers and as a way of embracing and organizing the Catholic faithful around the world. Despite the political upheavals that stripped Pius IX of the Papal States, this was a period of continuing concentration of papal power over the church throughout the world—a process that had begun in the mid-eighteenth century and accelerated in reaction to the French Revolution and the republican revolutions of 1848. Blanchet, his fellow bishops in North America, and Pius IX shared a worldview that saw the Catholic Church as a bulwark of supernatural power, with the pope as its central leader and symbol of eternal stability. The growing devotional fervor of Catholic laity and clergy alike during this period bolstered confidence in this vision and garnered compliance with the Holy See's concentration of power.

Nor should the intimacy with which Blanchet writes to the pope be surprising. As Luca Codignola notes, during this period all the bishops of the North Atlantic world knew "each other or of each other, were in regular contact, and felt they were part of an impressive clerical network within the Catholic Church."[4] So, while Blanchet's current situation, health-impaired and residing at a mission distant from major urban centers or long-settled agricultural communities, might seem far removed from events in Europe, to his mind it was not. Blanchet writes to the pope, seeking through his expression of sympathy and the narration of his own seemingly feeble missionary efforts to strengthen in his own mind the order, stability, and purpose of their shared mission—guiding and sustaining the church, a supernatural institution, divine instrument of salvation on earth.

LETTER CONCERNING THE PERSECUTION HE IS
SUFFERING AND THE IMMACULATE CONCEPTION
OF MARY[5]

Most Holy Father,

Given our distance from the Holy Apostolic See, it is only very belatedly
that we receive news of what is happening, and share in your joy or your
sorrow. Though we are distant in body, we are not in spirit & heart; and
every day we lift our prayers in unison with all the bishops to draw heavenly
favors down upon the Supreme Pontiff and divert the evil that the gates of
hell ceaselessly provoke against him and the church that he governs.

Your reign, M.H.F.[Most Holy Father] had begun with such good fortune.
From the moment you were elevated to the Chair of St. Peter, the people
of Rome, your cherished people, did not weary of exalting the greatness of
your views, the generosity of your sentiments, the liberality of your deeds;
and they portrayed you to the universe as the regenerator of Italy, and even
of all people. Could one have expected to see them turn against you so
soon? How very astonished we were on hearing of last November's events,
of the persecution that you have had to suffer, of your retreat from the Holy
City to a realm where your holy person could find freedom and safety.

Oh! M.H.F., how deep was our grief when we received the news
that those very individuals who had just blessed your reign in crying:
"*Benedictus qui venit in nomine Domini*," were no longer heard but saying:
"*Tolle, tolle, crucifige*"; and that some were not even hiding their vicious plan
to abolish the Church of J.C.[Jesus Christ], forgetting that its divine founder
had proclaimed: "that the gates of hell would never prevail."[6] How you must
have suffered, seeing so much malice & viciousness!

We share with all Catholics, M.H.F., your sorrow, your affliction. Upon
hearing the news, we hastened to raise our ardent prayers to heaven, we
summoned the clergy and the faithful of our diocese to pray that the Lord
decrease your time of tribulation, touch the hearts of the evil ones who
have flagrantly insulted you, and that He quickly restore you to your Seat.
Yes, M.H.F., here in Oregon, amid rocky mountains, you have humble,

submissive children, who are praying to God on your behalf with all the fervor of new Christians. These children are Indians. May this thought help sweeten the bitterness of the chalice that other corrupted children have offered to you! May the prayers of the Pastor and his flock rising as sweet-smelling incense to the throne of the All-powerful, move Him with pity!

Your Encyclical letter of February 2nd last, addressed to all the bishops, was sent to us. As with everything issued from the Holy Apostolic See, we received it with deference, M.H.F.; and we ordered public prayers for the Holy Spirit to inspire and direct you in your decision concerning the Immaculate Conception of the Mother of God.

We should, in response to your wishes, be telling you of how the clergy and the faithful of our diocese practice their devotion to the Immaculate Conception of Mary, and of the desire to see the Holy Apostolic See give a dogmatic decree on this matter; but it is to our deep regret that we can do so only imperfectly.[7]

First, the faithful of our diocese are comprised almost exclusively of Indian neophytes.[8] Although we can assure you that faith in Mary Immaculate is not lacking, we cannot discern if it is sufficiently understood for the importance of a dogmatic decree to be appreciated.

In addition, it takes several months to consult with our clergy, due both to the distance of most missionaries and the difficulty of travel during this season.

To put things simply, there is no doubt whatsoever that all members of the clergy are inspired with a tender devotion for Mary Immaculate. Your Holiness will readily understand this in hearing that the clergy is comprised of children of St. Ignatius[9] and Oblates of Mary Immaculate of Marseilles.

As for us, Most Holy Father, since our youth we have sung these words many times in the cathedral and other churches of the diocese: "*Tota pulchra es, Maria, et macula originalis non est in te.*"[10] And later, by virtue of a favor granted by Gregory XVI—a happy memory in the diocese of Montreal—we added the word "*Immaculata*" before "Conception," and the words "*sine labe concepta*" ["conceived without stain"] to the litanies of the Blessed Virgin Mary. It should be said, words reflecting the pious belief that Mary's conception was immaculate have always been pronounced with joy. We will most certainly consider the day a happy one when Peter, speaking through your lips, announces to the Catholic Church that "Mary, by virtue of a unique privilege, has not at any time been tarnished by the stain of original sin, that this is a truth of faith."[11]

While waiting for this solemn day, this day of glory for the Son and the Mother, please be so kind, M.H.F., as to bless us again, along with our clergy, the faithful confided to our care, and even the infidels, which we are charged to bring into the bosom of the Church of J.C. We will receive your apostolic blessing as a pledge of heavenly favors to come and as a glorious sign of Your Paternal Benevolence toward us.

The most obedient son of your Holiness
Aug. Magl. Al. Bp. of Walla Walla

AAS, A5: 77–80.

————◆————

1. Pope Pius IX, born Giovanni Maria Mastai-Ferretti (1792–1878), served as archbishop of Spoleto (1827–32) and was appointed bishop of Imola (1832–46) before being named cardinal in 1840. On June 14, 1846, was elected to the papacy over a more conservative opponent, installed on June 21, 1848, and served until 1878, making his the longest pontificate in history. His early papacy was marked by conciliatory policies toward the "Young Italy" reform movement, including the establishment of a council of lay representatives from the provinces of the Papal States and later, under pressure, a constitution. The pope's policies whetted the appetite of the republicans for more freedoms and unrest grew. His secretary of state was stabbed to death and a papal prelate shot. In November 1848 Pius fled Rome for Gaeta in the Kingdom of Naples, where he was joined by a number of cardinals. On February 9, 1849, just five days after the promulgation of the encyclical to which Blanchet refers in this letter, the revolutionaries abolished the temporal powers of the pope and established a democratic republic. In response, Pius IX appealed to France, which sent an army that restored order in Rome in June 1849. Pius IX returned to the Vatican on April 12, 1850. As political unrest continued and his temporal power waned further during the remainder of his papacy, Pius IX asserted more forcefully the supernatural character of the church and the spiritual power of the pope, including at Vatican Council I the pronouncement of dogmas such as the infallibility of the pope. Michael Ott, "Pope Pius IX," in The Catholic Encyclopedia; An International Work of Reference on the Constitution, Doctrine, Discipline, and History of the Catholic Church (New York: Robert Appleton, 1911), vol. 12; Encyclopaedia Britannica, s.v. "Pius IX."

2. Blanchet, Journal of a Catholic Bishop, 111.

3. Ubi Primum, http://www.saint-mike.org/library/papal_library/PiusIX/Encyclicals/Ubi_Primum2.html (accessed December 9, 2009). This letter from Pope Pius IX is written in the first-person plural, a common practice in papal letters.

4. Luca Codignola, "Roman Catholic Conservatism in a New North Atlantic World, 1760–

1829," *William and Mary Quarterly* 64, no. 4 (October 2007): 721. The network continued into the following decades.

5. *Immaculate Conception* is a theological term meaning that Mary was conceived without sin; that she was preserved even from original sin, which, following Augustine, the Catholic Church taught was transferred to each human at the moment of conception.

6. "Blessed be he who comes in the name of the Lord" and "Take him away! Take him away! Crucify Him."

7. By 1849, Pius IX was already preparing the dogma of the Immaculate Conception, which was proclaimed on December 8, 1854.

8. The term *neophytes* refers to beginners in the faith, persons who are in the process of preparing for baptism.

9. He is referring here to the Jesuit missionaries of the Rocky Mountains, working in areas under his jurisdiction, members of the religious order of the Society of Jesus, founded in the sixteenth century by Saint Ignatius of Loyola.

10. "You are most beautiful, Mary, and original stain is not in you."

11. Blanchet is referring to the understanding that, when the Pope formally declares Catholic teaching, he speaks for the entire church, continuing the apostolic faith symbolized in the apostle Peter, the first pope.

LETTER 12

To Ignace Bourget, Bishop of Montreal, February 6, 1850

Bishop Blanchet had spent four uninterrupted months at the mission of St. Peter at Waskopam when he wrote this letter. Residing at The Dalles, an important way station on the Columbia, allowed Blanchet to maintain contact with the outside world, despite the settlement's sparse Euro-American population. In October, officers of the newly arrived U.S. Army regiment visited him on their way to Vancouver, and he learned that a good half of the regiment was Catholic. In December, thirty destitute American immigrants remained two weeks, the river being frozen, until a Canadien neighbor, Raymond, led them by foot to the Willamette. And on the morning of November 15, the express made a scheduled stop with letters and newspaper articles from Montreal, including several warmly encouraging and thought-provoking pages from Ignace Bourget, to which Blanchet responded with this letter.[1]

The topics in Bourget's letter, dated April 28, 1849, gave Blanchet much to ponder. Political conditions in Montreal were so tense that Bishop Modeste Demers, seeking personnel and raising funds while en route to Europe, had been more afraid to sleep in Montreal than on the vast prairies of the Northwest or the banks of the Columbia. As for himself, Bourget wrote: "Believe me, dear *Seigneur*, the bishop's thorns here are longer and sharper than those in Oregon." A litany of troubles—famines in Ireland, ravaging plagues, devastating earthquakes, deluges of anti-religious and immoral writings, the persecution of religious personnel including the pope, languishing faith in Old Europe—all of these, Bourget feared, portended the coming of the end of the world and the final Judgment. With so many inhabitants of the earth being plunged into the darkness of death, he counseled Blanchet to hasten his work, in order to gather the good grain—the newly regenerated peoples (Indians of his diocese)—before the trumpet sounded. To this end, he was making every effort to organize and stimulate the Quebec Society for the Propagation of the Faith, in part to respond to the requests for assistance from fellow Quebec clergy in the northwest of Canada and in Oregon. And as for religious communities, he wrote: "when the time is right, you have but to cry out, and the one you select is yours."[2]

In this despondent response to Bourget's letter, Blanchet employs biblical imagery to extend the metaphor of thorns in recognition of the meritorious suffering of his mentor. He informs Bourget that his own missionary success is more comparable to a grain of mustard than to a harvest of wheat.

Aware that Bourget and others might use parts of this letter for publication in the annual reports of the Quebec branch of the Society for the Propagation of the Faith, Blanchet then devotes the greater portion to what might stand as ethnographic observations of Indians in areas with Catholic missions. Given his own suffering from malaria at the time, it is not surprising that this account appears to be based as much upon hearsay as on firsthand experience. Nuances of interest nevertheless emerge: though Blanchet criticizes practices of polygamy and medicine in familiar ethnocentric tropes—citing them as obstacles to baptism and therefore reasons for the lack of harvest—unlike many Protestant missionaries, he says nothing about a need for Indians to abandon their lifeways as hunters and gatherers and to become settled farmers in order to be Christianized.[3]

My Very Dear *Seigneur,*

Your letter of April last and Monsignor the Coadjutor's gave me great
joy. You cannot imagine how such words of consolation, of wisdom &
news—especially ecclesiastical news—gladden us, isolated as we are from
cultivated people for months at a time. We always wait impatiently for the
Montreal Express.

After reading of the thorns that troubles in your country have added to
your miters, my own have lost much of their sting. The crowns you receive
from our righteous Judge will be far more glorious and brilliant than mine.
So many good works are born of your thorns. They generate abundant fruit
on the vine that you cultivate;[4] they increase by a hundred fold the field
you water with the sweat of your labor, such that one day you will be able
to say with confidence to our Heavenly Father: "*Domine, quinque talenta
tradidisti mihi, ecce alia quinque super lucratus sum." Regi saeculorum
immortali, invisibili, soli Deo honor & gloria.*[5]

But me, what am I doing here? Alas! Here it has been almost two years
since I arrived, and I have accomplished almost nothing worthy of the Lord,
if not perhaps the desire to do his will, once He informs me of what it is.

As for the missionaries, they certainly long to do good, and some have
had the opportunity to acquire a lovely crown for the privations they are
suffering during this troubled time. If their work and their pains have
not met with success, it is surely because the moment of grace has not yet
arrived for the tribes they are evangelizing.

Here is the status of the missions in my diocese:

Of the four we began here, none have made great progress. St. Peter
among the Waskos (Waskopam), where Father Rousseau and I have been
living for twenty months, comprises several small camps within a twenty to
thirty mile circumference. With the exception of the Waskos (Waskopam)
who speak a different language, the Indians of these various camps speak
Wallawalla (Wallolla). Several families from one camp spent a good part
of last winter nearby, & Father Rousseau began instructing them, teaching
them prayers in their own tongue. The other camps still show no sign
of interest. The Waskos were indifferent during the first fifteen months,
but since last autumn, several have approached us, & now some thirty to

forty regularly attend catechism instruction, which is offered daily. Most have learned prayers and some Canticles in the tchinouk jargon. A good number attend mass daily and recite the rosary while they are there. I am hoping that several will receive the waters of regeneration come Easter.[6] So there, Monsigneur is our grain of mustard.[7] Trade with the whites has corrupted these Indians. They have a fairly bad reputation. But will grace not accomplish here what it has done elsewhere on so many occasions? I have no doubt whatsoever. I trust that one day they will all enter the fold of the Good Shepherd.[8]

A first obstacle that has prevented quite a number from coming to instruction is their practice of polygamy. Some have two wives, others three or even four. I say wives because this is the term they use, though I should say concubines. Ask them why they take so many wives, some will tell you that it is to their advantage, that the more they have, the more work gets done and the more food there is, for it is the woman who supplies food for the entire family and who is expected to carry the loads when she has no horses to carry them for her. Our Indians have no real sense of marriage. The man and the woman live together as long as one or the other finds pleasure, & after they separate, each enters into a new union, destined to be no more stable than the first. Such is their custom.

The vice of polygamy is not easy to eradicate, because the head of the family benefits, or at least thinks he benefits, from being better served; it is of little concern to him that quarrels often arise among these unhappy wives.[9]

Another obstacle to conversion is the practice of medicine. This so-called medicine amounts to blowing on the sick person, touching them, or squeezing the afflicted part with both hands and bringing the mouth to it, all the while putting on a thousand acts and uttering cries, while the assistants sing and beat on some pieces of wood. This scene goes on for quite some time. At the end, the healer [*reveals*] something he claims to have drawn from the afflicted part, but which he had carefully prepared in advance. Let it be understood that during the performance, the healer and the sick person are not always the most decently attired. Women practice this craft—or this art if you prefer—as well as men. But whatever the gender, after the performance, the healer demands several horses, blankets & so forth, and as a result, these doctors often live very comfortably. As medicine is profitable for them, they spare nothing to perpetuate faith in their power and ability, not only to heal the sick, but also to make whomever they please become sick and die, by means of their medicine or the spirit that empowers them.

From time to time the healers do the dance of the tamenoès (the spirit that empowers them), which can last three, four or five evenings. They invite everyone, men, women and children, and dance in complete nudity before the gathering. They are said to be surpassing the forces of nature. After this dance, or rather this infernal entertainment, presents are distributed to all the observers. Some return to their huts with a piece of blanket, others with a remnant of cotton, or another such item. As you can well imagine, the healer does not hesitate to extol his generosity, and the poor dupes think only of their next illness; but should they call upon him later, they will pay a hundred fold the piece of blanket or remnant of cotton that they received.

It must be said, however, that there are a number who have no faith in the medicine, and who attend the dance more out of curiosity than appreciation. It was the missionary who opened their eyes. As a result, healers who fear losing their practice do not hesitate to protest—just as a people of the East long ago evoked "Great Diana of Ephesus" against the preaching of St. Paul—but the healers do not arouse as much commotion.[10] Such, dear Seigneur, are the two great wounds that afflict many Indians in these lands.[11]

In addition to the Waskos, there are the Indians of the des Chutes, who live either next to the falls on the Columbia, or at the mouth of the des Chutes River, about twenty miles southeast of here; others are on a fork of the des Chutes River, twenty-five or thirty miles to the southwest. Their language suggests that these Indians are descendants of the Walla Wallas. They have not yet shown any sign of desiring instruction.

If all these Indians were gathered together at one spot, there would be enough to keep a missionary occupied, but these Indians, like the other nations, insist on remaining on their own land (their territory), so there is very little hope of bringing them here.

The Cayuse Mission of St. Anne was started in 1847 but abandoned in 1848 on account of the war. It has not been resumed, because the missionary went to California.[12] This mission had great promise. There is a fervent desire for the missionary to return.

The Yakama missions of the Reverend Father Oblates, to the north of the river and two or three (days by foot) from Waskopam, are languishing like the others, for lack of funds.

So there, Monsignor, is where we stand, after almost two years with the Indians of my diocese, strictly speaking. As you see, there is little to be proud of, but rather much cause for humility.

As for the missions of the Reverend Father Jesuits located in the Colville region, they are flourishing as they were before I arrived. Generous funding from the Society for the Propagation of the Faith has allowed the Fathers to forge ahead. They have four regularly established missions: the first among the Flatheads; the second, Sacred Heart, among the Coeur d'Alenes; the third, St. Ignace, among the Kalispels; the fourth, St. Paul, among the Kettles. Their neophytes are fervent; they have churches, houses, and barns. They cultivate the land for their own needs and to help out their neophytes as well.

And as for us, we have made little more progress materially than spiritually. With the exception of the rough plank floors that Father Rousseau laid, my "palace" is pretty much in the same state that it was when I last wrote. A chapel that will serve as "cathedral" remains to be built. As you are well aware, this is not due to a lack of will.

I believe that the Waskos are the poorest Indians of my diocese. In this country an Indian's wealth is measured by the number of horses he owns. We are told that some Cayuse chiefs have more than 1,500. Our Indians have very few. Until last year, they dressed quite poorly. One still sees children naked, old women wearing little, but I believe that this is as much the result of habit as want of clothing, because the girls and young women are more discreet. There is no lack, however, of bucks and hinds in our mountains, but the Indians are too lazy to hunt them; they prefer instead to spend the winter in their lodges, where they have no chores other than supplying wood, for during this season the women are freed from this duty. That is not to say that the women are idle; to the contrary, they are constantly working, either preparing meals or braiding mats, while the men are sleeping or smoking.

Dry salmon is a staple of our Indians and of all those who live close to the Columbia and its tributaries, from the ocean to the slopes of the Rocky Mountains. When not hindered by some obstruction, salmon return everywhere in abundance. In spite of innumerable rapids, they return in less than two months to the Snake River not far from Fort Hall, over 400 leagues from the mouth of the Columbia. This is a precious manna, without which our Indians would suffer from hunger.[13] The men do the fishing, using woven nets, but it is up to the women to clean, dry, and store them for winter. Some add camas onions to the dried salmon; others, roots or fruits such as blueberries or pears that the women collect or pick, & dry. Acorns are not spurned and they are put to good use. Those who live in the Rocky Mountains have buffalo or bison meat; but they risk their lives in procuring it, because the Blackfeet lie in ambush everywhere, waiting to massacre them.

As you see, the Indians do not lack food when they want to take the trouble to get it; but we have observed that dried salmon often gives them heartburn, due to the bile. To relieve them, we expend a considerable amount on salts.

I have decided to make my Episcopal See here (Waskopam) if Providence does not allow me to be transferred.[14] This station is commonly known as The Dalles, because the Columbia rapids are only a few miles to the east. It is located at the edge of the Cascade Mountains. There is every reason to believe that it will soon become important. It is no more than 120 miles from Oregon City, either by river or through the mountains, and the journey takes four or five days. My palace is about one mile from the former Methodist mission. Two Canadiens have settled a short distance from the Mission of St. Peter. There are no other whites here.

I need not tell you of the fevers that raged last summer in the California mines, carrying away a great number of Canadiens and Americans, for I assume that Monsignor the Archbishop will do so. Continue to pray and to ask others to pray for the missionaries; and in particular for your devoted colleague.

Aug. M. Al. Bp. of Walla Walla

P.S. If Your Lordship finds anything in this letter that may be of interest to the readers of the Reports of the Society for the Propagation of the Faith of Quebec, please pass it on to Monsignor de Sydime.

ACAM, FILE 195.133, 850–2; AAS, A3: 76–79.

———— • ————

1. The HBC established the Montreal Express as an annual mail delivery that spanned its overland trade route from the Montreal headquarters at Lachine to Fort Vancouver. "The Ex-

press passed by this morning bringing letters from Msgr. of Montreal, from his coadjutor & from Canon Paré . . . and some newspaper clippings." A. M. A. Blanchet, "Journal de l'Evêque de Walla Walla, depuis Montréal, capitale du Canada, jusqu'à Walla Walla," AAS, A1. We used the original statement of the bishop in this instance because of translation irregularities in the Kowrach edition, *Journal of a Catholic Bishop*.

2. Bourget to Blanchet, April 28, 1849, ACAM, Régistre des Lettres (RL), 5:186.

3. For a recent history of the Columbia River Indians, see Andrew H. Fisher, *Shadow Tribe: The Making of Columbia River Indian Identity* (Seattle: University of Washington Press and Center for the Study of the Pacific Northwest, 2010).

4. "The vine that you cultivate" is an allusion to the image of a faithful vinedresser from Luke 13:6–9 and contrasts with the evil vineyard keepers in Luke 20:9–17. More remotely, it alludes to the words of Jesus to his apostles in John 15:5, "I am the vine, you are the branches. Those who abide in me and I in them bear much fruit, because apart from me you can do nothing."

5. "Lord, you gave me five talents, here are five more that I gave rise to" is an allusion to Matthew 25:15–22, a parable in which a slave given money by his master worked to make more and was rewarded, and the slave who buried the money for fear of its being stolen was punished. The second sentence translates as: "To the immortal invisible King of the Ages, and only God, be all honor and glory."

6. "The waters of regeneration" refers to the sacrament of baptism, which for adults often occurred on Easter, the feast of the resurrection of Jesus.

7. "The grain of mustard" refers to Luke 13:19 and parallels, a parable in which Jesus compares the Kingdom of God to the mustard seed, a small seed that grows into a large shrub which shelters birds.

8. The Good Shepherd refers to Christ.

9. As marriage (as well as the last rites before death) was considered a once-in-a lifetime sacrament, the practice of monogamy was more than an ethical concern for Catholic missionaries. Evoking some of the same "obstacle" tropes to baptism in an earlier account of missionary work along the Cowlitz, Father Modeste Demers explained that polygamy was a custom deeply rooted since time immemorial and that a major reason for Indian opposition to abandoning all but one wife was concern that without the "illegitimate" wives, the family would suffer—a possible reference to the importance of clan networks in Indian culture, in addition to reliance on women's work. *Notice sur les Missions du Diocèse de Québec*, no. 3 (January 1841): 72.

10. The success of Paul's preaching against the worship of idols caused metalsmiths who made images of the goddess Diana to riot against him from fear that people would no longer purchase idols and that the goddess Diana would lose her "magnificence" (Acts 19:23–40).

11. Other missionaries at Waskopam also wrote accounts of their observations of these cures by object removal or exorcism. See Rousseau, "Caravane," 246–47; and Boyd, *People of The Dalles*, 120–27. The latter is an historical ethnography based primarily on documents written by Reverend Henry Perkins, Methodist missionary stationed at Waskopam from 1838 to 1844.

12. See letter 13 for Brouillet's stay in California.

13. The reference to manna connects the Indians' salmon to the food that sustained the Israelites as they wandered in the desert during the Exodus, the forty years of wandering after leaving Egypt (Exodus 16:15).

14. An episcopal see is a city where a bishop resides, the diocesan headquarters. Blanchet was still awaiting the pope's response to his request that he be transferred from the Diocese of Walla Walla to Nesqualy.

LETTER 13

To J. B. A. Brouillet, Vicar-General, March 9, 1850

From his exile in Gaeta, Pope Pius IX saw to the pastoral care of Catholic populations as well as to church dogma. Of particular concern to him was California. After three years of empire following independence from Spain in 1821, Mexico adopted a republican constitution in 1824. The federalists, who were in power when California became a territory of the Mexican Republic in 1825, secularized California's Franciscan missions, and the priests returned to Spain, creating a clerical vacuum; by 1849, most missions were closed. The United States annexed Upper California in 1848, and a year later an estimated eighty thousand people from around the world, many of them Catholic, were at work in the goldfields. Father Jose Maria de Jesus Gonzales Rubio, one of the later Franciscan missionaries and administrator, *Sede Vacante*, of Upper and Lower California, solicited American bishops to send priests, preferably English speaking, to serve this floating Catholic population.[1]

Vicar-General Brouillet was the first priest to respond affirmatively to this call. He spoke English, the prohibition on his return to his Mission St. Anne among the Cayuse was still in effect, and he was without a ministry in the Willamette Valley, most Canadiens having gone to California.[2] Brouillet remained in California from December 1848 to January 1850. He oversaw the building of a church on Vallejo Street in San Francisco and served as its first pastor; helped persuade the Sisters of Notre Dame of Namur and the Jesuits in St. Paul, Oregon, to relocate their schools to San Francisco; carried out pastoral tasks for Administrator Rubio; and solicited funds for the Archdiocese of Oregon.[3] With the 1849 movement to annex Quebec to the United States and news of riches to be had in California, Canadiens were migrating there as well; rumors spread among clergy in Quebec and Oregon that Brouillet himself was planning to remain there.[4]

When his bishop wrote this brief and terse letter, Brouillet had been back in Oregon for just two months. Blanchet had two immediate and not easily reconcilable needs to which he wanted Brouillet to attend: to replace the weakened Father Rousseau at Waskopam and to solicit funds in California. By permitting his vicar-general to return, but only briefly, to California, Blanchet reached a compromise, one that also tightened the leash on a valuable priest he feared losing. At the nadir of his episcopacy, events beyond his control led the bishop of Walla Walla to shed missionary idealism in favor of administrative pragmatism.

Oregon City, March 9th 1850

Vicar General,

Given the blessings that the Lord has deigned shower upon your efforts to seek funds for the impoverished missions of Oregon & your hope to collect considerably more, you may return to California and prepare to leave as soon as possible. But as the needs of my diocese are no less important than those of the Archbishopric—my lacking so much as a little chapel for proper services—you must work for us. The product of the collections you make will be split into two equal shares until Monsignor the Archbishop receives the equivalent of eight thousand piastres. If the Lord blesses our works in such a way that you receive still more, I reserve the right to decide, upon your return, how the split will be made.[5]

Given the difficulty in which I find myself, due to Father Rousseau's weak health, I can give you only two months for collecting subscriptions in California, & it is my firm intent that you not become involved in any other matter.

As soon as you return to Oregon, you will head for Waskopam for obvious reasons.

As in the past, my prayers will accompany you everywhere.

A. M. A. Bp. of W.W.

AAS, A5: 88–89.

1. Henry L. Walsh, S.J., *Hallowed Were the Gold Dust Trails: The Story of the Pioneer Priests of Northern California* (Santa Clara, Calif.: University of Santa Clara Press, 1947), 14–15. *Sede Vacante* means "with the see vacant"—"without a bishop."

2. Peter Burnett organized Oregon's first wagon company, led by Thomas McKay; at least two-thirds of the population capable of bearing arms left for California in the summer and autumn of 1848. Some went a second time to California in 1849, including members of a large company of Canadiens and métis, many of whom died from fever en route. Peter Burnett, *Recollections and Opinions of an Old Pioneer* (New York: D. Appleton and Company, 1880), 255–75, 325; Bancroft, *History of Oregon*, 2:43, 51; François Norbert Blanchet, "Historical Sketches," in *Early Catholic Missions in Old Oregon*, ed. Bagley, 1:144.

3. Marian Josephine Thomas, S.N.J.M., "Abbé Jean-Baptiste Abraham Brouillet: First Vicar General of the Diocese of Seattle" (master's thesis, Seattle University, 1950), 25–27; Blanchet, *Journal of a Catholic Bishop*, 138.

4. In the aftermath of the 1837–38 Patriote rebellions, Lord Durham, governor of British North America, in 1841 united the two colonies, French Canadian Lower Canada and anglophone Upper Canada, into the Province of Canada. The resulting unequal representation in the province's parliament aroused the anger of Canadien nationalists, and an unsuccessful movement began in 1849 to seek annexation to the United States, where greater equality was assumed. John Dickinson and Brian Young, *A Short History of Quebec*, 4th ed. (Montreal: McGill-Queens University Press, 2008), 182–85. Bishop Prince wrote to Brouillet that publication in the Montreal diocesan paper of his letter describing the riches of the mines in California produced a magical effect on all "our" Canadiens. He also stated that if annexation were not to happen, then too many people were emigrating, and he asked Brouillet to tell them the truth about the gold rush and whether the rumors were true that he was not returning at all to the Columbia. Prince to Brouillet, Montreal, November 1, 1849, box 6, folder 5, RG 820, AAS.

5. Blanchet reported to Bourget that he received a letter from Brouillet fifteen days after his arrival in San Francisco, in which Brouillet stated that he had nothing to do and that, in spite of the abundance of the mines, he despaired even of collecting enough to pay the expenses of his voyage, given the crisis in which he found the country (Blanchet to Bourget, July 21, 1850, ACAM, file 195.133, 850–4). Father François-Joseph Cénas, a secular priest who visited San Francisco en route from Montreal to Oregon, wrote that he had trouble finding the church run by Fathers Antoine Langlois and Brouillet and that no one was thinking of religion, all being plunged in material interests or debauchery. In the company of Vicar-General Brouillet and Father Michael Accolti, S.J., Cénas left San Francisco on July 8 aboard the steamer *Carolina* and arrived in Oregon City on July 15. Cénas to "Monsieur et bien digne ami," Oregon City, July 28, 1850, in *Rapport sur Les Missions du Diocèse de Québec*, no. 9 (March 1851): 58–65. A receipt dated September 6, 1850, signed by Richard Lane, agent for the HBC, for reception from "The Archbishop of Oregon City, through the hands of The Rev'd Mr. Brouillet, the sum of four thousand dollars in gold dust equal to two hundred and fifty ounces, being part payment of the debt owed by the Roman Catholic Mission to the Hudson's Bay

Company," indicates that Brouillet's second trip achieved a measure of success after all (receipt, Bishop's Correspondence, folder 7, RG 610, AAS). (In current value, the $4,000 would be roughly $115,000. The currency conversion is based on the consumer price index and is for the year 2010 [MeasuringWorth, http://www.measuringworth.com/uscompare].)

LETTER 14

To Ignace Bourget, Bishop of Montreal, November 22, 1850

By the time Blanchet again wrote Bishop Ignace Bourget, the fortunes of his episcopal project had improved. In mid-October, he received official notification from Rome that he had been appointed to the newly established see of Nesqualy. On October 20, he departed from his quarters at Mission St. Peter at The Dalles, leaving Father Rousseau in full charge. Seven days later he arrived at his new see. Here, on lands originally provided to the Church by the HBC, in sight of the pickets of Fort Vancouver to the southeast and the new U.S. military reservation to the northeast, the bishop presided. His new church was more recognizably a cathedral than had been the cabins at Tawatoé's camp or The Dalles.[1]

Blanchet saw opportunity for the Church in the growing number of settlers, some having claims in the newly platted township of Columbia City immediately to the west, later called Vancouver. While visiting his brother in Oregon City, Blanchet approached Bishop Bourget for personnel.

Oregon City, November 22nd 1850

Venerable Colleague,

Official news of my translation to the episcopal seat of Nesqualy arrived mid-October, and on the twentieth, I moved all my belongings downriver to the new diocese. After visiting the stations that appeared most promising, I settled here (Ft. Vancouver), as there is much good to be done, and also because it promises to become the most significant settlement in the Nesqualy region once the government of Washington purchases the property belonging to the Hudson's Bay Company.[2] It is already the most populous. There are Canadiens living here, as well as a fair number of Catholics among the troops on duty, for this is the main military post.[3]

As Bishop of Walla Walla, I didn't really have enough to do; I wished for more. Now, I can fulfill my zeal, and I hope to see much good achieved. A remarkable thing, there is not a single Protestant minister in the entire diocese; nor is there a tenth of the prejudice against Catholics that one finds in the archdiocese. Also, there is not a single Protestant school, although the Americans are ready to make sacrifices for the education of their children. Oh! May Providence come to my rescue and provide the means for bringing brothers, sisters for teaching, and Sisters of Charity! If I can avert the coming of Protestant teachers, I have every reason to believe that the taxes levied in each county for education will go to the teachers I bring in. I feel the impossible must be done to obtain teachers right away, so I am writing to Your Lordship, convinced that it will not be in vain.[4]

Initially, I will need sisters to teach. I have already cast my sights on the Community at Longueil. However, if you think that the sisters of the Congregation are more suitable, I have no objection. I rely on your judgment. Take note, however, that it is English, above all, that must be taught here.[5]

I also need brothers who can be placed here and there in small numbers (and even alone). You mentioned two years ago that the Brothers of St. Joseph were prepared to come. I would gladly welcome them provided that a few have some knowledge of English.

As for the Sisters of Providence, their place has been reserved for a long while, and they can prepare to come. Monsignor the archbishop also feels the need for having some in Oregon City, strictly for works of charity. For my part, I would like them to assume teaching the young as well, at least until we have a greater number of other sisters.

So there are my plans, Monsignor, and I will find a means to carry them out quickly. Perhaps the good sisters will find friends who are willing to help with the expenses of the voyage. In this way, at least those destined to teach the young will be able to set out for Oregon with Monsignor of Vancouver [Island].[6] Knowing that travel will become easier and less expensive, and wanting to avoid huge expenses that I cannot cover, we must be satisfied initially with the minimum number of sisters needed to constitute a foundation.

Letters from Canada arrive here in a month & a half. Please let me know what you think of my plans, & don't hesitate to mention any obstacles you may see to carrying them out. Once again, could you tell me if the government paid my portion of the indemnity, and see that *Les Mélanges religieux* or another good paper from Canada is sent here.[7]

My best respects to Monsignor the Coadjutor and members of the Chapter.

With respectful admiration, Monsignor,
I am your very humble and obedient servant
A. M. Al., Bp. of Nesqualy

P.S. Father Brouillet just informed me that he has already written to Father Laroque, requesting the *Mélanges religieux*; that will suffice.

ACAM, FILE 195.133, 850–5; AAS, A2: 141–43 (SHORTENED VERSION).

———•———

1. Blanchet's chapel was the second at Fort Vancouver. The first, located within the fort walls, had been outgrown. Factors James Douglas and John McLoughlin offered use of a tract of land to the north and west of the fort and donated the materials for a new church, St. James, opened and blessed by Father Peter de Vos, S.J., on May 31, 1846. Measuring 81 or 83 feet long, 36 feet wide, and 20 feet high, it contained a gallery, 12 feet in depth, that extended across the width of the building, and was reported to accommodate about five hundred persons. John A. Hussey, *The History of Fort Vancouver and Its Physical Structure* ([Tacoma]: Washington State Historical Society, 1957), 178–82, 208–9.

2. The third and fourth articles of the 1846 treaty fixing the United States–Great Britain boundary stipulated that "possessory rights of the Hudson's Bay Company and other British subjects who may be already in the occupation of land or other property lawfully acquired within said territory, shall be respected" until "transferred to said government at a proper valuation to be agreed upon by both parties" (Bancroft, *History of Oregon*, 1:592n). Though generally anticipated to take place within a few years, it was not until 1869 that the final sum for the purchase was agreed upon ($450,000 to the HBC and $200,000 to the subsidiary Puget Sound Agricultural Company) and not until 1870 and 1871 that the United States purchased the properties, including Fort Vancouver, in two equal installments (Hussey, *History of Fort Vancouver*, 114).

3. Although Fort Victoria on Vancouver Island had become administrative headquarters for the HBC Columbia District when Chief Factor Douglas took up residency there in May 1849, Fort Vancouver remained a financial center of the company's operations west of the Rockies until 1860, when it was evacuated. The mercantile business that gradually replaced the declining fur trade during these intervening years expanded as immigrants and miners increased. Canadien employees who handled much of the farm work, Hawaiians who were the backbone of the lumbering industry, English and Scottish skilled artisans, and Indian workers from diverse nations, all occupied dwellings outside the fort walls. In 1849, U.S. Army quartermaster Captain Rufus Ingalls executed an agreement with Chief Factor Ogden for rental of a few standing structures outside the walls and erection of others on the brow of the bluff overlooking the Vancouver settlement. In October 1850, arrangements were made for a military reservation, known then as Columbia Barracks, not to be confused with the HBC-owned Fort Vancouver. The army brought business to the company shops and mills and helped protect the lands from encroachment. Hussey, *History of Fort Vancouver*, 91–94, 101–4; David Lavender, "Part 2," in *Fort Vancouver, Handbook* 113 (Washington, D.C.: U.S. Department of the Interior, National Park Service, 2001), 9, 97; Douglas C. Wilson and Theresa E. Langford, eds., *Exploring Fort Vancouver* (Vancouver, Wash.: Fort Vancouver National Trust; Seattle: University of Washington Press, 2011), 12–13. Many recent male immigrants from Ireland and Germany, mostly Catholic, filled army ranks.

4. Since 1824, children of HBC employees had been instructed in fort schools north of the Columbia. In 1850, the Oregon Territory's legislative assembly established a system of free public schools and a tax of two mill (two-tenths of a cent) for distribution to local school districts in proportion to the number of children. With missionaries and their wives often serving as teachers, Blanchet assumed that schools operated by Catholic personnel would benefit from public funds as did schools operated by Protestants in the territory.

5. Longueil was home of the Sisters of the Holy Names of Jesus and Mary, established in Marseilles by Monsignor Eugène de Mazenod (founder as well of the male Oblates of Mary Immaculate), and in Lower Canada by Blessed Mary-Rose Durocher (beatified in 1843), to provide instruction for girls in rural areas. In 1848, Esther Blondin established the Congregation of the Sisters of Saint Anne in Lower Canada for teaching poor children. Both French Canadian institutions were under the patronage of Ignace Bourget. Marta Danylewycz, *Taking the Veil: An Alternative to Marriage, Motherhood, and Spinsterhood in Quebec, 1840–1920* (Ontario: McClelland and Stewart, 1987), 47; Louis Rousseau and Frank W. Remiggi, *Atlas historique des pratiques religieuses: Le sud-ouest du Québec au XIXe siècle* (Ottawa: Presses de l'Université d'Ottawa, 1998), 202–3. It was not until 1859 that twelve Holy Names sisters came west, to the Archdiocese of Oregon City, and several years later to Seattle, and that three Sisters of Saint Anne came west, to the Diocese of Vancouver Island (letter 30). Although the primary apostolate of the Sisters of Providence was charity, they taught in order to help fund their other ministries.

6. Modeste Demers, bishop of Vancouver Island, did not depart from Europe to return to his diocese until after March 1851 (Demers to Bourget, March 9, 1851, ACAM, file 255.108, 851–1).

7. In 1847, Lord Elgin, who was named governor of the United Provinces of Upper and Lower Canada, oversaw the formation of the local parliament that approved legislation allowing exiled Patriotes to return home, naming French as an official language, and signing into law

the Rebellion Losses Bill, which granted indemnity to Patriotes who had lost property during the rebellions (Dickinson and Young, *A Short History of Quebec*, 184). The name of A. M. A. Blanchet does not appear on the list of the indemnified. The *Mélanges religieux*, patronized by Bishop J.-C. Prince, was incurring financial difficulties at this time, and was not revived after the loss of the cathedral, the bishop's residence, and more than one thousand homes in Montreal's St.-Denis district during a devastating fire in 1852. Georges Aubin, "Correspondance de A. M. A. Blanchet, 1797–1887," 3:427nn4–5; Anne Gardon, *Eglises et sanctuaires du Québec / Churches and Shrines of Quebec* (Quebec: Messageries de Presse Benjamin, 1995), 5.

FORT VANCOUVER
and
VILLAGE

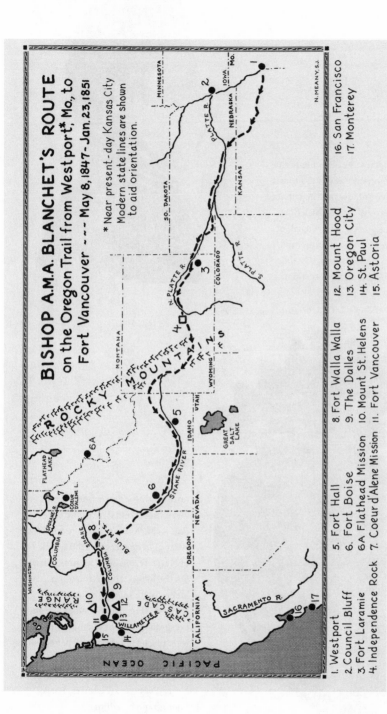

FIGURE 1. Route that Bishop A. M. A. Blanchet and his party took over the Oregon Trail, from Westport, Missouri, to Fort Walla Walla, May 8–September 5, 1847. Having moved to Fort Vancouver in October 1850, the bishop first reserved the sacrament in a tabernacle at Fort Vancouver's proto-cathedral on January 23, 1851, which explains the later date on this map. Map drawn by N. Meany, S.J., Archives of the Oregon Province of the Society of Jesus, 560.01.

FIGURE 2. Father A. M. A. Blanchet while incarcerated at Montreal's new jail, known as the Pied-du-Courant, during the Patriote insurrection of 1837–38. Sketch by fellow political prisoner, notary J. J. Girouard, of Saint-Benoît, Lower Canada. Photograph by Georges Aubin, L'Assomption, Quebec, courtesy of A. M. A. Blanchet descendants.

FIGURE 3. Memorial metal heart locket, representative of the type that A. M. A. Blanchet requested (in letter 1) to be placed in the Basilica of Notre-Dame des Victoires, Paris. On the locket, approximately 4 inches in diameter, the letter *M* refers to Mary. Most mementos, and presumably that of Bishop Blanchet, were placed behind the upper cornices of the church and remained there, inaccessible. Courtesy of the Archives, Notre-Dame des Victoires, Paris. Photograph by editors.

FIGURE 4. Map of the proposed Ecclesiastical Province of Oregon, as submitted for approval to Rome in 1846. Copy courtesy of the Archives of the Archdiocese of Quebec, 102 CM, Correspondance imprimée de Rome, 1:238.

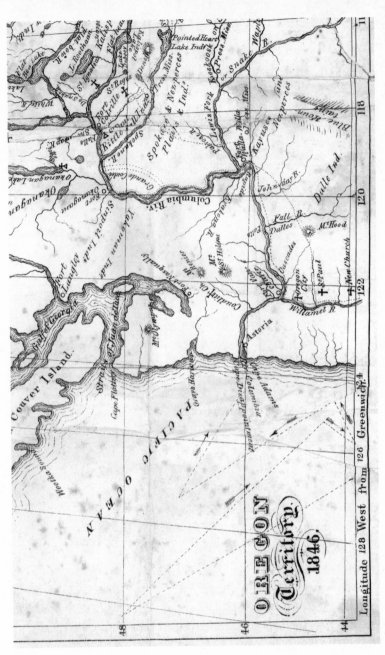

FIGURE 5. Map of Indian lands, missions, and Hudson's Bay forts in Old Oregon and parts of Rupert's Land, by Peter De Smet, S.J., 1846. Catholic missions and mission stations are indicated by a cross; Protestant missions on the Columbia Plateau are indicated by "Press. Miss." This map offers the perspective of Bishop Blanchet and his party upon arrival in the fall of 1847, with Fort Walla Walla and the Whitman Mission in the lower center. Early Washington Maps Collection, Manuscripts, Archives, and Special Collections, Washington State University Libraries, WSU 325.

FIGURE 6. Peopeomoxmox, head chief of the Walla Wallas. Sketch made by Gustave Sohon during the 1855 Walla Walla Treaty Council. Washington State Historical Society, 1918.114.9.64.

FIGURE 7. Joseph Joset, S.J., who served in the Jesuits' Rocky Mountain Mission from 1844 until his death in 1900. Replacing Peter De Smet as superior in 1845, he had hoped to establish a mission among the Cayuses and Nez Percés but lacked the resources. Taken during his later years, the photograph reveals Father Joset's legendary cheerful demeanor. Archives of the Oregon Province of the Society of Jesus, 1159.04.

FIGURE 8. Wecah-Te-na-Teo-ma-ny (Tawatoé), also known as "Young Chief," chief of a Cayuse band on the Umatilla River. Sketch made by Gustave Sohon during the 1855 Walla Walla Treaty Council. Washington State Historical Society, 1918,114.9.48.

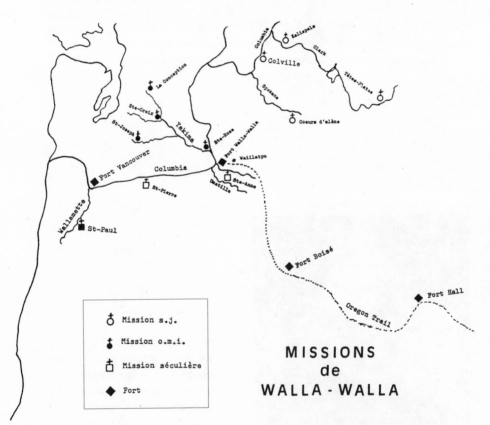

FIGURE 9. Catholic missions established in the Diocese of Walla Walla. The symbols indicate the three missionary groups in charge of each mission: Society of Jesus, Oblates of Mary Immaculate, and secular (diocesan) priests. Copy courtesy of Georges Aubin, L'Assomption, Quebec.

FIGURE 10.1. Front side of Immaculate Conception medal, less than one inch in diameter. The medal depicts Mary of the Immaculate Conception, a common artistic subject since the 1600s. Photo by editors.

FIGURE 10.2. Back side of Immaculate Conception medal depicting a cross with a bar, the letter M, twelve stars, and two hearts representing the "Sacred Heart of Jesus" and the "Immaculate Heart of Mary." Courtesy Providence Archives, Seattle, A-189.012

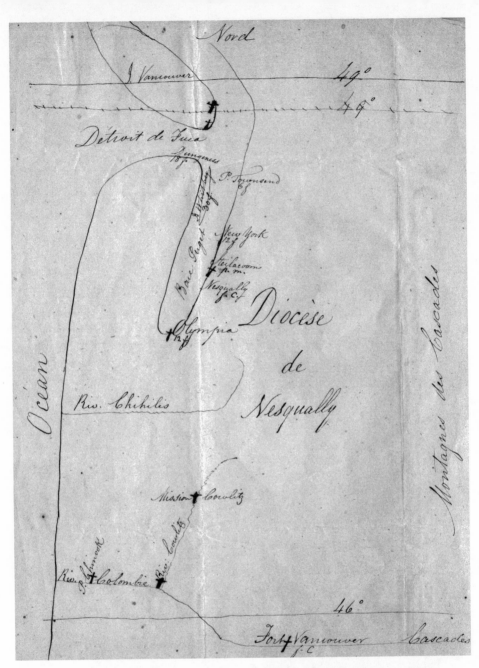

FIGURE 11. Hand sketch, in French, of the Diocese of Nesqualy, dated 1850, before lands east of the Cascades were added. This map depicts missions (with a cross) and early settlements, including New York (future Seattle). Spelling of the diocese with a double *l* and Chehalis River (Chihilis), reflects irregular spelling at the time. Archives of the Archdiocese of Seattle, RG 610, History, Maps, Diocese of Nesqualy.

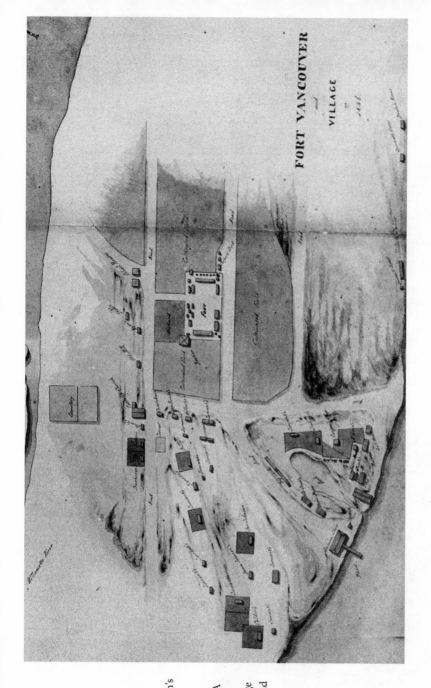

FIGURE 12.
Fort Vancouver
and village in
1846, portion
depicting the fort,
Catholic church,
and surrounding
neighbors' cabins.
By Richard
Covington. Hudson's
Bay Company
Archives, Archives
of Manitoba, HBCA
G.2/24 (N4179).
Details of this image
appear on pp. 88 and
166.

FIGURE 13. Fort Vancouver, Washington Territory, 1854. A view of the Catholic church and neighboring cabins in foreground, picketed Hudson's Bay Company Fort Vancouver, U.S Army's Vancouver Barracks (hilltop), Columbia River, and Mount Hood. Copy print from a lithograph by Gustave Sohon, published in 1860. Courtesy Providence Archives, Seattle, 22.E16.41.

FIGURE 14. Isaac Stevens, ca. 1856, governor of Washington Territory, Washington State Archives.

FIGURE 15.1. Father Charles Pandosy, O.M.I. Archives of the Oregon Province of the Society of Jesus, 03.01a.

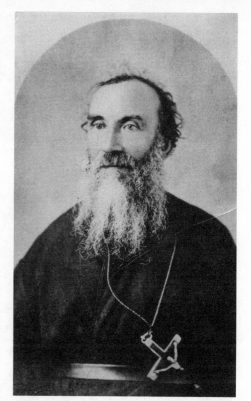

FIGURE 15.2. Fragment of musical notation and words adapted for Sahaptin-speaking Yakamas, in the hand of Father Pandosy. He spoke the language and adapted it to writing while serving the Yakama Indians. Archives of the Archdiocese of Seattle, RG 610, History.

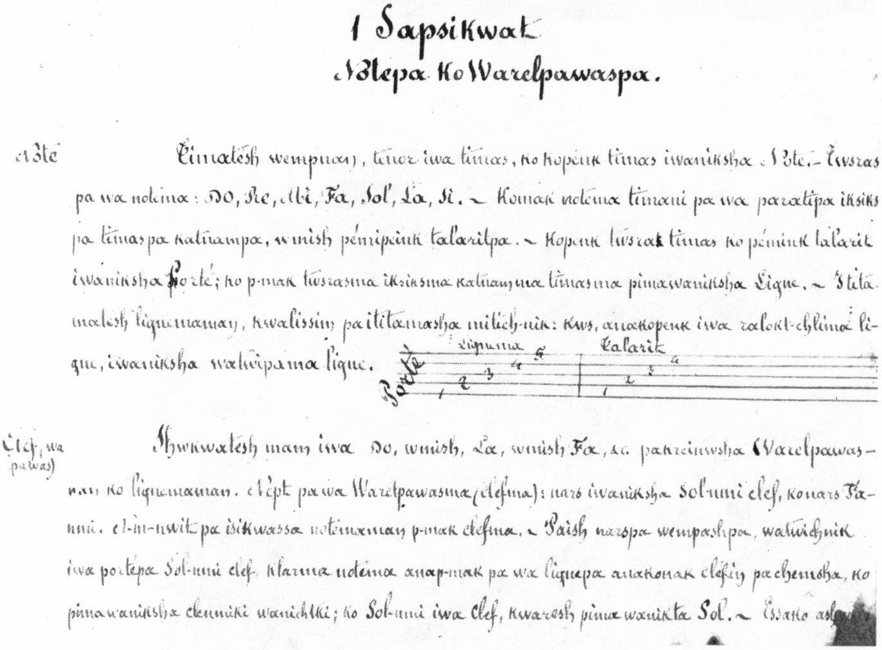

1 Sapsikwat
Notepa ko Warelpawaspa.

Note — Timatesh wempnay, tinoz iwa timas, ko kopenk timas iwaniksha Note. — Twsras pa wa notima: Do, Re, Mi, Fa, Sol, La, Si. — Komak notima timani pa wa paratipa iksiks pa timaspa katnampa, wnish pénipink talaritpa. — Kopenk twsrak timas ko pénink talarik iwaniksha Porté; ko p-mak twsrasma iksiksma katnamma timasma pinawaniksha Ligne. — Itita-matesh liqnemamay, kwalissiu paititamasha milich-nik: Kws, anakopenk iwa zalokt-chlima li-gne, iwaniksha wahvipama ligne.

Clef, wa pawas — Shwkwatesh mam iwa Do, wnish, La, wnish Fa, sa pakreinwsha Warelpawas-nan ko liqnemanan. Népt pa wa Warelpawasma (clefma): nars iwaniksha Sol-nmi clef, konars Fa-nmi. El-m-nwit pa isikwassa notimanan p-mak clefma. — Paish narspa wempashpa, watwichnik iwa poitepa Sol-nmi clef. Klarma notima anap-mak pa wa liqnepa anakonak cléfiy pa chemsha, ko pinawaniksha ckenniki wanichtki; ko Sol-nmi iwa Clef, kwaresh pima waniKta Sol. — Issako asl

FIGURE 16. Cross presented by "the passengers of the 'Star of the West,' Sep. 30 A.D. 1855 To the Rt. Rev'd Dr Blanchet, Bishop of Washington Territory. In testimony of his self sacrificing charity during great affliction on the voyage from California to New York. Received for aiding ship victims." Photograph by Georges Aubin, L'Assomption, Quebec, taken on October 3, 1987.

FIGURE 17. St. Ignatius Mission, panorama view, journal illustration. Archives of the Oregon Province of the Society of Jesus, 114.2.03a.

FIGURE 18. Sister Mary of the Infant Jesus with closest Flathead assistants, at second St. Ignatius Mission, founded on September 24, 1854, in today's state of Montana. On the left is Pe-na-ma, or Penama, most likely Sophie Finlay's mother, and on the right, Sophie Finlay (1842-1921), daughter of François (Penetzi) Finlay. The photograph was taken on the occasion of the fiftieth anniversary of the Providence Mission at St. Ignatius (begun in 1864); the location is probably the porch of the Holy Family Hospital. Courtesy Providence Archives, Seattle, 1914, 33.B1.2.

FIGURE 19. Sisters of Providence Mother House, Montreal, Quebec, used from 1844 to 1888. Courtesy Providence Archives, Seattle, SP1, B5.6.

Fondateur et Fondatrice des Soeurs de Charité de la Providence de Montreal.

FIGURE 20. Mother Emilie Gamelin, foundress, and Bishop Ignace Bourget, founder, Sisters of Charity of Providence, Montreal. Postcard published by Providence Mother House in honor of the centennial of the religious community in 1943. Widow Emilie Gamelin visited and assisted Father A. M. A. Blanchet during his imprisonment, 1837-38. Courtesy of Providence Archives, Seattle, SP1, A10.1.

FIGURE 21. Composite of portraits of the five founding Sisters of Providence, Northwest mission, in Washington Territory. *Front, left to right*, Praxedes of Providence, Joseph of the Sacred Heart, and Mary of the Precious Blood; *back, left to right*, Vincent de Paul and Blandine of the Holy Angels. Courtesy of Providence Archives, Seattle, 22. E19.1.

FIGURE 22.
May 1857 report submitted by Bishop A. M. A. Blanchet to the Society for the Propagation of the Faith, Paris and Lyons. Courtesy of the Archives des Oeuvres Pontificales Missionnaires (OPM), Lyons, France. Photo by editors.

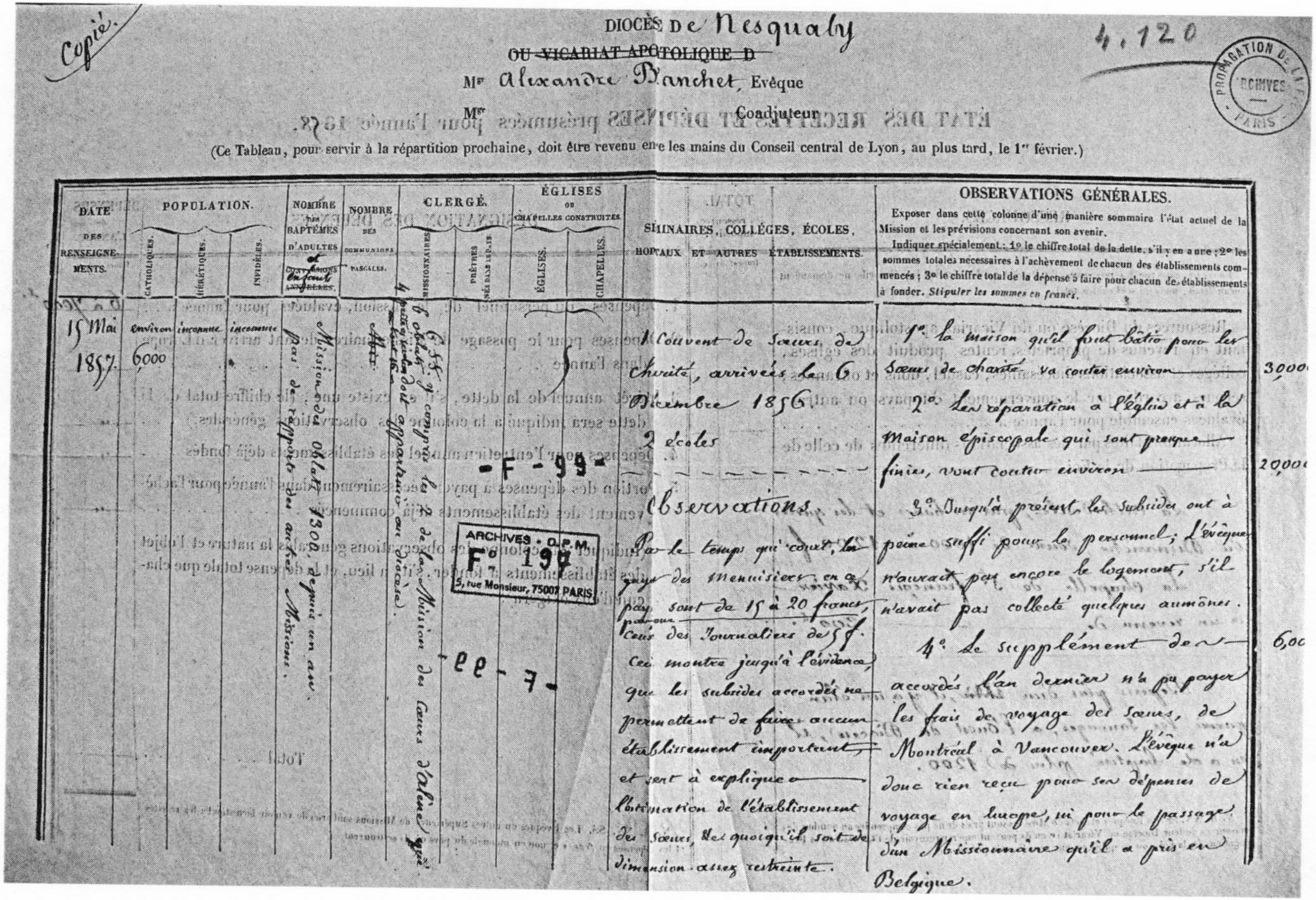

Copie.

DIOCÈSE de Nesqualy

~~OU VICARIAT APOSTOLIQUE D~~

Mgr Alexandre Blanchet, Evêque

Mgr Coadjuteur

ÉTAT DES RECETTES ET DÉPENSES présumées pour l'année 1858.

(Ce Tableau, pour servir à la répartition prochaine, doit être revenu entre les mains du Conseil central de Lyon, au plus tard, le 1er février.)

4,120

DATE DES RENSEIGNEMENTS	POPULATION. Catholiques	Hérétiques	Infidèles	NOMBRE DES BAPTÊMES d'adultes et enfants infidèles	NOMBRE DES COMMUNIONS PASCALES	CLERGÉ. Missionnaires	Prêtres indigènes	ÉGLISES OU CHAPELLES CONSTRUITES. Églises	Chapelles	SÉMINAIRES, COLLÉGES, ÉCOLES, HOPITAUX ET AUTRES ÉTABLISSEMENTS.	OBSERVATIONS GÉNÉRALES.
15 Mai 1857	environ 6,000	inconnue	inconnue	Missions des Oblats 1300 depuis un an. pas de rapports des autres Missions.	Abs	6 S.S. y compris les 2 de la Mission des Cœurs d'Alène qui doit appartenir au diocèse. 6 oblats 4 prêtres séculiers en tout 16				1 Couvent de Sœurs de Charité, arrivées le 6 Décembre 1856. 2 écoles	1° la maison qu'il fait bâtir pour les Sœurs de charité va coûter environ 3,000

Observations.

Par le temps qui court, les payes des menuisiers en ce pays sont de 15 à 20 francs, par jour ceux des Journaliers de 5 f. Ceci montre jusqu'à l'évidence que les subsides accordés ne permettent de faire aucun établissement important, et sert à expliquer l'estimation de l'établissement des Sœurs, lequel, quoiqu'il soit de dimension assez restreinte.

2° Les réparations à l'église et à la maison épiscopale qui sont presque finies, vont coûter environ 20,000

3° Jusqu'à présent les subsides ont à peine suffi pour le personnel; l'évêque n'aurait pas encore le logement, s'il n'avait pas collecté quelques aumônes.

4° Le supplément de 6,000 accordés l'an dernier n'a pu payer les frais de voyage des Sœurs, de Montréal à Vancouver. L'évêque n'a donc rien reçu pour ses dépenses de voyage en Europe, ni pour le passage d'un Missionnaire qu'il a pris en Belgique.

ARCHIVES · O.P.M. F° 199 5, rue Monsieur, 75007 PARIS

-F-99-

-99-7-

PROPAGATION DE LA FOI ARCHIVES PARIS

To Isaac Stevens,
Governor of Washington Territory,
October 20, 1854[1]

Rapid demographic, political, economic, and ecclesial change characterized the years immediately following Blanchet's translation to Nesqualy. By 1854, the bishop and his clergy had become increasingly entangled in defending Indian rights and maintaining peace.

By papal decree, on July 29, 1853, the Diocese of Walla Walla was suppressed and the Diocese of Nesqualy extended to include U.S. lands from the Pacific Ocean to the Rocky Mountains north of the Columbia River and the forty-sixth parallel. As a consequence Blanchet's diocese became contiguous with the territory of Washington, which had been approved by the Senate five months earlier. In July and August 1854, the bishop visited missions east of the Cascades. What he found prompted this letter to Stevens, the first of many complaining about the quality and behavior of Indian agents.

The bishop's travels took him to the Jesuit missions of St. Paul at Colville, St. Ignatius among the Kalispels and Pend d'Oreilles, and Sacred Heart among the Coeur d'Alenes. He also visited the Oblate missions of St. Rose among Canadiens in the Walla Walla valley and St. Joseph among the Yakamas on Ahtanum Creek, pastored by Fathers Chirouse and Pandosy, whom Blanchet had ordained shortly after the Whitman killings (see letter 2).[2]

At St. Ignatius, where Jesuit Father Anthony Ravalli had vaccinated against smallpox, Blanchet confirmed six hundred baptized Indians. At St. Rose, he was hosted for dinner by William McBean, who since mustering out of the HBC in 1851 had settled in the area; at Ahtanum, Blanchet was "charmed to see the piety, the fervent reverence of the Indians' prayer and participation in the holy services; he was amazed by the beauty of their chanting."[3] The bishop also left an impression. Father Pandosy, who accompanied him from Ahtanum back down to The Dalles, wrote to his superior in Olympia, Father Pascal Ricard, "En route, I found him to be a truly good man, an apostolic Bishop: simple, nondemanding, kind, pleasant, patient, & pious."[4]

Though pleased with the missions, the visiting bishop was rankled by the harm that traders, settlers, and agents brought to Indians. A year before Blanchet's visit to St. Rose, Father Chirouse had written to Governor Stevens, among other reasons, to complain of liquor traffickers and of the need to replace Oregon's Indian subagent Robert R. Thompson, who, acting outside of his jurisdiction, was allowing whites to encroach on lands of Washington Territory's Cayuses and Nez Percés.[5] While at Ahtanum among the Yakamas, Blanchet became aware of the behavior and influence of another Indian sub-agent, Andrew Jackson Bolon.[6] Troubled by what he had learned, the bishop wrote to Washington's territorial governor firmly requesting the agent's removal. His justifications incorporate detailed, written reports by resident priests Pandosy and Louis D'Herbomez.

Vancouver, October 20th 1854

Sir,

After congratulating you for your safe return to this territory, I am taking the liberty to draw your attention to an important matter.

It is with regret and in response to an urgent sense of duty that I find myself obliged to send you a few unfavorable remarks concerning a government employee under your jurisdiction. Mr. Bolon, deputy Indian agent to the section of this territory lying east of the Cascade Mountains, demonstrated, in my opinion, a complete inability to fulfill his position appropriately during the visits he made last summer to the Yakama Indians.[7]

1). He associated with and placed his confidence in the nation's most vile.[8]
2). He championed gambling, so very detrimental to the Indians.[9]
3). By unwisely rewarding thieves, he encouraged thievery among the Indians.
4). Contrary to their expectations of a government agent, he acted disgracefully toward the nation's missionaries.[10]
5). By virtue of his general behavior, he has lost the trust of all who are good among these Indians, to the point that, in my opinion, Mr. Bolon can no longer bring about the good for this nation that the government expects of an agent.

For these reasons, I believe it my duty to solicit his transfer.

I have the honor to be &c.
A. M. Bl. Bp. of N.

AAS, A2: 252.

---

1. Isaac Ingalls Stevens (1818–1862) was born in Massachusetts and graduated from West Point in 1839. While assigned by the U.S. Army Engineers to the Coast Survey of Washington City (1839–53) and serving on General W. Scott's staff in the Mexican War (1846–47), he cultivated important political relationships. On March 17, 1853, fellow New England Democrat President F. Pierce appointed Stevens to the intersecting tasks of serving as first governor of Washington Territory, superintendent of Indian Affairs, and chief of the Northern Pacific Railway Survey. Intent upon quickly leading Washington to statehood and advancing himself in the process, Stevens was "the first individual to seriously think of Washington Territory on an east to west basis" (Ficken, *Washington Territory*, 24). Anxious to extinguish Indian title to all lands in the territory before the fall arrival of the 1855 immigration, Stevens successfully petitioned Congress in person in August 1854 for approval to make treaties; he returned in early December.

2. By 1854, the Oblates of Mary Immaculate—strengthened in numbers by three priests and three brothers from France—had three remaining missions east of the Cascades, in addition to the motherhouse at today's Priest Point Park in Olympia: St. Joseph of Ahtanum in Yakama country, St. Anne among the Cayuses on the Umatilla, and St. Rose on Mill Creek in the Walla Walla Valley. Concern for the effect of solitude on missionaries who traveled seasonally with Indian clans had led to the closure of the stations of Immaculate Conception on Manashtas Creek, St. Joseph's on the Simcoe, and others among the Yakamas. Ahtanum remained as the main mission among the Yakamas. Yakama and Cayuse chiefs Kamiakin (Ahtanum and Simcoe), Teies and Owhi (Manashtas Creek and Moxee), and Five Crows (St. Anne and St. Rose) had invited the missionaries, provided lands, and frequently served as patrons and protectors from hostile bands. Métis had settled along Mill Creek and the Walla Walla River as early as 1820 (giving rise to the name of Frenchtown, today's town of Lowden) and intermarried with local indigenous populations. Young, "Mission of the Missionary Oblates," 81, 85, 91, 94–95, 115–21; Schoenberg, *Catholic Church in the Pacific Northwest*, 138–39.

3. Adrien Hoecken to Peter De Smet, in Hiram M. Chittenden and Alfred T. Richardson, *Life, Letters, and Travels of Father De Smet, S.J., 1801–1873* (New York: Francis P. Harper, 1905; New York: Arno Press and the New York Times, 1969), 4:1234 (page reference is to the 1969 ed.); Burns, *Jesuits and the Indian Wars*, 50. For Blanchet's visit to St. Rose, Chirouse to Ricard, August 5, 1854; for his visit to Ahtanum, D'Herbomez to Ricard, October 19, 1854, in Paul Drouin, O.M.I., *Les Oblats de Marie Immaculée en Orégon, 1847–1860: Documents d'archives* (Ottawa: Archives Deschâtelers, 1992), 2:466, 495.

4. Pandosy to Ricard, January 1, 1853, in Drouin, *Les Oblates*, 2:488. Well-lettered son of a French admiral, Father Pandosy learned the Yakama language for which he wrote a carefully developed grammar. He placed blame for any poor behavior and religious indifference among

the Yakamas entirely on the influence of whites, and dealt with a bad conscience for being white himself. Edward J. Kowrach, *Mie. Charles Pandosy, O.M.I, a Missionary of the Northwest* (Fairfield, Wash.: Ye Galleon Press, 1992), 58, 66.

5. Burns, *Jesuits and the Indian Wars*, 86–91; Chirouse to Stevens, October 28, 1853, in Drouin, *Les Oblats*, 1:359–60. Oblate superior Ricard chose not to communicate the letter, which Chirouse had sent to the Oblate mission in Olympia for translation and forwarding, to Stevens. Chirouse to Ricard, March 14, 1854, in Drouin, *Les Oblats*, 2:395.

6. Another Oblate missionary who helped found Ahtanum in 1852, Father Louis D'Herbomez, complained as well to Blanchet of Bolon when he passed through Vancouver on September 21 en route to the motherhouse in Olympia, having become ill with a chronic stomach ailment (Young, "Mission of the Missionary Oblates," 119, 128–29).

7. In March 1854, Isaac Stevens appointed Andrew Bolon (1825–1855) deputy Indian agent for the Central District, which extended from the Cascade Mountains in Washington to the Bitter Root Mountains in Montana. Stevens instructed him to prepare the various tribes for treaty councils and, in so doing, to throw the weight of his influence toward chiefs most partial to Americans. Though a physically strong frontiersman who knew the area east of the Cascades well, Bolon was not a tactful man, and one of his acquaintances claimed that he had "great contempt" for Indians. Bolon spent the summer of 1854 in Yakama country. Kent D. Richards, *Isaac I. Stevens, Young Man in a Hurry* (1979; rpt., Pullman: Washington State University Press, 1993), 212–13; Burns, *Jesuits and the Indian Wars*, 76.

8. Although Major Gabriel Rains, at the U.S. post of The Dalles, discouraged squatting until the Indian titles were extinguished, by 1855 Kamiakin's two brothers, Skloom and Chawaway, and their followers, according to Oblate priest Paul Durieu, were readily exchanging their lands for blankets supplied by "a sort of sub-agent living at Pescou [Pasco?], who distributed blankets to all those who would cede their lands," with the result that "except for Simcoe and Ahtanum, all the lands from the Dalles to the Naches belong to the Americans." Earlier, the two brothers tried to force Kamiakin to cede his lands as well, and his refusal occasioned a rupture in their relations (Durieu to Ricard, March 28, 1855, in Drouin, *Les Oblats*, 2:550). In a letter to Major Rains, Blanchet reported that Bolon had taken Skloom as his advisor and would like to make him head chief (Blanchet to Rains, September 22, 1854, AAS, A2: 241).

9. In their reports, Fathers D'Herbomez and Pandosy cite Kamiakin's and other Indians' censure of Bolon for distributing cards during his visits: "If he were chief, he would tell us, as would all chiefs, 'Indians, these cards are a source of disputes, quarrels, robbery, I prohibit you from playing.' But to the contrary, he has come to give us means to make us fight among ourselves, steal, to make us look on him as a chief." Pandosy, report; D'Herbomez, report; August 30, 1854, St. Joseph Mission, RG 700, AAS. Quotation from Pandosy's report.

10. In the same reports, the priests also cite what they heard Indians say regarding Bolon's visit to the Klickitats near Lake St. Helens and the Yakamas living near Camp Naches: that he did all in his power to have the Indians speak up against the missionaries, assuring them that they need not fear because the governor would likely visit the Indians in the fall, and the Americans would chase the missionaries back to their country. The same is repeated in a letter from Father D'Herbomez to George Gibbs, secretary of Steven's treaty commission. Copy submitted in D'Herbomez to Ricard, August 1, 1854, in Drouin, *Les Oblats*, 2:461–62.

To Jefferson Davis, Secretary of War, Washington City, D.C., December 28, 1854[1]

It took Governor Stevens, who was traveling in the east until early December, three months to reply to Blanchet's request to remove Agent Bolon. In his reply, dated December 21, the governor asked the bishop to send specifications with proofs substantiating his charges that "Mr. Bolon was unworthy to act as an officer of the Government." Without such proofs, Stevens added, Bolon was "entitled to the presumption of innocence till the charges against him are fully established."[2]

Before Stevens's response arrived at Vancouver, Blanchet appealed directly to then secretary of war Jefferson Davis, whose department included Indian Affairs. Davis had appointed Stevens as surveyor for a potential northern railroad route to the Pacific, one of four possibilities the United States was considering. Responsible for the choice of route and personally favoring a southern route through California, Davis was skeptical of Stevens's exaggerated claims for the northern route and impatience to clear the lands of Indian ownership.[3]

Rather than accomplish its end, it is possible that the following letter only strengthened the governor's resolve to retain Bolon, in spite of other growing concerns.[4] Nine months later, two young Yakamas killed Bolon. His killing contributed to the outbreak of the Yakima War.[5]

Vancouver, December 28th 1854

Honorable Sir,

I have the honor of sending you copies of two letters that I addressed to His Excellency Governor Stevens, Superintendent of Indian Affairs.[6] I have no doubt that you will recognize that my motives for writing them are just. For, Your Excellency understands that the duty of a Government

Indian Agent is to cement peace, to unify, to establish order, & not to create division or encourage evildoers. Instead of inspiring defiance or prejudice against missionaries who have sacrificed everything—their very health and even their life—for the well-being of the Indians, an agent of the government should support them when needed.

Were this the moment to tell you of the good that we are doing in our missions, I could easily provide the testimonies of several well-known persons in this country. I will simply say for now that Lieutenant Mullan, who spent last winter with the Flatheads at St. Mary's Mission, offered— in the presence of Colonel Bonneville—the most flattering praise of our missions, showing his willingness to publish it everywhere if need be.[7] This testimony seems sufficiently disinterested to inspire confidence.

I trust that Your Excellency will intervene with his authority, so that the good that is to be done among the Indians not be hindered, or obstructed, by agents whose very duty it is to promote such good.

With this trust, I have the honor of being respectfully &c.
Aug. M. Bl. Bp. of N.

AAS, A2: 263–64.

———•———

1. Jefferson Davis (1808–1889), a native of Kentucky, served as U.S. senator from Mississippi, secretary of war from 1853 to 1857, and president of the Confederate States of America.

2. Stevens to Blanchet, December 21, 1854, Records of the Office of Indian Affairs. Referenced as well in William Bischoff, S.J., "The Yakima Indian Wars, 1855–1856" (Ph.D. diss., University of Chicago, 1950), 73.

3. As senator from Mississippi, Davis had advocated the southern route; though he sought to avoid partisanship as secretary of war, Davis found what he considered to be a number of faults and exaggerations in Stevens's report of 1853, advocating the northern route (Richards, *Isaac I. Stevens*, 98, 139–42).

4. For this defense and for Stevens's half-hearted investigation resulting in no accusations against Bolon, see Bischoff, "Yakima Indian Wars," 73–74; and Richards, *Isaac I. Stevens*, 213.

5. Richards, *Isaac I. Stevens*, 237.

6. Shortly before writing to Davis, Blanchet sent a second letter to Stevens, expressing his disappointment in the governor's silence and failure even to acknowledge receipt of the first letter, and stating that he had no option other than to address himself to the appropriate person in Washington (Blanchet to Stevens, December 26, 1854, AAS, A2: 262–63).

7. Lieutenant John Mullan (1830–1909), explorer and road builder, spent the winter of 1853–

54 in western Montana marking a wagon and railroad route from Fort Benton on the Missouri to navigable waters on the Columbia River, living much of the time at the Jesuit mission of St. Mary's among the Flatheads, where, in the words of the Jesuit Father Peter De Smet, he "procured for me much valuable aid in founding this mission, and has all along taken a lively interest in its prosperity." In a subsequent letter to Belgium, De Smet cites from page 308 of Mullan's official report, *Explorations, etc., from the Mississippi to the Pacific Ocean*, concerning his stay with the Jesuits among the Flatheads: "I could never say enough of those noble and generous hearts among whom I found myself. They were pious and firm, men of confidence, full of probity, and penetrated at the same time with a lively and religious faith, to which they remain constant" (Chittenden and Richardson, *Life, Letters, and Travels of Father De Smet*, 4:1233, 1264). Colonel Benjamin Louis Eulalie Bonneville (1796–1878) was stationed at Fort Vancouver from 1852 to 1855.

LETTER 17

To William Leclaire, Missionary, Cowlitz Mission, May 15, 1855[1]

When Bishop Blanchet wrote this next pair of letters, Isaac Stevens was heading east of the Cascades for the treaty council with the Plateau Indians that Andrew Bolon, aided by James Doty, the governor's secretary, had been helping to prepare. The Oblate Fathers Pandosy and Chirouse, Jesuit Fathers Ravalli and Joseph Menetrey, and some métis settlers of the Plateau also would attend. The following two letters were occasioned by complaints from William Leclaire, the troubled priest of Mission St. Francis Xavier at Cowlitz, west of the Cascades.

The mission, founded in 1838, was the oldest in the old Oregon Country. It was located close to the Cowlitz River landing (today's town of Toledo), terminus of an eighty-mile, Indian trail and water route north from the Columbia. From this point, settlers moved north.[2] The mission also abutted the southeastern portion of an extensive farm of the Puget Sound Agricultural Company, a subsidiary of the HBC, which employed a rich ethnic mix of Indians, Canadiens, Scots, and Owhies (primarily from Hawaii).[3]

Since the 1850 opening of the Oregon Territory north of the Columbia River following congressional approval of the Donation Land Claim Act, Cowlitz inhabitants, mainly scattered bands of Indians and people of mixed descent, found their land particularly vulnerable to white migration to Puget Sound. Increasing numbers of Americans poached on their lands and staked out claims. The sale of liquor was widespread. The once praised St. Francis Xavier Mission had reached a nadir by 1855.[4]

Bishop Blanchet had visited the mission in 1853, and he was apprised of actions Vicar-General Brouillet had taken regarding Father Leclaire during the interim. He knew that Father Leclaire was sickly and wanted to leave, but having no replacement at hand, he needed to express support and encourage him to remain. At the same time, the growing population near the Cowlitz landing and portage also called for a shift in the character of the church, from a wilderness mission station supported by outside funding, to a self-sustaining Catholic faith community. In this letter, Blanchet balanced reassurance for his priest's personal support with a request for a copy of the mission's financial records that Leclaire was to be keeping.

Vancouver, May 15th 1855

Father

I just received your letter dated the day before yesterday, offering quite a sad picture of the temporal state of your mission. The grand vicar's report on the accounts of your fabric gives an even darker picture.[5] I hasten to respond at least in part to your request.

I had not committed to the sum of $150. When you informed me through the grand vicar that you "would stay at Cowlitz on condition that I give you the sum mentioned above," I did not respond, & I presume that you knew why. Your actions since lead me to believe that you understood my silence. You certainly will receive the amount I had intended to give you for your keep, &c before I received your proposal.

I was waiting to receive the report from the inspection of your fabric accounts before telling you from where to take funds, or sending you any. I received the report as requested; but now I would like something else, a detailed copy of the accounts showing revenue & expenses, with the balance that remains due for the rental of pews &c.[6] Send me this copy with the next mail run, if possible; for I do not want you to continue suffering for long.

I will also write to Marcel Bernier, to request an explanation for the way he is treating you. If the Cowlitz settlers cannot show greater appreciation for having a resident priest, they risk being deprived of this good fortune.

I am most cordially &c.
A. M. Bp. of N.

AAS, A2: 268–69.

—◆—

1. Subdeacon William Leclaire (1821–1893) of Montreal remained at St. Anne with Vicar-General Brouillet following the Whitman killings and was ordained by the archbishop in Oregon City on October 12, 1849. Assigned to serve Mission St. Francis Xavier in August, 1851, then under the jurisdiction of the archbishop, Leclaire had a record of poor health, a brief and unsuccessful novitiate with the Oblates of Mary Immaculate in Olympia, and a rumored bout of excessive drinking in public. Father Leclaire received his *exeat* from the Diocese of Nesqualy on October 21, 1857, and returned to Canada, where he continued an unstable clerical career. Brouillet to Leclaire, October 10, 1851; October 25, 1851; August 8, 1853, in J. B. A. Brouillet, "Cahier des lettres et correspondance de J. B. A. Brouillet, prêtre, pendant son administration du diocèse de Nesqualy, Mars 1851," 27–28, 30, 80–82, folder 4, Diocesan Priests, RG 820, AAS.

2. St. Francis Xavier, technically the first Catholic mission in the Oregon Country, was visited initially by Father François Blanchet in December 1838. He returned in March 1839 to give a mission, and while there he developed his famed "Catholic Ladder." Canadiens then living at the Cowlitz landing built a chapel and erected a lodge for the priest. Dr. McLoughlin provided personal funds for a larger church. Also having served the mission from its founding to this time were the Canadiens Fathers Modeste Demers, Jean-Baptiste Zacharie Bolduc, Antoine Langlois, and J.-B. Prétôt. For more, see F.N. Blanchet, *Historical Sketches of the Catholic Church*; Sister Letitia Mary Lyons, *Francis Norbert Blanchet and the Founding of the Oregon Missions (1838–1848)* (Washington, D.C.: Catholic University of America Press, 1940); M. Leona Nichols, *The Mantle of Elias* (Portland, Ore.: Binford and Mort Publishing, 1941); Schoenberg, *Catholic Church in the Pacific Northwest*; and Sister Mary John Francis Taylor, S.H.N., "St. Francis Xavier Mission, 1838–1880: Cowlitz Prairie, Washington" (master's thesis, Seattle College, 1948). There are some discrepancies in these sources regarding the dates for first use of the Catholic Ladder at the Cowlitz.

3. In 1832, Chief Factor McLoughlin and other officers issued a prospectus for a private joint-stock cattle-raising venture. HBC governor George Simpson and the committee in London reacted negatively, but appropriating the idea, they proposed a large-scale cattle-raising and agricultural venture on the Cowlitz portage and Nisqually plains, thus founding the HBC satellite enterprise known as the Puget Sound Agricultural Company. While bringing in some profit, it was hoped that, politically, the new company also would promote British colonization north of the Columbia. In 1839, an agreement was concluded for the company to supply the

Russian American Company with products. Fort Nisqually, under the direction of Dr. William F. Tolmie, became the main station of HBC operations north of the Columbia. John S. Galbraith, *The Hudson's Bay Company as an Imperial Factor, 1821–1869* (Berkeley: University of California Press, 1957), 192–202.

4. For the Donation Land Claim Act of 1850, see letter 10, note 8. Reporting to a friend in Quebec, Canadien Father Bolduc, who served in the Pacific Northwest from 1842 to 1850, wrote of his early visits to St. Francis Xavier: "'There are only thirteen inhabitants here, eleven of whom are Canadians [Canadiens], and the other[s] Indians. All are fairly good Christians; have much zeal for the religion and are very attached to their missionary. They wish that he lived with them continually. There are also a few hundred Indians still unbelievers." He wrote a few years later: "You will perhaps be surprised to see with what good taste the Indian women and especially the young mixed bloods (Métis) [*sic*], respect the solemnity of our ceremonies. One frequently comes across among them, rare and melodious voices." But, in 1852, Brouillet wrote discouragingly to his bishop that nothing could be expected of the residents of the Cowlitz or of Vancouver, a true malediction was weighing on the *race canadienne et métisse* of the region, and they were destined to live in crass ignorance, enslavement, and base mindlessness. Jean Baptiste Zacharie Bolduc, *Mission of the Columbia*, ed. and trans. Edward J. Kowrach (Fairfield, Wash.: Ye Galleon Press, 1979), 93, 102; Brouillet to Blanchet, February 6, 1852, in Brouillet, "Lettres et correspondance," 54.

5. *Fabric*, signifying a group of laypersons and their priest responsible for the construction and maintenance of religious buildings (the fabric), has existed since the first centuries of the Christian church. It provided a means for involving members in their local church and often served to limit the financial liability of the clergy. According to the rules for management of a *fabrique* in France, which J. B. A. Brouillet, standing in as administrator both for the Diocese of Nesqualy and the Archdiocese of Oregon City, sent to Abbé Prétôt, pastor of St. Francis Xavier in 1851, the *fabrique* was to receive funds from parishioner contributions, products and rent of church lands, marriages and burials, and it was to provide for upkeep of buildings and grounds, church ornaments, liturgical and sacramental supplies, and the pastor's sustenance. Father Leclaire was also serving at the mission at the time that Brouillet sent the instructions to Father Prétôt. Brouillet to Prétôt, April 1851, in Brouillet, "Lettres et correspondance," 12–18.

6. Charging rent for pews (seating spaces within churches) was a common practice in Catholic and other Christian churches into the middle of the twentieth century. Peter De Smet, former superior of the Jesuit missions of the Rocky Mountains, serving as assistant to the superior of the Missouri Province of the Society of Jesus, expressed the difficulty of getting priests to manage accounts, due to a twisted sense of the virtues of disdaining and therefore neglecting worldly affairs and to a lack of training in financial record keeping. This letter indicates that the problem of financial accountability was not limited to Missouri. John J. Killoren, S.J., *"Come, Blackrobe": De Smet and the Indian Tragedy* (Norman: University of Oklahoma Press, 1994; St. Louis, Mo.: Institute of Jesuit Sources, 2003), 215 (citations are to the 2003 edition).

To Marcel Bernier, Cowlitz Mission, May 15, 1855

At the heart of this letter is Cowlitz settler Marcel Bernier's failure to follow through on his commitment to Bishop Blanchet to help support Father
Leclaire. While Father Leclaire's troubled relationship with his mission likely
contributed to the situation, so too may have generational and cultural differences in conceptions of Catholic faith and practice.

Marcel Bernier (1819–1889) was born at the HBC fort on Spokane Falls.
His father, Julien Bernier (1794–ca.1849), had been a bowman on the Thompson and upper Columbia Rivers for the Northwest Company and the HBC.[1]
For first-generation *engagés* such as Julien, who had left eastern Canada before
or during the first decade of the nineteenth century, being religious meant
celebrating sacraments marking life's rites of passage and the liturgical cycle
of holy days in accordance with the seasonal cycle of work on the farm and
at lumber camps; it also meant praying to local saints for immediate material
needs and protection from disaster.[2] For boatmen who dealt regularly with
the natural forces of the rivers, overt religious devotion—planting crosses at
murderous river bends, reciting prayers to saints at set times of the day—had
become a way of expressing communal reverence, as well as ethnic and pro-
fessional identity.[3]

The heritage of these boatmen did not include regular support for a missionary priest on the occasions when one was present. They were accustomed
to the fur companies providing chapels and supporting priests financially
as a benefit to their Catholic employees. At the ecclesiastical district of St.
Boniface located at the central post of Fort Douglas on the Red River (today's city of Winnipeg), Bishop Joseph-Norbert Provencher and his priests
received allowances as well as tithes.[4] Julien's son, Marcel Bernier, was sent to
the parish school at St. Boniface in 1830, where he became an acquaintance
of Father Modeste Demers, a missionary there at the time. The Bernier family was living at this Red River settlement in 1841, the year when the family
migrated to the Cowlitz portage.[5]

In 1842, twenty-one-year-old Marcel is recorded as accompanying Father

F. N. Blanchet during his missionary tour among Indians of the Puget Sound region, where he rescued the boat and its passenger from a near-fatal accident on the Cowlitz and oversaw construction of a chapel on Whidbey Island. He also accompanied Father Demers on his first trip to Vancouver Island and Caribou. Returning in 1844, he married Cowlitz resident Cecile Bercier, granddaughter of a Cree woman, daughter of Pierre Bercier (late guide to David Thompson of the Northwest Company in 1808 and to Peter Skene Ogden in the Snake River Country), and sister of Pierre Bercier, Jr. (guide to U.S. commander Charles Wilkes in 1841 and Michael Simmons, founder of New Market [later Tumwater], in 1845).[6]

Though this métis family enjoyed financial stability and adapted to many elements of American settler life, neither Marcel nor his father appear to have experienced the sort of settled parish life known in eastern Canada and the United States, calling for support of a resident priest.[7] In short, cultural heritage may have played as large a part as the priest's apparent lack of commitment to his mission in creating the situation that evoked this letter.

Vancouver, May 15th 1855

Sir & Dear Son in Jesus Christ,

I received a letter from Father Leclaire, your good missionary, of a nature to grieve me deeply. He tells me, "that he receives nothing but a little meat & flour," which hardly suffices for his weak health; and he adds, "that for some time he has lived, so to speak, on bread and water alone." Trusting your word & your letter of last January that Father Leclaire brought me, I did not doubt for a moment that your missionary was being provided for in a manner fitting his position. Kindly tell me right away if you can give this good missionary what he has been deprived of for some time, so that I know what remains to be done to preserve his health.

I am most cordially &c.
A. M. Bp. of Nesq.

AAS, A2: 269–70.

1. M. W. Warner, trans., and Harriet D. Munnick, ed., *Catholic Church Records of the Pacific Northwest: Vancouver and Stellamaris Mission*, vols. 1–2 (St. Paul, Ore.: French Prairie Press, 1972), A6–7 (M. Bernier obituary); Watson, *Lives Lived West of the Divide*, 1:197.

2. Rousseau and Remiggi, *Atlas historique*, 145–53.

3. Daniel W. Harmon, *A Journal of Voyages and Travels in the Interior of North America* (New York: Allerton Book Company, 1922), 6, 9, 10, 236.

4. Brouillet to Blanchet, June 4, 1853, in Brouillet, "Lettres et correspondance," 73. In the letter, Brouillet quotes from George Simpson's *An Overland Journey Round the World: During the Years 1841 and 1842* (Philadelphia: Lea and Blanchard, 1847), 44: "Among the Catholics are a bishop & two or three priests, who, in addition to allowance from the Hudson's Bay Company, receive tithes amounting, as in Lower Canada, to the twenty-sixth bushel of all kinds of grains."

5. The need to renew its license, a sagging fur trade, and news of the imminent departure of the *Lausanne* for the West (part of Jason Lee's plan to colonize the Oregon Country by means of a reinforcement of Protestants), all lent to the British government's approval in 1838 of the HBC's plan to establish the Puget Sound Agricultural Company, to which retired servants from the Red River and the Willamette Valley would be induced to migrate, to work the farms and help influence British possessory rights north of the Columbia. The Bernier family was one of twenty-three in the 1841 Red River migration. Bancroft, *History of Oregon*, 1:176–77; Galbraith, *Hudson's Bay Company*, 193–212, 226; John C. Jackson, *Children of the Fur Trade: Forgotten Métis of the Pacific Northwest* (Missoula, Mont.: Mountain Press Publishing Company, 1996), 139; Watson, *Lives Lived West of the Divide*, 1:194. See also Jack Nisbet, *Mapmaker's Eye: David Thompson on the Columbia Plateau* (Pullman: Washington State University Press, 2005).

6. Schoenberg, *Catholic Church of the Pacific Northwest*, 33–34; Hubert Howe Bancroft, *History of Washington, Idaho, and Montana, 1845–1889* (San Francisco: History Company, 1890), 2; Warner and Munnick, *Catholic Church Records of the Pacific Northwest: Vancouver and Stellamaris Mission*, A6–7, A26.

7. In 1850, Marcel and his father both filed claims for their lands on the Newaukim Prairie, located along the major portage route from the Cowlitz landing to settlements on Puget Sound, some fifteen miles west of St. Francis Xavier Mission and other Canadien and métis claims near the Cowlitz landing. Marcel was summoned to serve on the grand jury convened in the wake of the 1849 killing of American Leander Wallace at Fort Nisqually. He represented Newaukim Prairie at the first Washington territorial convention. Daughters of the American Revolution, Washington State Society, "Early Records of Washington Pioneers" (Washington State Library, Olympia, n.d.), 22:226; 24:11; 50:160, 202; Bancroft, *History of Washington, Idaho, and Montana*, 49.

To Nicholas Congiato, Society of Jesus, April 26, 1856[1]

The muddy wagon roads of the Cowlitz mission and the log-hewn cabin of the Marcel Bernier family were a world apart from the avenues of Paris, Rome, Vienna, Prague, Brussels, and Montreal that Bishop A. M. A. Blanchet traveled from September 1855 to the end of the following year. In 1843 and again in 1853, Father Peter De Smet, S.J., founder of the Jesuit's Mission of the Rocky Mountains, had made rounds in Europe—promoting his missions, begging funds, and returning with clerics and sisters. Archbishop F. N. Blanchet and Bishop Modeste Demers also had made their tours. Though his 1851 trip to Mexico had been a financial success, Bishop Blanchet still needed funds, priests, and sisters. Now was his time to tour Catholic Europe and converse with church leaders, seminary directors, and potential benefactors.

Having appointed Vicar-General Brouillet as diocesan administrator in his absence, Blanchet set out for San Francisco, the first leg of his long journey, on August 28, 1855. On an overcrowded steamship between Nicaragua and New York, he cared for passengers stricken with cholera, undoubtedly remembering his late missionary, Godefroi Rousseau, who had died of the disease on the same route (see letter 9, note 23).[2]

This was a good moment for a French-speaking Catholic bishop to be in Europe: a garrison of French troops was protecting the pope, who had returned from exile to Rome; and under Napoleon Bonaparte III, the Restoration in France with resurgent Catholic sympathies was gaining strength. Blanchet's European itinerary brought him face-to-face with political and religious leaders, including Pope Pius IX and Peter Beckx, superior general of the Society of Jesus.[3]

This voyage marked a turning point in Blanchet's episcopal career. He garnered contributions, made connections for future personnel, and experienced being received as a serious leader—a different experience from the dismissive silences and acrid comments of many non-Catholic settlers in his own diocese. The voice of a confident bishop—in full stride and in control—comes through in this letter. Blanchet's proposal, to found schools at Jesuit Indian missions, would eventually become a reality.

Superior General Beckx took a more expansive view of Jesuit missions than had his predecessor. Blanchet leveraged Beckx's enthusiasm for the missions and the Jesuits' commitment to education. By offering financial support to establish schools at their missions, he sought to cement Jesuit presence in his diocese. In this way, he prefigured the successful negotiations of his vicar-general, beginning in 1859, for government contracts to support missionary-run Indian schools, beginning in 1859 (see letter 24).

Vienna, Austria, April 26th 1856

My Reverend Father,

At the end of December last, I wrote to you from Paris to share my desire to establish some schools in our missions, to ask you to consider the idea, & to let me know your thoughts. As for me, the more I think about it, the more I feel the urgent need for these schools. Not only would they assist our missionaries in their work wherever they are founded, they would also attract infidels who would see the good the schools are bringing about among their neighbors. While in Rome, I shared this idea with the Reverend Father General, who found it very appealing. I tend to believe that Your Reverence will agree as well. Given the urgency of this measure I took steps to see quickly to its solid establishment.

We should first consider the Mission of St. Paul among the Kettles, & the new Mission of St Ignatius. The white population of the first, if I know it well, will provide something for starting the school, which will allow us to allocate considerably more for the second.[4] As of now I can offer Your Reverence ten thousand francs (10,000 fr's) for this work. If this sum does not suffice for starting two schools, we will limit ourselves to one, while waiting for further subsidies.

Very well, My Reverend Father, there are my plans & my means at the moment for undertaking them. It remains for me to know all of your thoughts, your views on the best way to achieve this goal.

I will be pleased to find a response from Your Reverence upon my return to Montreal, Canada; for, if you were to concur with me, I would immediately go about finding missionaries & could perhaps bring them out myself.

A. M. Bp. of Nesqualy

AAS, A2: 280–81.

⎯•⎯

1. Nicholas Congiato (1816–1887), born in Sardinia, served as vice-president of the College of Nobles in Naples, Italy; of the College of Fribourg in Switzerland; and as president of St. Joseph College in Bardstown, Kentucky. He was superior general of the combined missions of the Rocky Mountains (Oregon) and California from August 1, 1854, to March 1, 1858, continuing as superior of the Rocky Mountain Mission until January 21, 1862. Congiato, who resided in San Francisco, visited the Indian missions of the Rocky Mountain Mission in 1856 and 1858. Burns, *Jesuits and the Indian Wars*, 55, 93; Schoenberg, *Catholic Church in the Pacific Northwest*, 146–47, 155, 162; Wilfred P. Schoenberg, S.J., *Paths to the Northwest: A History of the Oregon Province* (Chicago: Loyola University Press, 1982), 57–65, 588. On April 7, 1856, Blanchet arrived in Vienna, where he spent a month. A. M. A. Blanchet, "Journal de l'Evêque"; Seconde Partie; Voyage au Mexique; "Voyage en Europe, octobre 28, 1855–décembre 5, 1856," AAS, A1.

2. Ship passengers presented Blanchet with an engraved gold cross, in testimony to his charity.

3. Two generals directed the Jesuit Order during the period of 1840–80, Dutchman John Roothaan, until 1853, and Belgian Peter Beckx, until 1883. Whereas Roothaan sought to avoid overextension given the limited personnel and resources at the time, Beckx saw the order mushroom from ten to nineteen provinces, and from five thousand to almost twelve thousand priests. Burns, *Jesuits and the Indian Wars*, 44; Schoenberg, *Paths to the Northwest*, 56–57.

4. Blanchet is referring to the Jesuit mission of St. Paul, founded in 1845, at the invitation of local tribes, on Kettle (Chaudière or Swahniquet) Falls, a popular native fishing spot. The mission abutted the HBC's Fort Colvile (named after HBC governor Andrew Colvile), which functioned beginning in 1825 as granary, livestock, and provision depot for the interior posts; shipyard for constructing the lighter brigade and *express bateaux* for the lower Columbia; fur trading depot; and eventually supply depot for miners, causing unrest among neighboring Indians. As in Walla Walla, Vancouver, and Cowlitz, a considerable population of retired, largely Canadien employees and their families settled among both indigenous and immigrant populations, constructing their racial identity accordingly. Presumably, Blanchet is referring to these settlers. The U.S. Army's Fort Colville, located in the same vicinity, was not built until 1859, and the adjoining Catholic church, Immaculate Conception, not finished until 1861. James R. Gibson, *The Lifeline of the Oregon Country: The Fraser-Columbia Brigade System, 1811–47* (Vancouver: University of British Columbia Press, 1997), 99–100; Schoenberg, *Catholic Church in the Pacific Northwest*, 190, 786; National Park Service, Lake Roosevelt, St. Paul's Mission, http://www.nps.gov/laro/historyculture/upload/2007%20StPauls.pdf, (accessed October 20, 2009). The new St. Ignatius Mission, founded in 1854 by Adrien Hoecken, S.J., was located on Kalispel land just

below Flathead Lake in the Bitterroot Valley of today's Montana, an area more central to mission tribes and remote from settlement. It replaced the older mission on less fertile land among the Kalispels on the lower Pend d'Oreille River, some two hundred miles to the northwest (Burns, *Jesuits and the Indian Wars*, 85–86).

LETTER 20

To the Directors of the Society for the Propagation of the Faith, Paris, May 15, 1857

Having received substantial gifts and monetary collections for the diocese, Blanchet arrived in Montreal on August 9, 1856, physically exhausted.[1] While he was recuperating there, arguments flared over the bishop's request for a second party of Sisters of Providence for Oregon. Opponents pointed to the order's loss of sisters, first while caring for victims during the 1847 typhus epidemic, then during the 1852 cholera outbreak that, among thousands of others in Montreal, had taken the community's first superior, Mother Emilie Gamelin. During Blanchet's travels in 1852, a community of sisters had been bound for the Diocese of Nesqualy, but never got to Fort Vancouver due to communication problems, poor weather, and the low morale of sisters and clerics who hosted them in Oregon City. They eventually established a foundation in Chile. In 1854, the community established a house in Burlington, Vermont, and many now thought their remaining ranks too thin to care even for pressing needs in Montreal. Supporters of Blanchet's request, including Mother Emilie Caron, Bishop Bourget, and Sister Joseph, finally prevailed. Bourget formally bestowed on Sister Joseph the obedience of superior— Sister Servant in the parlance of the community—and the new name of Sister (Mother) Joseph of the Sacred Heart. On November 3, Blanchet departed by ship for Oregon, along with three professed sisters, two postulants, servant Moïse Loiselle, and Abbé Louis Rossi, who while Blanchet was in Belgium had offered his services to the diocese.[2]

The voyage west was an unusual adventure for the young religious women. Dressed in secular garb to avoid drawing attention in a Protestant country, they sailed across Lake Champlain. At the Irish-Catholic-run Hotel Delmonico in New York City they found shelter from election-day street violence and anti-Catholic Know-Nothing Party members on the day James Buchanan was elected president. In Acapulco they were strengthened "by the holy bread of angels" and breakfasted on biscuits and hot chocolate in the cathedral rectory. The Irish Sisters of Mercy hosted them warmly in San Francisco, where they also visited other communities of women religious and churches.[3]

The party departed San Francisco on December 5. On December 8—their ship having outrun a violent Pacific storm and crossed the bar of the Columbia—the relieved women gathered on deck to sing the Stabat Mater, accompanied by Sister Blandine on an accordion donated by the Sisters of Mercy. Only Moïse, the servant, was absent, having missed the boat while running to buy popcorn and candy for the two youngest women. When they stepped onto the solid bank of Fort Vancouver later that day, they were met by a party that included Vicar-General Brouillet, a distinguished man with long gray hair, hardly distinguishable in dress from the other men on the shore.[4]

In the following annual report dated six months after his return, Blanchet writes to an audience of pious businessmen whose faces he had come to know. Though echoes of his 1849 funding request reappear—the need for new buildings, the high cost of carpenters, travel expenses—the contours of a diocese transformed by shifting populations emerge. As might be expected, Blanchet does not mention the success of his collections in Mexico and Europe, or recent Indian-white conflicts in the territory.

Vancouver, W.T., May 15th 1857

Gentlemen Directors,

It is my honor to send you the diocesan report explaining some of our needs. As the contacts I had last year with the Presidents & some members of the two Councils were such as to thoroughly inform you of our needs, it would be useless for me to emphasize them again here.[5]

I will take this opportunity to express my gratitude for the supplement of 6,000 [francs], granted last year, which covered only a part of the expenses for my voyage and that of Abbé Rossi & the Sisters of Charity whom I brought from Montreal, in Canada. Should I receive enough, I will not fail to bring in brothers for teaching the young.

For over a year now, the Indians in the west of the diocese have shown real enthusiasm. More than 1,200 of all ages have been baptized. These Indians have such a great desire to be taught to pray that they willingly undertake voyages of several days to reach the missionaries.[6] Please join me in blessing the Lord who deigned to bring about such marvels for these indigenous tribes who at first showed nothing but indifference for our holy religion.

I have the honor &c.
Aug. Magl. Al. Bp. of Nesqualy

Diocese of Nesqualy, W.T.

A. M. A. Blanchet, Bishop

Date: May 15th 1857

For 1857–58

Population:

Catholics: about 6,000

Heretics: unknown

Infidels: unknown

Number of baptisms: Missions on the Sound: 1300

No reports from the other missions that belong to the diocese

Paschal Comm.: No report

Clergy:

Missionaries:

      6 Society of Jesus;

      6 Oblates, including two from the mission of the Coeur d'Alenes;

      4 secular[7]

      Born in the country: [none]

Churches or Chapels: 5

Seminaries, Colleges, Schools, Hospitals &c.:

      1 convent of the Sisters of Charity, arrived December 8th 1856

      2 Catholic Schools[8]

Observations:

      Presently carpenters in this country are paid from $3 to $4 (15 to 20 francs) a day; day workers, from 5 to 6 frs. &c. From this, it is evident that the subsidies granted us are inadequate for any substantial construction; it also explains the estimate for the sisters' premises, even though the dimensions are quite modest.

General Observations:

1. The house to be built for the sisters will cost about 30,000 frs.

2. Repairs of the church and bishop's house will cost about 20,000 frs.

3. Until now subsidies from the Society Prop. F. have barely sufficed for personnel;the bishop would still be without lodging had he not made collections.

4. The supplement of 6,000 frs. granted last year could not cover passage of the 5 Sisters of Charity from Montreal to Vancouver. So, the bishop has not in fact received anything from the Society, as supplement, for the expenses of his trip to Europe!! Nor for the passage of Abbé Rossi whom he brought from Belgium.

Presumed Income and Expenses for 1857–58:

Revenue: The cathedral brings in from 1,000 to 2,000 frs. a year from its pews & Sunday collections.

Revenue from St. Fr. Xavier Chapel is about 300 frs.

Designated Expenses: For diocese personnel: from 6,000 to 7,000 fcs.

ARCHIVES DE LA PROPAGATION DE LA FOI, PARIS (HEREAFTER CITED AS APFP), F-99, FOL. 97, DEPOSITED IN OPM; AAS, A2: 285–87.

———•———

1. Blanchet, "Journal de l'Evêque," "Voyage en Europe, octobre 28, 1855–décembre 5, 1856," AAS, A1.

2. For a detailed description of these negotiations, see "Chronicles, 1856–1857," in "Chronicles of the Providence House, 1856–1875," 40–52 (22), Vancouver, Washington Collection, Providence Archives, Seattle. Luigi Angelo Maria Rossi (1817–1871), an Italian convert from Judaism, ordained in 1843, was a member of the Passionist order, living in communities in Italy and Bordeaux, France, until he left the order to become a secular priest. Father Louis Rossi served in the diocese for six years.

3. Ibid., 60–74; Sister Mary McCrosson of the Blessed Sacrament, in collaboration with Sisters Mary Leopoldine and Maria Theresa, *The Bell and the River* (1956; rpt., Palo Alto, Calif.: Pacific Books, 2006), 84–87, 94–96, 104.

4. "Chronicles, 1856–1857," in "Chronicles of the Providence House, 1856–1875," 71–76; McCrosson, *The Bell and the River*, 100–105.

5. Suggesting an increase in annual allocation, the Council of Paris on August 13, 1857, wrote to the Council of Lyons with regard to information the bishop of Nesqualy had furnished them in person during his passage: "There is no doubt, and on this point we have the authority of Baltimore, that this diocese is among those that most justly claim our aid. The bishop himself is a man full of modesty and his word left us with absolutely no doubt when he explained the impossibility he faced of doing the minimum to bring about the salvation of his flock, lacking resources to found schools, construct chapels, maintain existing stations, and certainly to establish any new ones" ("Procès verbaux," 1857, 252, OPM).

6. Blanchet also wrote to Bourget of the remarkable enthusiasm among Indians on Puget Sound; of the Oblate Fathers having baptized more than twelve hundred, including a good number of adults; and of the Indians' willingness to walk two or three days to reach the Fathers' residence in order to learn to pray. At the time, there were no other Indian missions west of the Cascades (Blanchet to Bourget, May 22, 1857, ACAM, file 195.133, 857–1).

7. Secular priests were Fathers Brouillet, Leclaire, Rossi, and King. Oblate priests, Ricard (superior), Chirouse, D'Herbomez, Jayol, and Richard, were all at the motherhouse in Olympia; Pandosy and Durieu, of the Ahtanum mission, were initially sheltered at the Jesuit's Coeur d'Alene mission during the Yakima War. Blanchet lists seven Jesuit priests for 1857: Joset, Hoecken, Gozzoli, Taddini, Ravalli, Vercruise, and Menetrey. A. M. A. Blanchet, "Notes sur les diocèses de Walla-Walla et de Nesqualy," AAS, A4.

8. The two schools were Brouillet's academy in Vancouver and the Oblates' St. Joseph Indian school in Olympia.

LETTER 21

To Emilie Caron, Superior, Sisters of Providence, Montreal, June 16, 1857[1]

In 1857, Fort Vancouver and its environs was an ethnically diverse, multi-national settlement. According to the possessory rights guaranteed by the British-American Treaty of 1846, the HBC technically owned the lands. It was through special arrangements with the company that the terrain and buildings of the Catholic Church and the U.S. Army garrison were legally occupied. American settlers had begun poaching on the HBC lands as early as 1846 and making claims in 1850. Though the army prevented many from actually occupying their claims, on January 23, 1857, the city of Vancouver was incorporated, based on the notion that the treaty granted the HBC a right only to its improvements, not to the soil itself.[2]

During this time of transition in Vancouver, the safety net that the HBC, particularly under Chief Factor John McLoughlin, had extended to immigrant settlers and its own employees, unraveled. The five women constituting the Providence congregation and their few assistants stepped into this void by responding immediately to the education, health, and other social needs of their new community. With American, British North American, and indigenous populations of varying religious orientations seeking their aid, the sisters' duties outstripped their numbers. These circumstances led Bishop Blanchet to write this first of many requests to the Providence Motherhouse in Montreal, for additional personnel.

Blanchet wrote using the trope of dutiful daughters of the Church. He wrote with a patronizing fondness understandable for one who had been involved in the institute's founding and had served as the community's chaplain. However, it is crucial to recognize that most professed Providence sisters came from established Canadien families and were, for their era, well educated. They understood themselves as part of a centuries-long tradition in which women influenced society by engaging in corporal and spiritual works of mercy. Hence the sisters had a greater sense of their own agency and autonomy than is apparent in Blanchet's letter.[3]

In it, Blanchet had to negotiate the tension between his desire to show that the sisters' tasks were too great for their number and, at the same time, his need to assure Mother Caron that the sisters' living and working conditions were sufficient to allow for a life conducive to their spiritual advancement.

Vancouver, W.T., June 16th 1857

Reverend Mother,

It is time to break the silence. I would not have kept it for so long had no one else been occasionally sending you news about your most beloved daughters, & all that has happened since the moment they departed from the Community. Thinking now that you will find what I have to say a pleasure, I decided to write.

Let me say first that the sisters continue to sacrifice themselves generously, never flagging for a moment nor letting up in their devotion to all of your works. To be sure, there was a little discouragement, as one would expect, but virtue puts an end to such problems, as it does to others that are unavoidable, given our human weakness.[4] In a word, I think that everything is going as well as I could have hoped for.

Given their new premises, the new establishment, and the very particular circumstances the sisters found themselves in when they arrived in the diocese—circumstances you are well acquainted with—one could not expect to see everything run smoothly.[5] On the contrary, some disorder, additional difficulties, and weariness were to be expected. This has occurred, and was not unforeseen. Now, by God's grace, life is more regular, detachment more evident; they are getting their bearings; great progress has clearly been made.[6]

Caring for elderly invalids, for orphans, the poor, teaching the young, overseeing the sacristy &c. keeps the little community quite occupied, without a moment to give in to the demon of idleness, were that ever a challenge.

The two older sisters are unfailing in virtue; the youngest is not lacking, & given her desire to advance, she will in time ascend a number of steps on the ladder to perfection. The two novices also seem to be of good will, & I trust that they will persevere with courage.[7] To sum up in a few words, I am pleased to see the best of dispositions in all of them, the most perfect devotion to works for which they left everything behind, detached themselves from all that was dear to them in this world.

Their presence alone has done much good: trust in them can only increase, resulting in greater piety among Catholics and less prejudice among non-Catholics.

Whatever may have been said, & is perhaps still being said in some places, the diocese urgently needed such a community. All the Catholics I have spoken with since my return have expressed great satisfaction with the new Mission; & the Canadiens, as can be expected, are thrilled to have Canadien sisters in the country. Had my wishes been carried out four years ago, we would be much further along; as you know, I am not to be blamed if we are behind, nor is the Providence community.[8]

I have given my lodging to the sisters so that they can do their works more easily and on a greater scale, while they wait for their own house to be built, which will allow for further growth.[9]

The sisters' main occupation for some time will be teaching the young. It is important that they be trained to teach to the extent that your Institute rules will allow. To carry this out as soon as possible, we need a sister with experience, that is to say, a sister who has already been teaching successfully for some years, e.g., three or four, & above all who knows English well. I know that some in the community would be suitable. My goal in making this request is to provide the best possible instruction to our young Catholics, so that they will not be obliged on leaving here to further their education at Protestant schools & thus run the risk of being lost.[10]

I recently had the honor to explain this need, which I see as urgent, to Monsignor of Montreal. It is my hope that you will be able to do what was not possible last fall after classes had begun at the missions. The flame of devotion has not died out since then; several will still feel inspired to make a sacrifice that will be most pleasing to God. I would guess that upon the first mention of my request, several will step forward, & even yearn to set out. So, please consider my request, in accord with the advice of Monsignor of Montreal. We will pray here that God inspires you to grant this request.

I was delighted to hear that your novices all wanted to be missionaries in the Diocese of Nesqualy. Please tell them that in a few years there will be room for several of them. For now, if there is someone who can play the harmonium at public services, she could accompany the sister I just described. Sister Blandine has a good taste for music and has already taken some lessons, but with her other duties, she hardly has time to practice; and as the sergeant who has been playing for two years will be leaving soon, we will find ourselves without music, to my deep regret.[11]

I conclude in expressing my hope that the Lord bring ever greater numbers to your dear community, that religious virtues continue to be nourished, that zeal for far-off missions be preserved, transmitted from age to age, from year to year, & that your pious and worthy founder be preserved for many years to come, for your consolation, & for the benefit of souls entrusted to me.

I am most cordially, in the Sacred Hearts of Jesus & Mary, &c.
Augustin M. Bl. Bp. of Nesqualy

AAS, A2: 287–90.

———•———

1. Emilie Caron (1808–1888) was born in Rivière-du-Loup-en-Haut, in the Diocese of Three Rivers, to Ambroise Caron and Josephte Langlois, modest farmers. She benefited from excellent

local schooling, helped her family financially through the art of plaiting straw, served as a rural school mistress, and was one of the seven foundresses of the Providence community. Known to be frank, generous, and gifted, she was appointed superior of St. Elizabeth (the third Montreal Providence house, dedicated to education and care for the elderly) in 1849; from 1851 to 1858, she served as superior of the motherhouse; and eventually as superior general of the Sisters of Charity of Providence, which expanded to include five provinces, located in Canada and the United States. She did not take a religious name. Rev. Elie-J. Auclair, *Life of Mother Caron: One of the Seven Foundresses and Second Superior of the Sisters of Charity of Providence, 1808–1888*, trans. Anna T. Sadlier (Montreal, 1914).

2. Galbraith, *Hudson's Bay Company*, 256, 267, 281; Ted Van Arsdol, *Vancouver on the Columbia* (Northridge, Calif.: Windsor Publications, 1986), 23.

3. With the large network of lay confraternities of noble women, known as *charités*, inadequate to address the rampant pauperism resulting from the collapse of feudal estates, the first religious order of the Daughters of Charity was founded in mid-seventeenth-century France by Louise de Marillac, with the support of Vincent de Paul. To accomplish its apostolic call, professed sisters in the new organization took only simple vows and were among the few non-cloistered religious women of the period. Separated from these French women by two centuries and the Atlantic Ocean, widow Emilie Gamelin of Montreal had exhausted her wealth organizing a lay confraternity of women modeled on the earlier Charités of France, when in 1843, with the assistance of Ignace Bourget, she founded the Sisters of Charity of Providence. To this end, she spent several months with the Daughters of Charity community in Emmitsburg, Maryland (founded by Elizabeth Ann Seton). She brought back on loan an authenticated manuscript of the Rules of St. Vincent de Paul. A. M. A. Blanchet made an official copy of the Rules. He had served as confessor to the new foundation for almost a year when he was consecrated bishop of Walla Walla. Blanchet thus knew the sisters well, including Emilie Caron, who was one of the first to make final vows and so be fully professed. Barbara B. Diefendorf, *From Penitence to Charity: Pious Women and the Catholic Reformation in Paris* (Oxford: Oxford University Press, 2004), 210–16; Sisters of Charity of Providence, *The Institute of Providence: History of the Daughters of Charity, Servants of the Poor Known as the Sisters of Providence*, vol. 2, *Heroic Years, 1845–1852* (Montreal: Providence Mother House, 1930), 51, 95; McCrosson, *The Bell and the River*, 10.

4. Letters from Mother Joseph to Montreal provide details: the sisters were initially overwhelmed by domestic tasks, difficult living conditions, fear that the heart-chilling religious indifference of the people would lead to discouragement and loss of piety, and regrets and longing for their community, offset only by an inner sense of doing God's will; by the time Blanchet writes this letter, they were caring for four orphans, visiting sick women, had prepared a "métisse" for Communion, were teaching a group of young girls from Brouillet's academy, had hosted local Canadien visitors, and had made a retreat led by Father Rossi. The two postulants had taken their vows, and servant Moïse had arrived from San Francisco. Mother Caron was asked to send not only biographies of several saints for the novitiate but also a spindle, a flange, and some wire for making a spinning wheel, as "it is hard to get woolen stockings here, but we can get all the wool we need at low cost." Mother Joseph of the Sacred Heart to Mother Caron, October 21, 1856; May 1857; Mother Joseph to Bishop I. Bourget, December 29, 1856; January

27, 1857; Mother Joseph to Vicar-General A. F. Truteau, April 19, 1857, Mother Joseph of the Sacred Heart Personal Papers Collection, Providence Archives, Seattle.

5. Brouillet, not anticipating the sisters' arrival, had not prepared their living quarters despite the bishop's request that he do so. A vocal and disquieting brush between the vicar-general and his returning bishop had ensued ("Chronicles, 1856–1857," in "Chronicles of the House of Providence, 1856–1875").

6. Two traditional signs of a successful religious community, since the medieval era, are (1) regularity, the hourly rhythm of work and prayer that lends to spiritual advancement, and (2) individual detachment, the transcendence of temporal and self interests through communal and spiritual fulfillment. According to this report, the sisters had adapted to their circumstances with remarkable grace and speed.

7. The three professed sisters were Mother Joseph of the Sacred Heart (Esther Pariseau), Sister Praxedes of Providence (Desanges Lamothe), and Sister Blandine of the Holy Angels (Zephyrine Collins). The two postulants were Adelaide Theriault, professed as Sister Vincent de Paul, and Helen Norton (born in New York), professed as Sister Mary of the Precious Blood. These five women are considered the foundresses of the Providence Sisters in Washington.

8. Blanchet is referring to the first group of sisters who had arrived in response to his initial request in 1853, while he was still in Mexico. See introduction to letter 20.

9. Living quarters not having been prepared before they arrived, the women slept the first eight nights in the front room of a partitioned attic of the bishop's residence, where they put order to the pell-mell of vestments and sacred objects occasioned by use of the residence as refuge for Indians and whites during the Indian wars. For want of privacy, they then turned a servant's unused ten-by-sixteen-foot room adjoining the kitchen into their dormitory-refectory-community room, where they skillfully fashioned five narrow bunks, a table hinged to the wall, storage boxes that also served as a chair for each, and an altar from an exquisitely embroidered linen image of the Sacred Heart of Jesus, a gift to the bishop during his travels, lit by an improvised vigil light. On Ash Wednesday they moved to a neighboring sixteen-by-twenty-four-foot, two-story cabin that Blanchet, embarrassed by their awkward reception, had had built for them; but in May, with additional room needed for their expanding works of charity, including the care of four orphans, they took over the entire bishop's residence, and the priests moved to other quarters, to wait until the cost of workers was low enough to build a convent. "Chronicles, 1856–1857," in "Chronicles of the House of Providence, 1856–1875"; McCrosson, *The Bell and the River*, 109–10, 117.

10.Blanchet, like all other Catholic bishops at this time, perceived the Protestant bias in U.S. public schools as a danger to the faith of Catholics. The rules of the Institute viewed teaching only as a means of support for other charitable works.

11.In addition to the accordion she had received in San Francisco, Sister Blandine played the harmonium, a metallic reed organ, for the church, and Blanchet taught her to sing plain chant. "Chronicles, 1856–1857," in "Chronicles of the House of Providence, 1856–1875," 74; McCrosson, *The Bell and the River*, 100, 103.

To William Archbold, U.S. Army Sergeant, Fort Steilacoom, W.T., July 28, 1857[1]

While Blanchet waited for a response from Mother Caron regarding his request for more sisters, he acknowledged an important event in the growth of his diocese: the construction of a Catholic church at Fort Steilacoom, the major U.S. Army installation on Puget Sound.[2]

Continuous Catholic clerical presence on the Sound had begun with visits from the earliest missionaries, Fathers Modeste Demers and F. N. Blanchet, in 1839, during which they evangelized Indians and held a mission at the HBC's Fort Nisqually. Clergy visited and provided services at the Cowlitz mission regularly from 1839 forward. In 1848, F. N. Blanchet, by this time the archbishop of Oregon City who was responsible for this area, assigned a resident priest to the Cowlitz mission with responsibility to work with Indians and residents around Fort Nisqually, the settlement at Steilacoom, and points north. During that same year, the Oblate superior, Pascal Ricard, established the Oblate motherhouse on today's Budd Inlet, four miles north of New Market (later Tumwater), from where fellow Oblates would serve Indians of Puget Sound, HBC employees at Fort Nisqually and its environs, and settlers near Steilacoom until the spring of 1853 (see letter 20, notes 6 and 7).

In July 1854, A. M. A. Blanchet, now in charge of the area as bishop of Nesqualy, assigned Father Michael King, recently arrived from Ireland, to reside at Steilacoom and serve the Sound. Illness cut short his work, and he returned to Vancouver before that year ended. In August 1855, with King's health improved and having received indication that the settlers, primarily in Olympia, would support a priest, Blanchet again appointed King as missionary to the Sound, to reside in Steilacoom and to maintain a regular presence in Olympia. King was at his assignment only a short time when he removed to Vancouver during the Indian-white conflict that began in the fall of 1855, and then to California for reasons of health. During the absence of a resident diocesan priest, the Oblates again served Steilacoom and Fort Nisqually. The next diocesan pastor to be appointed to Puget Sound, to reside at Steilacoom, was Father Louis Rossi, who arrived in the fall of 1857.[3]

The newly built church was located inside Fort Steilacoom and not in the town of Steilacoom. This fact reflected the reality of Catholic presence and development on the Sound. It also exemplified the challenges Blanchet faced in securing from the population both the fiscal and personal commitment that were essential to establishing and maintaining religious institutions in a region of rapidly expanding and highly mobile settler population.[4]

The vast majority of the Catholic population that was not Indian or Canadien consisted of current and former U.S. Army personnel. At Fort Steilacoom, over half the garrison's soldiers and officers were Catholic. They provided most of the money to build the church. The record shows that over two years of collections, 1855 and 1856, citizens contributed $78, soldiers $445, and the bishop $100 to the construction of the church.[5] The dates of the collection and a January 1857 letter from Sergeant Archbold to Vicar-General J. B. A. Brouillet suggest that construction began at the earliest in 1855 and was completed in 1857.[6] In this letter, Bishop Blanchet thanks Sergeant Archbold for his efforts.

Vancouver, July 28th 1857

Sir,

I have received your letter of the 12th of the present, with the list of the contributors, and the expenses incurred, for the new church at the F. Steilacoom.[7]

You deserve certainly more than an ordinary praise for the zeal and the perseverance with which you have conducted that affair all long [*sic*]. I am happy to find the present opportunity to acknowledge it, and to offer you the expression of thankfulness.[8]

Please to tell all the contributors to your good work that I appreciate very much the sacrifices they have made so generously, thus proving once more their attachment to their Mother, the holy Catholic Church. No doubt, the Lord and the blessed V. Mary, conceived without the stain of original [sin], in whose honor this church is built, will reward an hundred fold, you and all the individuals who forwarded the enterprise. And, for that end, I will not fail to address to them my prayers.

I am always disposed to place a Missionary in the Sound, as soon as the

Catholics will be able to support him, or at least to pay the greatest part of the expenses.[9]

I am cordially and with great regard, Sir, your . . .
A. M. Blanchet, Bp. of Nesqualy

AAS, A2: 292–93. LETTER WRITTEN IN ENGLISH.

———•———

1. William H. Archbold, a native of Kilkenny, Ireland, served as ordnance sergeant at Fort Steilacoom from his arrival in 1856 until his death in April 1868. Early Missionary Records for Puget Sound, vol. 1, pt. 2, 114, RG 1000, AAS.

2. Under the command of Brevet Major Samuel Hathaway, Captain Bennett H. Hill, and two company of artillery established Fort Steilacoom in August 1849. The U.S. Army rented the land, part of the HBC's Puget Sound Agricultural Company, from William F. Tolmie, head of the HBC's Fort Nisqually trading post. The fort was located about a mile south of the Steilacoom River (now known as Chambers Creek) and about one and a half miles from the town of Steilacoom. The U.S. Army's Fort Steilacoom, its soldiers and its officers, played a key role in mediating Indian-white relationships and conflicts between 1855 and 1861, including defending Chief Leschi in the trial that led to his execution. Herbert Hunt and Floyd C. Kaylor, *Washington, West of the Cascades; Historical and Descriptive; The Explorers, the Indians, the Pioneers, the Modern* (Chicago: S. J. Clarke Publishing Company, 1917), vol. 1, 170–75; George Dickey, "The Founding of the 11th Military District, Oregon Territory," and Robert E. Ficken, "The Three Party Conflict: The Army and the Indian on the Pacific Northwest Frontier," in *Military Influences on Washington History: Proceedings of a Conference; March 29–31, 1984, Camp Murray, Tacoma*, ed. William Woodward and David Hansen (Tacoma: Washington Army National Guard, 1984), 39–78; Gary Fuller Reese, "A Documentary History of Fort Steilacoom" (Tacoma Public Library, March 1978).

3. Sister M. Caroline Ann Gimpl, S.H.N., "Immaculate Conception Mission, Steilacoom, Washington" (master's thesis, Seattle University, 1951), 1–20; D. Moriarty to Blanchet, October 27, 1852, Diocesan Correspondence (Blanchet, A. M. A.), 1850–87, RG 610, AAS; Schoenberg, *Catholic Church in the Pacific Northwest*, 169–71.

4. The town of Steilacoom in 1857 was the seat of Pierce County and a contender to be the capital of Washington Territory. It housed the first sawmill on Puget Sound and was a major shipping site for lumber to California. Reese, "Documentary History of Fort Steilacoom."

5. Correspondence 1849–1974, box 131, folder 3, Steilacoom–Immaculate Conception, RG 700, Parishes, AAS; Gimpl, "Immaculate Conception Mission," app. 3.

6. Archbold to Brouillet, January 8, 1857, Correspondence 1849–1974, box 131, folder 3, Steilacoom–Immaculate Conception, RG 700, Parishes, AAS; Gimpl, "Immaculate Conception Mission," 27–28.

7. Immaculate Conception Church in Steilacoom, completed in 1857, is the oldest Catholic church building still standing in Washington State and continues to be used for services.

8. As ordnance sergeant Archbold was attached to the fort and not to an army company. He lived with his wife in a cabin apart from the fort. And, when the other regular army soldiers departed to fight in the Civil War, Archbold remained at Fort Steilacoom. Priests who came to serve the Catholic soldiers at the fort often stayed at his home. Archbold and his wife appear as sponsors for baptisms in the records of Immaculate Conception Church. Father Louis Rossi, who resided at Steilacoom and Olympia while serving the Puget Sound, had a low opinion of Archbold. Gimpl, "Immaculate Conception Mission," 24–26; Louis Rossi, *Six Years on the West Coast of America, 1856–1862*, trans. and annotated by W. Victor Wortley (Fairfield, Wash.: Ye Galleon Press, 1983), 129–31.

9. As discussed regarding the Cowlitz mission (see letter 17), monetary support for resident priests and upkeep of a church were not obligations that local populations accepted gladly. In a January 8, 1857, letter to Vicar-General Brouillet, responding to a query about the people of Steilacoom and the Sound supporting a missionary, Sergeant Archbold reports that of sixteen Catholic citizens in the vicinity he was able to secure donations for construction of the church from only five of them. Further, he notes that while the soldiers would support a priest, the local citizens showed no interest in those priests who did visit the fort (Archbold to Brouillet, January 8, 1857).

LETTER 23

To Eugène-Casimir Chirouse, Oblate of Mary Immaculate, March 12, 1860[1]

Much had changed on Puget Sound in the three years since the completion of the Catholic church at Fort Steilacoom. Indian-settler clashes on the Sound had largely subsided. News of allegedly rich deposits of gold on the Fraser River had remade Whatcom on Bellingham Bay into a nascent San Francisco. In March 1859, the Senate approved the treaties Governor Stevens had negotiated in 1854–55, including the one that designated Tulalip, where Father Chirouse was residing, an official reservation.[2]

Oblate missionary activities also had moved north. Conflicts of 1855–57 had forced the closure of their missions among Yakamas and Cayuses east of the Cascades, and the scattering of their missionaries. Louis D'Herbomez was named Oblate superior, replacing Pascal Ricard, who was recalled to France, and in 1858 the motherhouse was moved from Olympia to Victoria on Vancouver Island.[3] Pandosy, whose life was endangered west of the Cascades due to suspicions of his support for Yakama resistance, remained among the Jesuits of the Rocky Mountains until he was reassigned in the summer of 1858 to a new mission on Lake Okanogan in British Columbia.[4] Fathers Durieu and Chirouse and Brother Verney brought the experience they had gained east of the Cascades to their new mission on the Sound.[5]

On September 25, 1858, these three clerics, upon the invitation of local Indians, planted their tent in woods of the Sénéomus (Snohomish), at the mouth of a river by this name, where they subsequently built two cabins. On May 30, 1859, Indian agent Michael Simmons met formally with the Indians to announce Senate approval of the Point Elliott Treaty, and four months later, he authorized Chirouse to erect buildings, including a chapel and school, on the Tulalip Reservation a few miles to the north of their mission. By October 29, the Oblates, with their own funds and help from a neighboring Canadien, were building a log cabin at the location Agent Simmons had designated, and in response to agent orders they had procured spelling books so they could teach Indian boys the little English they possessed.[6] Father Jayol and Brother Blanchet held the rearguard at the former motherhouse on Budd Inlet (located at today's Priest Point Park in Olympia) until it was closed in 1860.

In spite of these shifts of locale, the Oblates did not lose contact entirely with Yakama Indians they had befriended, some of whom appear to have visited them in their new missions.[7] Nor did they lose contact with one another. A rich web of correspondence that reached geographically from Bishop Blanchet in Vancouver, W.T. to Oblate Superior D'Herbomez in Victoria, enabled in part by Lummi and other Indian and métis carriers, molded this far-flung enterprise into a community. The correspondence focused on the missionaries' internal spiritual practices, catechetical and sacramental life among Indians, and day-to-day temporal matters. The trail of letters also reveals domains of responsibility between the Oblate superior and the bishop: the superior oversaw the placement of his clergy, their religious and material life, and general pastoral approaches; the bishop had the last word on matters related to catechesis and the sacraments, including baptism and marriage, and he played a role in seeing that contracts for the newly emerging schools on reservations (negotiated by his vicar-general when in Washington, D.C.) were fulfilled in his diocese.

This letter communicates the crucial role the missionaries thought that sisters should play in their work with Indians. As well, it provides a candid glimpse into issues of cultural encounter and liturgical practice that the missionaries and their bishop confronted on the territory's nascent reservations.

Vancouver, March 12th 1860

Most Reverend Father,

I received your letter of February 16th last describing the means you have adopted for instructing the Indians. May the Lord be blessed for inspiring them with a desire to learn and to practice their religious duties. I congratulate you for the blessings He bestows upon your works.[8] I very much liked your remark concerning sisters. Every mission must have some sisters, no matter what its size. I am convinced of this. Otherwise you will be unable to fulfill the government's aims with respect to the Indians. Once the superintendent receives money for buildings, there will be no problem with establishing sisters at your mission. As soon as I know if Congress has provided the requested funds, I will write to Montreal to be sure that a sufficient number of sisters are sent.
Now I reply to your questions.

1st. With regard to the indult that allows an infidel Indian who converts to take whichever wife he pleases unless the first wishes to convert . . . &c.
   Response. As missionaries generally consider marriages of infidel Indians to be null, to be concubinage, there are no grounds for the terms of the indult, if I am not mistaken & the converted person is free to take the wife he likes the most. However, if one of them wishes to convert, I think it would be wise for him to marry her rather than another.[9]

2nd. What should be done about Indians who were baptized in the cradle & who are found with several wives?
   Response. If they had no dispensation for one of them, they are free.[10]

3rd. Should one baptize or absolve *in art. Mortis,* persons who are left unconscious in the act of the sin of *tamanwas*?[11]
   Response. If this superstition is considered a serious sin, I see no grounds for administering sacraments, assuming that the Indian understands its enormity.

4th. The same question for drunkards, dying while inebriated, assuming they have . . . &c. The same response.[12]

I am . . . &c.
Aug. M. A., Bp. of Nesqualy

AAS, A5: 111–13.

———•———

1. Eugène-Casimir Chirouse (1821–1892) was born to a farming family in Hostun, in the Drôme region of France; he completed five years of classical studies, made his Oblate novitiate at Notre-Dame de l'Osier, and vowed perpetual oblation on September 14, 1844. Bishop Eugène de Mazenod described Chirouse as charming, adroit, and intelligent. Ordained by Bishop A. M. A. Blanchet on January 1, 1848, Chirouse remained attached to the Diocese of Nesqualy until 1878 (Young, "Mission of the Missionary Oblates," 59).

2. The Treaty of Point Elliott was signed on January 22, 1854, by some seventy-five Indians, including Chief Seattle (Duwamish), Chief Patkanim (Snoqualmie), and Chief Chow-its-host (Lummi), and seventeen whites. Article 1 called for ceding the rights of about twenty-five hundred Indians to lands south of the United States border, west of the summit of the Cascades, east of a line roughly through the eastern limits of Puget Sound, and north of those lands ceded by the Nisqually, Puyallup, and other tribes of the Medicine Creek Treaty. In addition to establishing the Port Madison and Lummi reservations (each comprising two sections or 1,280 acres), Article 3 established the Tulalip Reservation (of thirty-six sections or one township) north of the mouth of the Snohomish River and including Tulalip Bay, on which there was to be an agricultural and industrial school. Charles J. Kappler, ed., *A Life beyond Indian Affairs: Laws and Treaties*, vol. 2, *Treaties, 1778–1883* (Washington: Government Printing Office, 1904), 659–71.

3. Louis-Joseph D'Herbomez, of Spanish ancestry, was ordained in Marseilles on October 19, 1849; arrived with two Oblate brothers in August 1850; and was sent to St. Joseph of Ahtanum, where he served until September 1854, when he returned to Olympia. Bishop de Mazenod described him as sensible, capable, and scholarly, one who inspired respect and confidence. Correspondence reveals that D'Herbomez was instrumental in maintaining internal harmony among the Oblates and with the local bishops. Pascal Ricard, weak in health, was formally recalled to France on November 11, 1855, and departed March 15, 1857. D'Herbomez, who had been acting as superior, was named provincial superior of the Oblate Vicariate of Oregon in 1858, and on April 14 of the same year, the General Council of Marseilles decided to move the Oblate motherhouse to Vancouver Island. Young, "Mission of the Missionary Oblates," 101, 119, 137, 139, 145.

4. Father Pandosy, who felt he was edified by the Indians among whom he lived, left Yakama Immaculate Conception Mission in 1851, to serve followers of Chief Teies at Holy Cross Mission in Moxee. By 1852, he was with other Oblates at Ahtanum, where he developed a close friendship

with his patron Yakama chief Kamiakin, who regularly attended prayer gatherings and would see to the baptism of his children throughout his life and eventually his own baptism before his death in 1877. Along with Father Durieu, Pandosy was forced to flee Ahtanum mission when volunteer forces, convinced of Oblate collusion with the Yakamas, burned it to the ground and desecrated Pandosy's liturgical vestments in mid-November 1855. Initially expelled from the Yakama country by Governor Stevens, Pandosy stayed at the Jesuit missions near Colville and Coeur d'Alene, where he continued to minister to local Indians and visiting Yakamas. In 1856, he returned to Immaculate Conception Mission and also served as chaplain to Colonel Wright's troops during a temporary peace with the Yakamas. In the summer of 1858, he was assigned to begin a new mission in Okanogan, British Columbia. Richard D. Scheuerman and Michael O. Finley, *Finding Chief Kamiakin: The Life and Legacy of a Northwest Patriot* (Pullman: Washington State University Press, 2008), 20–21, 48–51, 96, 100, 108, 110; Kay Cronin, *Cross in the Wilderness* (Toronto: Mission Press, 1960), 38–42; Young, "Mission of the Missionary Oblates," 105, 116, 118, 134–35.

5. In 1852 Father Chirouse had restored the Cayuse mission of St. Anne on the Umatilla and in 1853 established Mission St. Rose on lands donated by Cayuses on the Yellow Hawk and Walla Walla confluence. He departed for Olympia in spring 1856, both missions having been destroyed during Indian-white conflicts (see letter 28). Father Pierre Paul Durieu, O.M.I., arrived from France in December 1854 and served briefly among the Yakamas. Munnick and Munnick, introduction to "Missions of St. Ann and St. Rose of the Cayouse," in *Catholic Church Records of the Pacific Northwest*, vol. 7; Young, "Mission of the Missionary Oblates," 119–24.

6. Chirouse to Blanchet, July 10, 1859; Durieu to D'Herbomez, May 30, 1859; Simmons to Chirouse, October 10, 1859; Chirouse to D'Herbomez, October 29, 1859; Durieu to D'Herbomez, October 29, 1859, in Drouin, *Les Oblats*, 3:889, 876, 919, 925. Blanchet had also invited the Oblates to establish a mission at Steilacoom and serve both whites and Indians on the Sound, but the Oblates ultimately did not accept the conditions of his proposal. D'Herbomez to Blanchet, May 8, 1860, in Drouin, *Les Oblats*, 3:1031.

7. Pandosy's former cook at his Yakama mission, "Muksi" (Moxee?), visited Father Durieu at the Snohomish mission and told him that their chief, Teies, and his family, still frightened, were hiding from soldiers among the Snoqualmies; that Yakama chief Kamiakin had fled to British Columbia; and that most Yakamas were wintering at Sylla (Zillah or Selah?). Durieu to Pandosy, March 25, 1859, in Drouin, *Les Oblats*, 3:852.

8. We were unable to locate this letter, but others suggest its content. Chirouse sent two lengthy epistles the same month to his superior, Louis D'Herbomez, telling of 830 Indians, "elites" (the "elect") from sixteen neighboring tribes, who took up residence five months earlier with the Oblates. The Oblates follow a schedule of morning mass, including prayer and catechism, at the chapel built by visiting Lummi; afternoon lessons in English, singing, and catechism for children; and evening prayer and recitation. In addition, there are fixed times on weekends for confession, a meeting on Sundays for those preparing to marry, afternoon processions on feast days, and a year-long catechumenate followed by an exam in accord with the provisions set by the Council of Trent. Chirouse also obtained permission from Blanchet during this time to use a catechism he had written and was translating into Salish. Chirouse to D'Herbomez, February 3, 1860, in Drouin, *Les Oblats*, 3:959–67; Blanchet to D'Herbomez, March 12, 1860, AAS, A5: 108–9.

9. An indult is a special privilege or exception granted by an ecclesiastical authority. *Concubinage* as used here is a technical term, implying a union of a nature that can become grounds for marriage by a priest when circumstances, on the part of both parties, are met. Priests did not consider such indigenous unions to be marriages, because, among other reasons, they were often prearranged by parents without consent of the interested parties, they lacked lifelong vows, and they allowed for polygamy. Pandosy, in opposing the validity of indigenous unions, wrote that he had observed during his missionary years tribal ostracism of girls who objected to a forced union, resulting on occasion in famine, suicide, or abusive treatment by a neighboring tribe (Pandosy to D'Herbomez, March 30, 1867, in Drouin, *Les Oblats*, 3:1046).

10. A dispensation is the relaxation of a law in a special case; the most common at the time was a dispensation from a marriage bann (a public proclamation of proposed marriage, to allow for objections based on known impediments, such as already being married). If such a dispensation had been granted, the marriage would be legitimate.

11. "At the moment of death." The most common spelling is *tamenoès* (see letter 12).

12. Article 10 of Governor Stevens's treaties excluded ardent spirits from reservations; the federal Indian Intercourse Act also barred the sale of liquor to Indians, as did Washington territorial law. Nevertheless, with many Indians continuing to live and work both on and off the reservation, with alcohol readily available, and with the territorial government lacking the means to fully enforce its laws, drinking among indigenous peoples was difficult to prevent or control. Indians on the Tulalip Reservation experienced confusion between the missionaries' opposition to alcohol and peddlers' encouragement in defiance of the laws. Brad Asher, *Beyond the Reservation: Indians, Settlers, and the Law in Washington Territory, 1853–1889* (Norman: University of Oklahoma Press, 1999), 81–90; Fisher, *Shadow Tribe*, 67–70; Alexandra Harmon, *Indians in the Making: Ethnic Relations and Indian Identities around Puget Sound* (Berkeley: University of California Press, 1998), 97–101.

LETTER 24

To Edward R. Geary, Superintendent of Indian Affairs for Oregon and Washington Territories, October 7, 1860[1]

As the previous letter to Father Chirouse indicates, Indian agent Simmons on Puget Sound had requested that the Catholic missionaries already located on the Snohomish near Tulalip assume the responsibility of teaching at the newly established Tulalip Reservation. Bishop Blanchet expected that Catholics would staff the school at the newly established Yakama Reservation as well, priests having maintained missions among the Yakamas since 1847, except when forced to absent themselves for brief periods because of conflict between settlers and Indians (see letter 23, notes 4 and 7).

The location for the agency and the school in question in this letter, Fort Simcoe, was a former Indian gathering spot. In response to Kamiakin's petition of July 1848, Father Chirouse had opened Mission Saint Joseph of Simcoe there, with the approval of Bishop Blanchet.[2] The site, one of several camps associated with Chief Kamiakin's bands, was located some thirty miles south of the Yakima Valley (and future Ahtanum mission, another Kamiakin camp). The U.S. Army created a strategic fort at this location in 1856, in an initial attempt to prevent hostilities between Indians and Governor Stevens's volunteer troops. With the crushing of the territory's armed Indian resistance on the Columbia Plateau in September 1858 and the close of the Yakima War, the fort was decommissioned and turned over to the Bureau of Indian Affairs on May 26, 1859, to serve as the headquarters for the Yakima Indian Agency.[3]

In seeking the resumption of Catholic presence among the Yakamas, Blanchet found his plans blocked, however, by a patronage system of appointments heavily informed by long-standing anti-Catholic prejudice. That prejudice had been reenforced during the Yakima War by the rumor that Father Pandosy and other priests assisted Indian combatants. Reverend Henry Harmon Spalding, former missionary among the Nez Percés at Lapwai and from 1850 to 1853 an Indian agent in Oregon, continued to repeat his accusations that Blanchet and his priests were responsible for the Whitman massacre (see letter 2).[4] Further, difficult negotiations to resolve the boundary dispute between Britain and the United States, occasioned by the Pig War of 1859 (on today's San Juan Island), were under way. Superintendent Geary and others feared the influence of the HBC—with which he associated the Catholic Church—on the Indians should those negotiations go awry.[5]

So, while Bishop Blanchet considered continuation of the interrupted Catholic missionary work among the Yakamas to be a logical result of the federal government's implementation of the reservation system, Superintendent Geary saw it differently. Geary accepted the recommendation of Simcoe agent Richard Lansdale and appointed the Reverend James H. Wilbur as superintendent of teaching on the Yakama Reservation. At the time of his appointment, Wilbur served as senior elder of the Methodist Church's entire Columbia District, which included Portland and all of the Great Columbia Plain. To Geary, the appointment of a fellow Protestant minister, far more than that of a priest, held the possibility of moving the Yakamas in the direction of civilization, understood as conversion to Protestantism and acceptance of a life of settled farming.[6]

Bishop Blanchet knew of Wilbur's Methodist zeal and his abhorrence of Catholicism. But the bishop could not know that Wilbur's appointment to Fort Simcoe was the beginning of a nearly two-decade conflict between Wilbur and himself. That conflict exemplified a larger struggle between Protestants and Catholics in the United States over appointment of Indian agents and teachers and access of missionaries to reservations, a struggle that continued into the 1880s.[7]

Vancouver, October 7th 1860

Sir,

I have received your answer to my letter of the 3rd inst. You say in the last part of it, "That there is no authority, on the part of this (your) office to interfere with the religious tenets of the Indians, when happily they have any, or debar them from the privileges and consolations to be obtained through the ministers & rites of the religion of their choice."[8]

I am very well pleased with this part of your letter; it is entirely conformable to my ideas. But the other part has, on the contrary, greatly astonished me, after your repeated protestations that all the tribes formerly instructed and christianised [sic] by the Catholic Clergy, should be placed again, when on their reservations, under the care, & in the charge of the same Catholic Clergy, as to their litterary [sic] and religious training.[9] You have, several times, gone so far as to say that the litterary & religious instructions of none but two or three reservations at most would be entrusted to the Protestant Clergy; these were the Nez Percé, the Spokanes, and *perhaps* the Grand Round.[10] All the other reservations, you said, should fall to the care of the Catholic Clergy, namely the reservations of Puget Sound, Yakima, the Warm Springs, the Umatilla & Pend d'Oreille. Surely, when you declared that such were your determination you knew well that, during the thirteen years past, the Indians of Yakama country have been evangelised [sic] only by the Cath. Missionaries, and never by the Protestant ministers.[11] Now you seem to have changed your mind, and you say that you are determined to approve the appointment of a

Methodist Preacher to the Superintendency of teaching on the Yakama Reservation,[12] and this you do, after the assurance given a few months ago to you by Very Rev. J. B. A. Brouillet, V.G. that we would be prepared for supplying the wants of all the reservations allotted to us, as soon as the Department was ready, provided we were notified some time in advance. You will perceive at once, Sir, that I cannot but regret sincerely to see such a sudden and unaccountable change of principles in regard to a matter of so great importance in a public officer of your high standing. And you will allow me, I hope, to beg you to postpone your approval of the above stated appointment, and to take time to reconsider the matter at leisure.

I have the h . . . resp. &c.
A. M. A. Bl., Bp. of Nesq.

AAS, A5: 135–37. LETTER WRITTEN IN ENGLISH.

————•————

1. Edward Ratchford Geary (1811–1886), born in Washington County, Maryland, became a Presbyterian minister. In 1851, after a successful thirteen-year tenure at a congregation in Fredericksburg, Ohio, the Board of Education and Domestic Missions of the Presbyterian Church sent him as a missionary to Oregon, charged with establishing both schools and congregations. Without sufficient population in Oregon to sustain either congregations or schools, Reverend Geary engaged in his ministry and in various civil occupations. He became secretary to the superintendent of Indian Affairs for Oregon and Washington, Joel Palmer, in 1853, and so was present at the negotiating and signing of Oregon's treaties. In late 1855, the Rogue and Yakama Indian wars under way, he resigned the position and moved to Linn County to begin churches in Corvallis, Calapooia, Brownsville, and Diamond Hill. In 1858, he was elected superintendent of schools for Linn County. In March 1859, Geary was appointed superintendent of Indian Affairs for Oregon and Washington, a position he resigned in 1861. He then returned to Brownsville, where, in addition to preaching, he aided in establishing a woolen mill. Geary was one of the founding members of the Presbytery of Oregon. Clifford M. Drury, "John White Geary and His Brother Edward," *California Historical Society Quarterly* 20, no. 1 (March 1941): 12–25; *Memorial of Edward R. Geary, D.D., Late of Eugene City, Oregon* (San Francisco: Occident Printing House, 1887); Alban W. Hoopes, *Indian Affairs and Their Administration, with Special Reference to the Far West, 1849–1860* (Philadelphia: University of Pennsylvania Press, 1932), 128.

2. Chirouse to Ricard, January 12, 1849, in Drouin, *Les Oblats,* 1:39; Young, "Mission of the Missionary Oblates," 83. Article 5 of the 1855 Yakama Treaty provided for the establishment of two reservation schools, one of which was to be an agricultural and industrial school located at the agency, to employ one superintendent of teaching and two teachers. The assumption of

the time that schools, for Indians or for whites, would incorporate Christian teaching made them sectarian by nature.

3. See D. W. Meinig, *The Great Columbia Plain: A Historical Geography, 1805–1910* (Seattle: University of Washington Press, 1968), 161–67; Clifford E. Trafzer and Richard D. Scheuerman, *Renegade Tribe: The Palouse Indians and the Invasion of the Inland Pacific Northwest* (Pullman: Washington State University Press, 1986), 60–92; Prucha, *The Great Father*, 1:407–9; Hoopes, *Indian Affairs and Their Administration*, 117–18, 120–22, 126–28; and Albert Culverwell, *Stronghold in the Yakima Country: The Story of Fort Simcoe, 1856–1859* (Olympia: Washington State Parks and Recreation Commission, 1956), 3–9, 14–15.

4. Henry Harmon Spalding, *Letter from the Secretary of the Interior: communicating, in compliance with the resolution of the Senate, information in relation to the early labors of the missionaries of the American Board of Commissioners for Foreign Missions in Oregon, commencing in 1836 . . .* (Washington: Government Printing Office, 1871). For a history of these accusations and rebuttals, see letter 9, note 20; also, Peter J. Rahill, M.A., *Catholic Indian Missions and Grant's Peace Policy, 1870–1884* (Washington, D.C.: Catholic University of America Press, 1953), 55–56.

5. In his first report to the commissioner of Indian Affairs, September 1, 1859, Geary noted, "The influence of the Hudson's Bay Company, and of the British name, over the Indians in a large portion of this superintendency, is well understood; and our present threatening relations with Great Britain have already had a perceptible influence on the Indians of Washington Territory, bordering the coast and Puget's Sound." Edward R. Geary, *Report of Edward R. Geary, Superintendent of Indian Affairs for Oregon and Washington, to the Commissioner of Indian Affairs* (Washington, D.C.: Office of the Commissioner of Indian Affairs, 1859), 383; online at University of Washington Libraries, American Indians of the Pacific Northwest Collection, http://content.lib.washington.edu/u?/lctext,2045 (accessed December 1, 2009). See also C. F. Coan, "The Adoption of the Reservation Policy in the Pacific Northwest, 1853–1855," *Oregon Historical Quarterly* 23, no. 1 (March 1922): 25–26. On the Pig War, see Clinton A. Snowden, *History of Washington; The Rise and Progress of an American State*, 6 vols. (New York: Century History Company, 1909), 4:50–69.

6. Maurice Helland, *There Were Giants: The Life of James H. Wilbur* (Yakima, Wash.: M. Helland, 1980), 63–74; Rahill, *Catholic Indian Missions and Grant's Peace Policy*, 116, 305; Robert L. Whitner, "Grant's Indian Peace Policy on the Yakima Reservation, 1870–1882," *Pacific Northwest Quarterly* 50, no. 4 (October 1959), 137–38. All speak to Wilbur's attitude toward Catholics. For a clear presentation of the theory of Protestant mission work and the notion of civilization, see Jeffrey's *Converting the West*. Useful background is also given in Robert H. Keller, Jr., *American Protestantism and United States Indian Policy, 1869–82* (Lincoln: University of Nebraska Press, 1983), 1–45.

7. See Francis Paul Prucha, *Indian Policy in the United States: Historical Essays* (Lincoln: University of Nebraska Press, 1981), 479–83, 501–33; Rahill, *Catholic Indian Missions and Grant's Peace Policy*, 44; Robert L. Whitner, "The Methodist Episcopal Church and Grant's Peace Policy: A Study of the Methodist Agencies, 1870–1882" (Ph.D. diss., University of Minnesota, 1959); and Keller, *American Protestantism and United States Indian Policy*, 46–71, 167–87.

8. The bishop is quoting from Geary's letter to him of October 4, 1860 (AAS, A5: 133–34).

9. In his letter to Blanchet of October 4, Superintendent Geary claimed that in appointing

persons to reservations, he could "officially make no distinctions on account of religious tenets or connections."

10. Blanchet is acknowledging the long tenure of Protestant missionaries to the Nez Percés, beginning with Henry Harmon and Eliza Spalding, two of the original ABCFM missionaries sent to Oregon, and of the work among the Spokanes of Cushing and Myra Fairbanks Eels with Elkanah and Mary Richardson Walker, from 1838 to 1848. Multiple tribes gathered on the Grand Ronde reservation had encountered both Protestant and Catholic missionaries.

11. Blanchet was correct that the Yakamas had been evangelized only by Catholic priests from 1847 until 1860. Superintendent Geary, however, in his 1859 report to the commissioner of Indian Affairs, referenced the early work of both Protestant and Catholic missionaries east of the Cascades as having a "salutary effect" on Indians in the region (Geary, *Report*, 397).

12. See letter 2 for an account of Wilbur's presence in the Walla Walla region at the time of the Whitman killings; see note 21 of the same letter for biography. Wilbur had welcomed Geary to Oregon upon his arrival in 1851. The adamantly anti-Catholic Wilbur held Blanchet and his clergy responsible for the killings at Waiilatpu. Wilbur continued in his capacity as Methodist elder and missionary to all the Indians of the Columbia District even after he became superintendent of instruction at Simcoe. See Keller, *American Protestantism and United States Indian Policy*, 178; Helland, *There Were Giants*, 63–69; and Whitner, "Grant's Indian Peace Policy," 135–42.

LETTER 25

To Allen McLeod,
March 6, 1862

For Bishop Blanchet, educational institutions served multiple functions. They provided continued contact with Indians who, for various reasons, sought Catholic presence. In recent settlements such as Vancouver they generated income for other ministries of the Sisters of Providence, and they were ideal nurseries not only for future Catholics but also for the formation of future priests and sisters. And, often, especially in the fluid situation of the frontier, they became refuges for orphans.

On March 3, 1860, Blanchet wrote to Father Thomas Soulard, one of the many priests who served briefly in the Cowlitz and Puget Sound areas. In the letter, Blanchet raised the issue of support for three Cottnoire children from the Cowlitz, stating that the mother had left them at the Sisters of Providence orphanage in Vancouver. In the same letter, he added: "tell McLeod that the Sisters should be able to take his daughter in a while, I hope."[1] Two years later,

Blanchet returned to the matter of the McLeod child. Records indicate that an Allan McLeod, probably of Stornoway, Scotland, joined the HBC in 1847 on a five-year contract and appeared in the Columbia region in 1848–49. He deserted on February 24, 1849, likely to the goldfields of California; he was back working as a laborer on the Cowlitz Farm in 1850 and quit for a final time in 1852. The 1857 Lewis County census records list an Allen McLeod of Scotland, farmer, living in the region.[2]

Blanchet's brief response to Mr. McLeod is intriguing. First, the location of the letter's recipient suggests that the safety net provided by the sisters—only nine in number at the time of this letter—extended well beyond the geographical boundaries of Vancouver. There was also the matter of ethnicity. Given the presence of other Scotland-born McLeod fathers with Indian wives and mixed-heritage children living in the region, and Allen McLeod's own marriage to a woman born in Washington, it is reasonable to assume that any children he may have had were also of mixed descent.[3] According to the sisters' "Vancouver Chronicles" of 1859–60, "métis children" were to be pitied, because they received less compassion than others, and girls were victims of the immorality of whites who perverted them even at a young age.[4] Of the forty-one girls listed in the combined registry of Vancouver's Providence boarding school and orphanage, from the March 24, 1856, opening to September 1861, at least fifteen were from well-known Canadien families, including ten from the Cowlitz. (Three other children were listed as Indian.) Among these were Philomène Bercier (who went by her mother's last name), daughter of Marcel Bernier, and two others for whom Mr. Bernier was listed as guardian.[5] Assuming the McLeod child was also of mixed ethnic heritage—though apparently Scottish rather than Canadien—the sisters and their bishop may well have been particularly anxious to provide for her care.

This letter also raises questions about who at the time was considered an orphan. The fact that a parent is writing to ask permission to leave his daughter at an orphanage suggests that the McLeod child would probably have been considered a semi-orphan, a child who had at least one parent, but one who was unable to care for the child at the time. Records also indicate a considerable blurring of lines between the categories of orphans and boarding students at the Providence establishments in Vancouver. Given the frequent practice at the time among children of Indian heritage of taking the mother's name, and the lack of available records about this mother, we are unable to ascertain if the McLeod child ended up in the care of the Sisters of Providence.[6]

Despite the many unanswered questions this letter provokes, it stands as testimony to the influence of the passion to get rich in the mines and its affect on the lives of some of the most vulnerable children in the Pacific Northwest.

Vancouver, March 6th 1862

Sir,

I have received your letter of Febry [*sic*] 19th wherein you express your wish of placing your child under the care of the Sisters of Charity, and beg to be informed whether they can admit her at the orphan asylum. I reply.

The Sisters are always disposed to receive every orphan, and especially female, at the asylum. But, unfortunately, their means of providing of the board and other wants of such children do not agree with the dispositions of their hearts. Far from it. Nevertheless, relying on Providence, they will not refuse any orphans whose parents are too poor to pay for their board &c. If you belong to that class, your child will be received heartily. Yet, as you intend to go to the mines, I presume that your intention is to get some money for the maintenance of your child at the asylum. You are certainly commendable for doing so.[7]

A. M. A. Bp. of Nesq.

AAS, A5: 183–84. LETTER WRITTEN IN ENGLISH.

---

1. Blanchet to Soulard, March 3, 1860, AAS, A2: 359–60. Two Cottnoire boys and one Cottnoire girl, from Cowlitz, appear in the Providence orphanage records of the time. "Register of orphan boys admitted to House of Providence, Vancouver, WA, from its foundation, March 24, 1857, to September 1916"; "Register of orphan girls admitted to House of Providence, from its foundation, March 24, 1857, to September 1916," Personnel-Student Records, Providence Academy, Vancouver, Wash., RG 22, Providence Archives, Mother Joseph Province, Seattle.

2. Watson, *Lives Lived West of the Divide*, 2:667. The 1878 and 1879 Pierce County census also lists an Allen McLoud (age fifty), of Scotland, a farmer. *Pierce County, Washington Territory Auditor's Census for 1878 and 1879* (Tacoma, Wash.: Tacoma–Pierce County Genealogical Society, 1997).

3. John McLeod, retired sheep farmer for the Puget Sound Agricultural Farm, was one of the

Muck Creek homesteaders whom Governor Stevens confined to Fort Nisqually, and one of the seven he eventually had imprisoned, for allegedly hosting nine Indians at his home on Christmas night 1855 and, a few weeks later, for forwarding a message from Chief Leschi indicating that he wanted hostilities to cease. John McLeod appears to have had children by two Indian women, Cowlitz and/or Puyallup. Richards, *Isaac I. Stevens*, 274–87; "The McLeod/McCloud Family at Nisqually and Puyallup," *Sequalitchew*, no. 8 (October 8, 2006); Steve A. Anderson, "A Crofter's Tale: Adventurous John of the Clan McLeod," *Columbia: The Magazine of Northwest History* 24, no. 2 (Summer 2010): 32–33.

4. "Chronicles," July 1, 1859–July 1, 1860, Providence Academy, Vancouver, Wash., RG 22, Providence Archives, Mother Joseph Province, Seattle.

5 "Register of orphan girls admitted to House of Providence, from its foundation, March 24, 1857, to September 1916."

6. Jennifer S. H. Brown, "Woman as Centre and Symbol in the Emergence of Métis Communities," *Canadian Journal of Native Studies* 3, no. 1 (1983): 39–46.

7. On August 30, 1889, an Allan McLeod received a patent to portions of sections 8 and 17 of township 18, range 4E, Pierce County, Washington, land he had claimed in 1862. If he was the letter's recipient, he eventually had some stability. Interestingly, according to the General Land Office Survey maps of 1871 and 1873, there was a footpath leading directly from this claim location to Puyallup, and wagon roads accessing the nearby home of John McLeod on Muck Creek, suggesting the likelihood of communication between the two McLeod families. U.S. Department of the Interior, Bureau of Land Management, General Land Office Records, http://www.glorecords.blm.gov (accessed May 2, 2011). Lawrence D. Anderson, historian of Graham, Washington, brought this claim and its location on the maps to our attention.

LETTER 26

To the Central Council of the Society for the Propagation of the Faith, April 15, 1862

Need for the care of children like the McLeod daughter, combined with the lack of hospitals, of homes for the destitute elderly, and of schools, all led to the rapid growth of Providence institutions in Vancouver and to the call for additional sisters. Clerics were wanting as well, as a result of the gradual departure of most Oblates of Mary Immaculate by 1860, the death of some diocesan priests, and the growing Catholic population. The construction of buildings and the travel of new religious personnel to staff the churches, institutions, and schools were costly matters. Knowing that the limited annual allocations from the Society for the Propagation of the Faith were readily transferred to pay the passage of priests and sisters from Europe and Montreal, Blanchet focused in this report on his need for personnel.

Among topics of particular interest in the report is the American College of the Immaculate Conception in Louvain. While in Belgium in 1856, Bishop Blanchet had subscribed to the foundation of this seminary for the formation of diocesan priests to serve in the United States.[1] This timely visit placed him in a position to incorporate some of the first graduates into the Diocese of Nesqualy, including Fathers Aegidius Junger and Jean-Baptiste Auguste Brondel. These exceptionally able men figured in the next generation of bishops in the Northwest's expanding Catholic Church.

Vancouver, April 15th 1862

Gentlemen

There has been little change since my last Report to the Central Councils on the state of the Diocese.

I have, however, experienced a great loss. Of the four priests I had, I have lost two. God has taken them in the prime of life, in the space of four months. May his Holy name be blessed![2] To fill the void caused by their death, I will send for the two subjects from Louvain who are already incorporated into the diocese, & on the verge of completing their studies in theology.[3] The cost of their transportation from Louvain to Vancouver can be estimated at about 2,000 francs each. I trust that you will kindly consider this additional expense in your next allocation.

In spite of the these difficult times, our religious establishments continue to prosper, with the exception of the debts that will burden them for some time, that is to say, until it pleases divine Providence to come to their assistance.[4]

The orphanages have about fifty children of each sex. About one hundred students are attending our schools.[5]

The Sisters of Charity, of which there are thirteen, are no longer sufficient in number for their ongoing works. I am expecting ten others. They will come, I hope, sometime next summer, if it pleases Providence to provide for their transportation. One should not figure on less than 1,500 francs per person for the trip from Montreal, Canada, here to Vancouver.[6]

Finally, if I can acquire the needed personnel, I will open a Latin class at the academy, come autumn. There are some pupils at the academy & at the orphanage with much promise. They will, I dare hope, be the first fruits of an indigenous clergy. For some time, the formation of this clergy has been a preoccupation of mine.[7]

May it be the Lord's pleasure to bless the projects I am undertaking for his glory, & to shower ever more of his favors upon the Society that will help us accomplish them!

A. M. A. Blanchet, Bp. of Nesqualy

OEUVRE DE LA PROPAGATION DE LA FOI, PARIS (OPFP), F-99, FOL. 52, OPM; AAS, A5: 193 (SUMMARY).

———•———

1. Unlike the United States, where there was a severe shortage of priests to serve the increasing numbers of Catholic immigrants, Catholic Europe, in the midst of a deep revival of piety, was experiencing a boom in vocations. In Belgium alone, the number of priests tripled between 1829 and 1856, resulting in more candidates for ministry than demand. At the American College, dedicated exclusively to the formation of European men for American missions, students took their courses at the venerable Catholic University of Louvain and studied English. The United States provided a rector, and individual U.S. bishops paid the board and room for those students who were incorporated into their dioceses at the start of their studies, as well as their travel expenses, once their studies were complete. Kevin A. Codd and Brian G. Dick, *The American College of Louvain: America's Seminary in the Heart of Europe* (Louvain, Belgium: American College, 2007), 13–27.

2. Following the departure of Father Rossi for reasons of health in December 1859, Father Thomas Soulard of Quebec served briefly at the Cowlitz mission and on Puget Sound. He died September 20, 1861, in Vancouver (Blanchet to Soulard, March 3, 1860; September 22, 1860; October 6, 1860, AAS, A5). We are unable to confirm the identity of the second priest who died.

3. The two incorporated seminarians to whom Blanchet refers were Aegidius Junger and Paul Antoine Mans.

4. Blanchet provided funds from his collections in Mexico and Europe for the refurbishment and construction of buildings, but day-to-day costs of sustaining works of mercy were greater than available revenue, this despite income from schools. As a result, the sisters were obliged to hold bazaars and make collections.

5. School registries and annual reports in the Providence chronicles indicate that this second figure included orphans of age for schooling and boarding and day pupils. The two

orphanages, known as St. Genevieve for girls and St. Vincent for boys, also served at the time as residences for boarding pupils. "Chronicles, July 1861–July 1862" in "Chronicles of the House of Providence, 1856 to 1876."

6. Sisters Jean de Dieu (Elmire Pinard) and Marie-Pierre (Louisa Cousack), and postulant Mathilde Fissiault, arrived October 6, 1858; Sisters Agnès (Honora Slate) and Pudent (Vitaline Laroque), and postulant Emilie Guimond arrived October 21, 1859, along with two sisters and a postulant of the Sisters of St. Anne for Victoria, and twelve Sisters of Holy Names of Jesus and Mary for the Archdiocese of Oregon City (Sisters Mary Florence, Mary of the Visitation, Mary Alphonse, Mary of Mercy, Mary of Calvary, Mary Arsinius, Mary Margaret, Mary Agathe, Francis Xavier, Mary Febronia, Mary Perpertua, Mary Julia). They were accompanied by Vicar-General Brouillet, Archbishop F.N. Blanchet, newly incorporated clerics Fathers Charles-Louis Augustin Richard and David-Joseph Halde (for Nesqualy), and F.X. Blanchet (for the archdiocese). In arriving at the figure of thirteen sisters, Blanchet is including three postulants from Vancouver (see letter 31). "Régistre de l'Institut des Soeurs de Charité Servantes des Pauvres et des Malades depuis la fondation le 16 mars 1843," Personnel, Sacred Heart Provincial Administration Records, Providence Archives, Mother Joseph Province, Seattle; "Notes sur le diocèse de Nesqualy," AAS, B6; "In Union with My Companions: Oregon's Twelve Foundresses," at www.holynamesheritagecenter.org/exhibits.html. Accessed March 3, 2013).

7. By *indigenous*, Blanchet most likely means U.S.-born, and of either Indian or non-Indian heritage. Historically, a reason for creating apostolic vicariates and dioceses in remote missionary areas, including New France and the Far East, was to assure the presence of a bishop to ordain indigenous (native-born) clergy, this being considered the sign of a successful, self-sustaining missionary diocese. Blanchet is referring to the Academy of Holy Angels that Vicar-General Brouillet had opened in 1856; it was attended by some of the fifty boy students who figured among the one hundred reported above. Pupils on the registry included sons of Canadiens, of military officers, of recent American settlers, and of Indians. "Student Account Ledgers, 1857–89," Personnel-Student Records, Providence Academy, Vancouver, Wash., RG 22, Providence Archives, Mother Joseph Province, Seattle.

LETTER 27

To Major Pinkney Lugenbeel, Commanding Officer, Fort Vancouver, May 22, 1862[1]

In addition to funds for building and supplying their growing charitable works, Vancouver's Sisters of Providence needed food for the eighty-plus people they provided for, many of whom were orphans and school boarders.

Blanchet had given the sisters several acres of land on the Catholic claim for their use, purchased fruit trees, and had an orchard planted. In 1860, Mother Joseph purchased a four-acre farm a few miles from the Catholic establishment for $1,200, to provide additional food, work for pupils, and income from the sale of extra produce. The winter of 1861–62 was unusually harsh, and by the time Blanchet wrote this letter, it was evident that the spring seedlings and potato plantings on the farm had all been lost to flooding. Given the dire circumstances, every hog belonging to the sisters was needed.[2]

In this letter, Blanchet diplomatically assumes that the commanding officer's order to kill wandering hogs was not intended to include those belonging to the sisters. In doing so, he recalls the harmony and mutual support that had existed during the early 1850s among the neighboring officers of the HBC, the U.S. Army, and the Catholic Church in staving off the tide of poaching settlers. By 1860, however, under new command, and with the Pig War playing itself out on the United States–Great Britain border, the army's hostility toward the HBC had become such that remaining HBC personnel of all ranks, just fourteen of the two hundred once present, left Fort Vancouver and moved to Fort Victoria.[3] With the departure of the HBC, the final pieces of the first colonization movement in the U.S. Pacific Northwest came to a close, and Vancouver's Catholic establishment became increasingly enmeshed in the affairs of neighboring U.S. Army personnel and American settlers.

Blanchet had another reason to assume that the commanding officer did not intend for his order to include the Sisters' of Charity hogs: Major Lugenbeel's two daughters, Irene and Attie, were day pupils at the Providence School.[4]

Vancouver, May 22nd 1862

Sir,

A report is communicated to me that the soldiers of this Post have received from the Commanding Officer the order to kill the hogs that are straying. Whether the order is given to kill the hogs straying within or without the fence of the Post, it is not said. Be that as it may. There is another report that some soldiers have taken advantage of it, to drive some hogs within the fence to kill them. Now, Sir, I wish to let you know that the Sisters of

Charity have a certain number thus at large, because they cannot feed them properly otherwise, and they are destined to feed the poor orphans of both asylums, no less, presently, than forty-eight in round number. I regret, therefore, that the order may cause such damage to a charitable institution so dear to every sensitive heart. I am quite sure that it is against the intention of the Commanding Officer, and that he will not hesitate, an instant, to put a stop thereto.

I have the honor to be respectfully, Sir,
Your most obedient humble Servant
A. M. A. Blanchet, Bp. of Nesqualy

UNIVERSITY OF WASHINGTON LIBRARIES, ACCESSION NO. 4614–001. LETTER WRITTEN IN ENGLISH.

1. Major Pinkney Lugenbeel (1819–1886) was a career military officer who served in the campaign against the Yakamas and commanded Fort Vancouver and later Fort Cascade.

2. Loretta Zwolak Greene, "Sisters of Providence Farm at Providence Academy, Vancouver, Washington, 1860–1935" (paper presented at the Washington Heritage Conference, Olympia, Wash., February 27, 1999).

3. Hussey, *History of Fort Vancouver*, 99–109.

4. Other officers' children listed in the registries of the ethnically integrated schools included those of Colonel George Wright—Marcella-Agnes, Marie Amelia Elizabeth (who became a Providence sister), Henry, and Edward. "Day Scholars attending school from April 15, 1857–Sept. 1, 1867" and "Student Account Ledgers, 1857–89," Personnel-Student Records, Providence Academy, Vancouver, Wash., RG 22, Providence Archives, Mother Joseph Province, Seattle.

LETTER 28

To Caleb Blood Smith, Secretary of the Interior, Washington, D.C., June 16, 1862[1]

Sustenance for the pupils at Vancouver and funds to defray travel costs of new personnel were just two among many concerns that preoccupied Bishop Blanchet. Equally troublesome was the state of affairs at Simcoe, the Yakama Reservation. The Catholic missions among the Yakamas, the longest continuous and most successful venture in Indian work of those begun when Blanchet first arrived in Walla Walla, was blocked. Superintendent Geary had approved the appointment of a Methodist minister, James H. Wilbur, as superintendent of instruction for Simcoe, an act Blanchet considered to be a violation of Geary's stated intent and an injustice against the Yakama people and the Catholic Church. Further, after what had been a series of short-term appointments, the elderly and ineffectual Anson A. Bancroft now held the post of agent and was not up to the task of dealing with an incompetent reservation physician or the corruption that was rife in the procurement system (see letter 24). By the time Bishop Blanchet penned this letter of frustrated appeal to the secretary of the Interior, Caleb Blood Smith, Catholic priests did not have free movement on the reservation and Agent Bancroft supported Reverend Wilbur's efforts to block Catholic Indians from leaving the reservation to attend Catholic services at the Ahtanum mission. As well, Reverend Wilbur used distribution of goods to pressure Catholic Indians to attend Methodist services, and all Indians in the school he ran were taught the Methodist form of Christianity.[2]

Blanchet understood himself to be an advocate for Catholic Indians and, therefore, picks up in this letter on Indian discontent stemming from the corruption and sectarian biases of Yakama Reservation agents. He uses those complaints to press his own case for Catholic agents and educators for Simcoe. That case needs to be understood in the context of steady, ongoing conflict between Catholics and Protestants in the United States at this time.

Both Blanchet and his adversaries envisioned helping Indians adapt to reservation life in terms of their own convictions regarding religion and human well-being. Whatever expectations Blanchet may have entertained fifteen years earlier about how Indians would continue to maintain most of their lifeways when they became Catholic, those expectations had changed. Brutal wars and the ensuing restriction of many to life on reservations had shifted his focus to survival achieved through adaptation to imposed Euro-American lifeways. If Blanchet did not necessarily share the Protestant view that farming was integral to being Christian, he seems increasingly to have assumed that Christianity and education were integral to the Indians' survival. At this point, neither Blanchet nor his Methodist opponents address the question of the rights of reservation Indians to practice shamanic and other indigenous faith and healing traditions, though those practices were alive and would gain potency in growing Indian revitalization movements. By the early 1880s, such indigenous practices on the Yakama Reservation would be explicitly prohibited.[3]

With the Civil War now under way, concerns about the well-being of Indians were not primary in Washington, D.C. At the time Blanchet wrote, Vicar-General Brouillet was in Washington, to accomplish, among other tasks, the procurement of contracts for Catholics to provide teachers for schools on reservations in Oregon and in Washington Territory where Catholics historically had engaged in mission work. Blanchet sent this letter to Brouillet, to present to the secretary of the Interior.[4] Notably, Blanchet uses the Protestant trope "civilization" to gain a sympathetic hearing.

Vancouver, W.T., June 16th 1862

Sir,

On February 5th of last year I sent a letter to the secretary of the Interior explaining my views on what the government could do to achieve its desired goals with respect to the Indians. There was no response to this letter. Given all the troubles that arose at about the same time, it may easily have been overlooked, were it received.[5]

I wish once again to call the government's attention to this letter, which proposes what in my opinion is a sure means for bringing about the civilization of the Indians. Convinced of its value, I am taking the liberty to refer you to it, if received; if not, I will see that you get a copy.

You can easily obtain useful information on this important subject from Father J. B. A. Brouillet, vicar general of this diocese, who is presently in Washington, D.C. This gentleman, whose devotion to the civilization of the Indians is surpassed by none, will be able to unfold the story of certain abuses, which unfortunately are all too common on various reservations.

But I would like, Sir, to call your attention especially to what has happened to one of the missions in this diocese, from which you can easily surmise what could ensue on others.

Since the start of 1848, I have been placing missionaries in the country comprising the watershed of the Yakima River, north of the Columbia. The missionaries continued their apostolic work among the Indians there until 1855, though not without great sacrifices & privations of every sort. When war broke out that year between the whites and the Indians, they were forced to withdraw for their own safety. [See letter 23, note 4.] The mission, however, was not abandoned. Far from it. Since then it has been visited every year, to the great satisfaction of the Indians in general, and especially those who were drawn to the missionaries' instructions. At the time we had no competitors, life was nothing but sacrifice, and hope for reward in the afterlife was the only recompense for our apostolic works.

In 1859, however, the treaty that had been drawn up with the Indians in 1855, was ratified. Immediately thereafter, competitors suddenly began to show up, appearing to be devoured by an *entirely new zeal* for the well being of the Indians of our mission! For various reasons that you can well surmise, the superintendents and agents acted to support their interests. Individuals were placed on our mission, which we alone have cultivated for eleven to twelve years, individuals who not only are incapable of carrying out our work, [but] who also—let it be said—are inclined to wiping it out if they could. A minister and others are placed on the reservation, installed in the houses belonging to the military post at Simcoe, receive subsidies from the government!! and as for us . . . !!⁶

This, Sir, is how we are treated here by the agents of a liberal government, of a government whose first principle is the equal treatment of all religious denominations, preference for none, protection of each, justice for all. As Catholics, we do not request any privileges on the part of the government. We do not seek to take possession of the Indian missions established by other religious denominations; it is simply the Indians' desire to have Catholic missionaries that prompts us to hasten to their side.⁷ Surely the Indians will not be denied the right to choose the Catholic religion in preference to any other. Should this be their preference, they can without doubt expect the government to provide the protection it gives to all other Christian denominations. Sir, you have the power to rectify your agents' mistakes.

The government's views with respect to the Indians are good, Sir, its intentions are charitable, there is no doubt; but if they are to bear fruit, in my opinion, the local administrations must be reformed. You are fully aware that not just any sort of person should be placed on the reservations.

It is common knowledge here that certain government agents, far from working for the civilization of the Indians, have, more than any others, contributed to the corruption of their ways.[8] To avoid such disorder, only married men of honorable repute, particularly in matters touching on morality, should be placed on the reservations. It is truly disheartening to all upright persons to see the government sacrifice considerable sums of money only to result in the deteriorating conduct of our poor Indians. This assuredly would not be the result of such sacrifice if the government were to determine that religious denominations take on the direction of their respective missions, leaving the appointed ministers to select individuals responsible for initiating the Indians on each reservation to civilization.[9] With less expense, I am convinced, the government would retrieve more abundant fruits from its sacrifices, the Indians would be more virtuous, God less offended.

In presenting these comments to you, Sir, I am in good conscience fulfilling an important duty to God and the government. May the Lord bless my intentions, fulfill my wishes!

I have the honor of being . . . &
A. M. A. Blanchet, Bp. of Nesq.

AAS, A5: 198–201.

———•———

1. Caleb Blood Smith (1808–1864), a multi-term congressman from Indiana, was secretary of the Interior when Blanchet wrote this letter. Smith served in the post from March 1861 through December 1862. Smith's appointment came, in part, as a result of his role at the 1860 Republican convention in leading the uncommitted Indiana delegation to vote in Lincoln's favor. *American National Biography*, s.v. "Smith, Caleb Blood."

2. Keller, *American Protestantism and United States Indian Policy*, 178; Schoenberg, *Catholic Church in the Pacific Northwest*, 228–231; Helland, *There Were Giants*, 77–113; Whitner, "Grant's Indian Peace Policy," 139–41; Rahill, *Catholic Indian Missions and Grant's Peace Policy*, 43–45.

3. For agency policing against indigenous practices on the Yakama Reservation starting in 1883, see Fisher, *Shadow Tribe*, 123–24. Fisher does not differentiate between denominational groups with regard to the use and preservation of Indian languages and differences of attitude toward assimilation.

4. Blanchet to Brouillet, June 17, 1862, AAS, A5: 201.

5. The phrase "all the troubles" refers to the opening of the Civil War. The unanswered letter

to which Blanchet refers made three proposals. First, that "every-where all the natives be left free as to the choice of their religion and Missionaries." Second, that "on every Indian reservation, the religious and litterary [*sic*] training of the natives be entrusted to the religious denomination which has brought them previously to the knowledge and practice of Christianity, unless a majority of the said natives should oppose it." And, third, that "however, this latter provision should not be understood, as refusing any other denomination the privilege of starting, on the same reservation, with the agreement of the Indians, any private religious and literary establishment of their own" (To the Honorable ___, Secretary of the Interior, February 5, 1861, AAS, A5: 148–50). Blanchet goes on in the letter to argue that agents need to be men who are not biased by sectarian principles and are not themselves ministers. His effort in this letter is to frame policy that will provide the Catholic Church a presence on Indian reservations. Interior Secretary Jacob Thompson resigned the position in January 1861 when the vessel *Star of the West* was dispatched to relieve Fort Sumter. President Buchanan offered the position to Commissioner Alfred Greenwood of Indian Affairs in early February. The position remained unoccupied, however, until Caleb Blood Smith was appointed in March 1861. So, when Blanchet wrote his letter of February 5, 1861, the position of secretary of the Interior was vacant. Robert M. Kvasnicka and Herman J. Viola, eds., *The Commissioners of Indian Affairs, 1824–1977* (Lincoln: University of Nebraska Press, 1979), 85–86, 90; Prucha, *The Great Father*, 1:322, 2:1213.

6. Blanchet is referring to the work of Reverend James Wilbur, the Methodist minister, who, by this point, had served for two years as superintendent of instruction for the Yakama Reservation (see letter 24). Wilbur, like the Catholic missionary-teachers at Tulalip, who incorporated religious instruction into classes, did not distinguish between his work in education and his work in converting the Yakamas to Protestantism. Wilbur went further, however, by lobbying in the territory and nationally to keep Catholic clergy from having access to Yakamas who were already Catholic (Whitner, "Grant's Indian Peace Policy," 139–42).

7. One of Reverend Wilbur's major admirers noted that in subsequent years, after he had been appointed agent at Simcoe, his conflation of roles as agent and missionary was driving Indians from the reservation (Whitner, "Grant's Indian Peace Policy," 141–42).

8. The position of Indian agent was sought by most for its remuneration. The positions generally were awarded in response to political favors or in deals. Competence was not a major requirement for agents. At the time Blanchet wrote Smith, the Yakamas had been subject to a series of poor agents. R. H. Lansdale was ousted in 1861, to be followed briefly by Wesley B. Gosnell, Charles Hutchins, and finally, in September 1861, the elderly Anson A. Bancroft, who would remain through 1864. Four agents in six months. Even Blanchet's nemesis, Reverend Wilbur, complained to Washington, D.C., that the situation was intolerable. Wilbur himself was ousted in October 1861 by the new superintendent of Indian Affairs, B. F. Kendall, in part for having complained about the agency physician, Dr. L. H. Roberts, whom he and others accused of drinking excessively and of "lascivious conduct" (Helland, *There Were Giants*, 79). Blanchet may also be alluding to Roberts when he refers to agents who corrupt rather than civilize Indians.

9. Blanchet's suggestion shows that he was aware of the discussion then under way about the best way to provide agents of good character and sound ethics to work on reservations. Keller, *American Protestantism and United States Indian Policy*, 1–30; Prucha, *The Great Father*, 1:463–78.

To Aegidius Junger,
Missionary of Walla Walla,
November 6, 1862[1]

On All Souls' Eve, 1862, Aegidius Junger and Paul Mans, the first in a series of graduates from the American College of Louvain to serve in Washington Territory, stepped onto the shores at Vancouver City (see letter 26). Within a week, a relieved bishop had assigned each: Father Mans to teach at Holy Angels Academy in Vancouver, Father Junger to see to the building of a church in the booming town of Walla Walla and to serve Canadiens at Mission St. Rose on the Yellow Hawk. The geography, ethnicities, and recent histories of Walla Walla and neighboring Canadien settlements were sufficiently challenging to make this a hefty task for a recently graduated seminarian from Europe.

Father Junger arrived in Walla Walla on January 13, 1863, a year after the town received its charter. Plotted soon after General William S. Harney lifted the ban on settlement east of the Cascades, on October 29, 1858, the town grew rapidly. When gold was discovered on Nez Percé lands in 1860, Walla Walla became the last outfitting point before the mines.[2] Once a collection of tents and shacks anchored to Fort Walla Walla, it was now a feverish boomtown, populated by cattle ranchers, miners, land speculators, and shop and saloon keepers. While Blanchet saw newer Catholic immigrants to the region from Ireland, French Canada, and continental Europe as potential sources of support for building the Catholic Church in Walla Walla, his primary concern seems to have been for those Catholics who had long resided in the region—Indians and Canadiens who had lost land and influence in the process of armed conflict and economic and political realignment in the area.

No note or cover letter accompanies this list of instructions in the letter-book. Written just a week after the young Father Junger arrived, and while he was still in Vancouver, it is possible that Blanchet delivered this list to him in person. The thoroughness and detail would have assisted in orienting someone as new as Junger to life on the American frontier, where customs and laws were considerably different from those of Europe. The third-person nature at the start of the list and allusions to "the Missionary" suggest that

Blanchet began the list before he gave the assignment specifically to Father Junger. However it was used, the document is a valuable portrait of the early Catholic Church in the Walla Walla area.

Vancouver, November 6th 1862

INSTRUCTIONS:

1. When he arrives in Walla Walla, he can consult with Mr. Simms who has a mill a short distance from town, in order to find adequate lodging for the moment. He is a good Catholic, an influential man. He can be of service to the Missionary on many occasions.[3]

2. The Catholics of W.W. must take immediate steps toward building a church. The Missionary will not fail to encourage them in this.

3. To this end, it will be necessary to start a subscription. When he does this, the Missionary should have an influential, local citizen accompany him.

4. It will be necessary to make, or have made, a drawing of the building, for the bishop's approval. The priest's quarters should be at one end of the church and attached to it, unless a house completely separate from the church is preferred.

5. Construction will not begin until there are sufficient pledges to fund all of the exterior.

6. Following a Sunday mass, the Missionary will gather the Catholics together to elect three persons from the group; they will make the purchases and oversee the work under his direction, in such a way, however, that he (the missionary), acting as treasurer, is responsible for nothing other than the money that he will receive from the subscribers.

7. As for the location of the church, there are two pieces of land under consideration, one offered by Mr. Barron, the other by Mr. Cain, both on the little river. The first would seem preferable, because it is closer to the military post, thus enabling the soldiers to get there more easily. I would like at least two acres of land, and an additional piece for the Catholic cemetery.[4]

8. Before beginning the church, it will be necessary to procure a good title to the chosen site. If several people have a claim to the land, each must give a *Quit-claim*. The title should be signed over to the "Corporation of the Catholic Bishop of Nesqualy, W.T." and sent to me after it is registered. Once these formalities are taken care of, it will be time to build, according to the approved plan.

9. As for the land where the shack that has served as chapel is located, I must say

that it concerns me. I do not have the title to it. However, I would like it to be kept for the mission, if possible. It could be used for other establishments later on.[5]

ANOTHER TEMPORAL MATTER:

You will soon hear talk of the Saint Rose Mission on the Walla Walla River. The section on which the mission was founded belongs to the Catholic Church. Encroachers are occupying parts of it. If you meet someone who wants to buy it, and who offers 2,500 dollars for all but the 40 acres on Mr. Wm. McBean's line, you can sell it; but in a manner that does not obligate me to evict the people occupying it. If you are made an offer below this sum, please write to me.

Mr. McBean is a good Catholic with a zeal for serving the church, but he is poor in spite of owning one of the best pieces of land in the area.[6]

NOW FOR THE SPIRITUAL:

You will have much to do with regard to several families of Canadiens settled on the Walla Walla River, some as far as nine miles from town. You can choose a centrally located house for assembling the children for catechism lessons, for Mass, &c. Mr. McBean's house has been the former meeting place, but it is not central. You will find several Canadiens in a state of deplorable degradation, weakened in faith. Your fervent zeal will, I believe, bring them back to the path of salvation.[7] Finally, after having planted and watered, you will patiently wait for God to make things grow in his own time, and I am certain that He will. "*Insta opportune, importune; argue, obsecra, increpa in omni patientia et doctrina. In omnibus labora, opus fac evangelistae, ministerium tuum imple.*"[8]

I am, . . . &c.
A. M. A. Bp. of Nesq.

AAS, A5: 214–16.

1. Aegidius Junger (1833–1895) was raised in Aachen, Germany; worked six years in a carriage maintenance shop to support his mother and five siblings after the death of his father; and entered the American College of Louvain in September 1859, graduated, and was ordained in 1862. "Intelligent, pious and of robust constitution," he aspired from a young age to the ecclesiastical state and missionary work in North America. Letter from the bishop of Aachen, cited in Kevin A. Codd, "The American College of Louvain and the Catholic Church in the North Pacific Coast of North America, 1857–1907" (master's thesis, Catholic University of Louvain, 2002), 58. Junger succeeded Blanchet as second bishop of the Diocese of Nesqualy, August 6, 1879.

2. Meinig, *The Great Columbia Plain*, 201–4, 202; Lancaster Pollard, *A History of the State of Washington* (New York: American Historical Society, 1937), 1:302–4; Bancroft, *History of Washington, Idaho, and Montana*, 139–40; Snowden, *History of Washington*, 4:74–83. See also Chester C. Maxey, *The Historical Walla Walla Valley* (Walla Walla, Wash.: Inland Printing Company, 1934); and W. D. Lyman, *Lyman's History of Old Walla Walla County, Embracing Walla Walla, Columbia, Garfield, and Asotin Counties* (Chicago: S. J. Clarke Publishing Company, 1918).

3. John A. Simms (ca. 1827–1890) traveled in 1850 from his home in Maryland to California, in the wake of the gold rush, and to Oregon in 1851; he was in The Dalles, in conversations with the resident priest regarding the welfare of Fathers Pandosy and Chirouse, still among Yakama bands during the uprising of November 1855. In 1858, he moved from The Dalles to the nascent settlement of Walla Walla, where in partnership with A. H. Reynolds and F. T. Dent (brother of Mrs. Ulysses S. Grant), he built and operated the first flour mill of the region. From 1861 until 1862 or 1863, he was a member of the nine-man Territorial Council (upper house) where he represented Clark, Skamania, Walla Walla, and Spokane counties. Simms raised cattle and was regarded as a quiet, intelligent, and scrupulously honest man. During the 1870s, he assumed the position of principal agent at the Colville Agency. "Biographical Sketch," John A. Simms Papers, 1858–1881, Washington State University Libraries, Manuscripts, Archives, and Special Collections, Pullman, http://www.wsulibs.wsu.edu/holland/masc/finders/cg213.htm (accessed May 15, 2012).

4. Joseph Barron, a Walla Walla banker, provided land for the Academy of the Sisters of Providence and for the hospital (see letter 37). Northwest commander Colonel George Wright, in carrying out the U.S. Army policy of preserving the Columbia Plateau east of The Dalles as Indian country, sent Colonel E. J. Steptoe in September 1856 to replace the volunteer militia and stave off further hostilities. Steptoe, with nearly eight hundred troops, constructed the fort. In June 1858, the U.S. Army, having shifted to an offensive position against the inland Indians, including the Yakamas, subdued indigenous forces from Colville to Walla Walla, thus ending large-scale Indian-white conflict on the Columbia Plain. Meinig, *The Great Columbia Plain*, 160–67; Ficken, *Washington Territory*, 50–57.

5. Colonel Steptoe's chaplain, Father Toussaint Mesplie, a priest of the Archdiocese of Oregon City, constructed a small chapel, St. Patrick, at the fort, consisting of poles stuck in the ground and covered with shakes. The first Walla Walla election for county officers was held in July 1859 at the chapel. Munnick and Munnick, introduction to *Catholic Church Records of the Pacific Northwest*, vol. 7.

6. William McBean, who had hosted and assisted the Blanchet party on its arrival in 1847 (see letter 3), retired from his position as factor of Fort Walla Walla in 1851 and settled with his

family on Yellow Hawk Creek, a branch of the Walla Walla River located a few miles south of the future town of Walla Walla. Since 1824 or earlier, HBC retirees such as McBean had been settling in the Walla Walla valley as "guests" of the Waiilatpu and Wallulapam (Cayuse and Walla Walla) Indians, whose permission they sought and with whom their children often intermarried. The log cabins of Canadien settlers were scattered among Indian camps for over fifty square miles—hence the name Frenchtown—and relative peace among the ethnic groups prevailed. In 1853, with the Cayuse War over and the region again open to missionaries, McBean helped returning Father Chirouse make a land claim and build a chapel (St. Rose) next to his home. Chirouse and other Oblate clerics who joined him enjoyed two years of relative peace among neighboring Cayuses and Canadiens. Frenchtown Partners, "Frenchtown," http://www.frenchtownpartners.org/5. html; "St. Rose Mission," http://www.frenchtownpartners.org/8.html; "Battle of Walla Walla," http://www.frenchtownpartners.org/7.html (accessed April 20, 2012).

7. Confrontations and rumors that the Indians of the Yakima and Walla Walla areas had formed an alliance led to the forced evacuation of whites and Canadiens from the area in October 1855. December 7–10 of the same year, Oregon volunteers laid siege to Indian forces near Walla Walla, during which they killed and mutilated the body of Walla Walla chief Peopeomoxmox. Chirouse, who was in hiding with followers, wrote to Father Mesplie, then at The Dalles, of the volunteers' continued despoiling of the country and requested protection from the U.S. troops. By June 2, with St. Rose Mission in cinders and the upper Plateau country again closed to all whites, including missionaries, by order of General John Ellis Wool of the U.S. Army, Father Chirouse had moved down to Olympia. Chirouse to Mesplie, January 15, 1856, in Drouin, *Les Oblats*, 2:601. The editor's note in the volume states that Brouillet translated the letter into English and forwarded it to General Wool; the Brouillet translation is located in the Wool papers, New York State Archives.

8. "Be diligent. Pursue in season and out of season; censure, entreat, rebuke in all with patience and erudition. Exert yourself in everything, do the work of an evangelist, fulfill your ministry." Modeled on 2 Timothy 4:2, 4:5.

LETTER 30

To J. B. A. Brouillet,Vicar-General, March 20, 1863

With Father Junger now serving the challenging mission of Walla Walla and Father Paul Antoine Mans at Vancouver's Academy of Holy Angels, Blanchet again was able to spare his vicar-general for a short while. In mid-February 1862, Brouillet departed on a second voyage east, in order to attend to diocesan matters in Washington, D.C., and recruit additional sisters and clergy from Montreal.

Missionary Brouillet had already witnessed major events in the American West: it was he who first came upon the scene of the Whitman killings; while making collections and building the first Catholic church in San Francisco, he experienced firsthand the effects of the California gold rush on the city; as diocesan administrator during Blanchet's voyage to Europe, he dealt with repercussions on missions resulting from the Colville gold discoveries, the Bolon killing and ensuing military incursions among the Yakamas, and the Battle of Walla Walla. Now, on this second trip to the nation's capital, he found himself within a few miles of major Civil War battles.

On December 17, 1862, writing from Washington, D.C., to a friend in Montreal, he reported on the most recent battle that had taken place to the south of the capital: "Last Saturday the 13th at Fredericksburg we were beaten hollow: we lost no less than 25 to 30 thousand men; it is not yet reported in the papers, but this is what people from everywhere are reporting. Entire regiments were nearly annihilated. There is mention of one that came back with only 50 men, companies coming back with but 7 or 8, one with only a corporal in command. The Irish regiment, the 69, has almost entirely perished. It was all a matter of a few hours."[1] (Isaac Stevens was among those who survived the battle.) Two months earlier, Brouillet had written to the same friend of an impending battle between the Army of the Potomac and General Robert E. Lee's Confederate forces, of his profound concern for the two hundred thousand to three hundred thousand Catholic soldiers of the Union army, there being but seven to eight Catholic chaplains.[2] Despite the catastrophic events on his doorstep, Brouillet, seasoned to death, corruption, ineptitude, prejudice, and violence, complied with his bishop's request that he pursue routine diocesan matters.

Vancouver, March 20th 1863

Monsieur,

On the fifteenth of this month I sent a letter to your address, by means of the office of the *Express*, Wells Fargo & Co. to tell you that on February 8, I had written to you of Mr. Hale's objections to the Oblates' contract, which he refused to sign; to inform you that I requested Monsieur Certes, Treasurer, Propagation of the Faith, to send five thousand francs to Vicar General Truteau in Montreal, to help pay for the passage of the Sisters of Providence.[3] I told him that in requesting ten sisters I had anticipated that Monsignor of Montreal would see to providing the greater part of the expense; that since this has not occurred, I am back to my original thought of limiting the number of sisters to six, that I will pay the expenses for three, so as not to be plunged in debts;[4] that the 5,000 francs & the thousand piastres from the Holy Childhood will be used for passage of the priests and sisters;[5] that if the collection that you announced and began in Washington succeeds, you can bring as many sisters as the House of Providence gives you; likewise if Dr. Henry's decision is confirmed in Washington.[6] Finally I spoke to you of the voyage by way of Fort Benton & the Mullen Road, etc., and told you not to carry any greenbacks, because they have no more value here than in the East. I wanted to inform you of all in this letter which will be going by land or sea.[7]

All that I wrote on the 15th still holds. Only, it seems more and more likely that the decision of the Secretary of the Interior will be favorable, & and thus that you will be able to bring a greater number of sisters. In our opinion, the decision will take place within the month. Saint Joseph has been solicited, urged to see to a favorable outcome, and we are confident that he will not fail.

Congress's establishment of the new Territory of Idaho provides an additional motive for placing sisters in the east of the diocese. Should this be Walla Walla or Lewiston, I cannot now say. However, at the moment, this latter city appears to offer more resources and it would be more central to the two territories. If I do not have enough sisters for two new missions, that is to say, one on the Sound, & the other in the east, I will give a preference to the latter location, its being much more important.[8] So you need to make every effort to procure the money needed to pay for passage of sisters and the priest, over what I can offer myself, which is not likely to be more than 2,000 piastres. If on top of this you also collect in Washington, you should be in position to provide for needed expenses. It is my hope that after this year we will no longer need to rely on the Mother House for subjects, as I presume that the two missions under consideration will bring in a sufficient number of postulants & novices to meet the needs, except possibly for the Indian missions. As for the state of health here, there is nothing new to report.

I am, etc. A. M. A. Blanchet, Bishop Nesq.

———•———

1. Brouillet to a Friend, December 17, 1862, ACAM, 421–009, 862–3.

2. Brouillet to a Friend, October 20, 1862, ACAM, 421–009, 862–2.

3. Wells Fargo & Company opened in San Francisco and Sacramento, California, in 1852, to buy gold, sell paper bank drafts, and deliver gold and other valuables. By the 1860s, the company was sending items to major cities throughout the United States by the fastest means possible—stagecoach, steamship, railroad, pony riders, or telegraph—and was known for reliability. For Blanchet's earlier correspondence regarding the problem with the Oblates' contract, see letter 28. Having followed up on the issue in the capital, Brouillet wrote that President Lincoln, the commissioner of Indian Affairs, and the secretary of the Interior all found Bishop Blanchet's recommendation reasonable and were submitting the memorial to the cabinet. (For the recommendations, see letter 28, note 5.) By December, Brouillet had obtained two government contracts for reservation schools, one for the Oblates of Puget Sound and the other for the Jesuits of the Rocky Mountains. The first contract provided $3,000 annually for board, room, and instruction of forty children; the second, $2,000 for the same, for twenty-eight children. Territorial Superintendent of Indian Affairs Calvin H. Hale signed the contract for the Jesuits, but refused to sign the same for the Oblates of Tulalip, objecting to the stipulation that the priests finance and construct their own schools and that, upon termination of the contract, the buildings revert to the government on the grounds that treaties had committed the government to these expenses. Blanchet subsequently wrote Hale to inform him that he would forward the signed contract to the Jesuits and that he shared the superintendent's concern about the Tulalip contract. Brouillet to a Friend, October 20, 1862, ACAM, 421–009, 862–2; Blanchet to Brouillet, June 17, 1862, AAS, A5: 101–2; Blanchet to F. N. Blanchet, November 26, 1862, Archives of the Archdiocese of Portland (AAP), B11, F11, 34; Blanchet to D'Herbomez, February 2, 1863, AAS, A5: 223; Blanchet to Hale, February 6, 1863, AAS, A5: 223–25.

4. Vicar-General Brouillet was unable to obtain a loan from the Diocese of Montreal to help cover the sisters' travel expenses, the banks of Canada refusing to release capital on account of the American Civil War (Bourget to Blanchet, November 28, 1862, ACAM RLB-12, 629); consequently, Blanchet had a part of his annual allocation from the Society for the Propagation of the Faith in France transferred directly to the Diocese of Montreal, to help cover the expenses (see letter 26).

5. Monsignor Charles de Forbin-Jansen, bishop of Nancy, France, led vast revival campaigns in Lower Canada and Europe during the early 1840s, in part to counter Protestant evangelists. In 1843, he founded the Oeuvre de la Sainte Enfance (Association of the Holy Infancy) on the model of the Propagation of the Faith, to help inspire children, through education, with a missionary conscience and vocation, and especially to provide material assistance and education to children in the neediest regions of the world. Known today as the Enfance Missionnaire, the association has branches in more than 150 countries and, like the Society for the Propagation of the Faith, is under the umbrella organization of the Oeuvres Pontificales Missionnaires in Lyons, France.

6. Dr. Anson G. Henry of Springfield, Illinois, a close friend of Abraham Lincoln, emigrated to Lafayette, Oregon, in 1852; he served in the Oregon legislature, in the Rogue River Indian War, as physician on the Grand Ronde Reservation, and as surveyor of Portland. Upon election in March 1861, Lincoln appointed Henry surveyor general of Washington Territory, thus involving him in Catholic Church land claims. Henry departed for Washington, D.C., early in 1863, to aid in the organization of Idaho Territory, and was a guest at the White House. The St. James Mission land claim of Vancouver, which Blanchet thinks the land commissioner will approve, was in fact not resolved until 1905. Harry C. Blair, "Dr. Anson G. Henry, Physician, Politician, Friend of Abraham Lincoln," president's address, Fourteenth Annual Meeting of the Western Orthopedic Association, Portland, Ore., October, 1950.

7. Blanchet is responding to Brouillet's earlier plan to return with his recruits by land in order to avoid potential danger raised by recent incidents of Confederate piracy. To offset the depletion of federal reserves of gold used to pay for the war, Congress passed the first Legal Tender Act on February 25, 1862, authorizing the printing of $150 million in Treasury notes, printed with green ink, to be used as legal tender for most transactions. The value of these notes deflated with Union army losses and was well below par at the time of this letter. Brouillet and the recruits, having been assured of safe passage, eventually traveled to Oregon by sea.

8. On March 4, 1863, Congress passed the act to establish the Idaho Territory out of that portion of Washington lying east of Oregon and the 117th meridian of west longitude. Lewiston, a commercial mart centrally located with regard to the whole Snake River country, served as Idaho's capital until 1865, when borders were readjusted and Boise was designated territorial capital. Bancroft, *History of Washington, Idaho, and Montana*, 262–63.

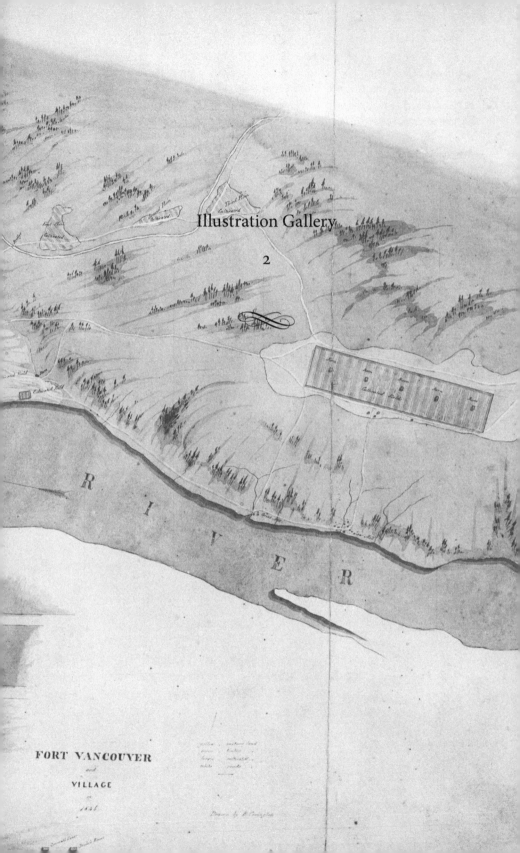

Illustration Gallery

2

FIGURE 23. Multicolored embroidery of the
Sacred Heart, donated to Bishop A. M. A.
Blanchet during travels in Mexico, found by
Sisters of Providence in the bishop's storage
in 1856. Names of all Sisters of Providence
who served in the Northwest until 1906
encircle the heart, on gold-ink-decorated
white paper, in the form of a clock,
framed. (See letter 21, note 9.) Courtesy of
Providence Archives, Seattle, 22.008

FIGURE 24. Spinning wheel made by Mother Joseph. She had written to Mother Caron of the Montreal motherhouse to request a spindle, a flange, and some wire to make a spinning wheel, because wool stockings were difficult to come by, but wool was plentiful. (See letter 21, note 4.) Courtesy Providence Archives, Seattle, A.SP0013.053.

FIGURE 25. Eugène-Casimir Chirouse, O.M.I. Archives of the Archdiocese of Seattle, RG 840, Missionary Oblates of Mary Immaculate.

FIGURE 26. St. Anne Mission, Tulalip Reservation, including a church and schools for boys and girls, completed in 1868. Archives of the Oregon Province of the Society of Jesus, 17.01a.

FIGURE 27. A. M. A. Blanchet, c. 1866. Photograph from the Seminary of Quebec. Kindly loaned by Georges Aubin, L'Assomption, Quebec.

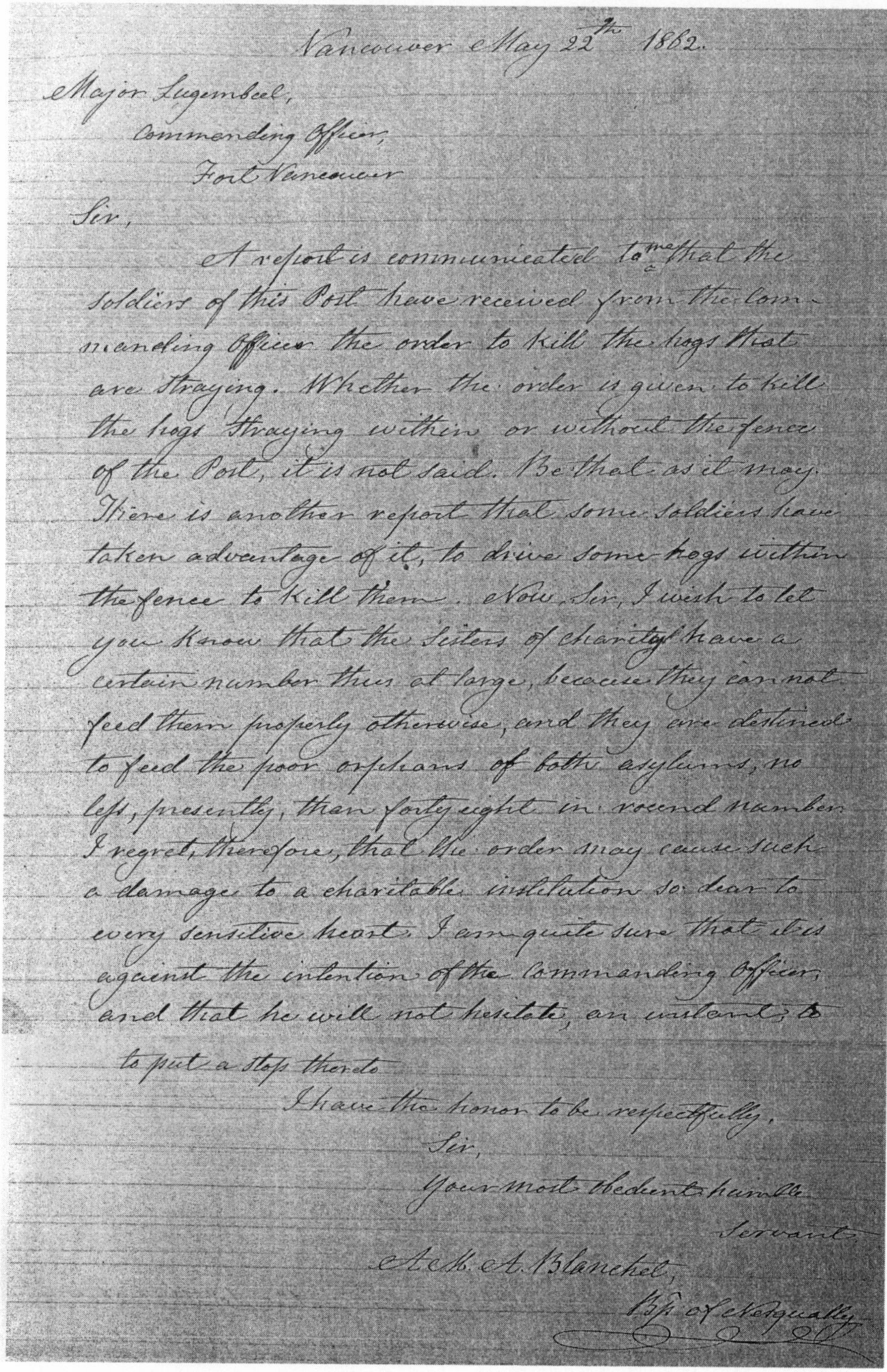

Vancouver May 22th 1862.

Major Lugenbeel,
  Commanding Officer,
    Fort Vancouver

Sir,

   A report is communicated to me that the soldiers of this Post have received from the commanding Officer the order to kill the hogs that are straying. Whether the order is given to kill the hogs straying within or without the fence of the Post, it is not said. Be that as it may. There is another report that some soldiers have taken advantage of it, to drive some hogs within the fence to kill them. Now, Sir, I wish to let you know that the Sisters of charity have a certain number thus at large, because they can not feed them properly otherwise; and they are destined to feed the poor orphans of both asylums, no less, presently, than forty eight in round number. I regret, therefore, that the order may cause such a damage to a charitable institution so dear to every sensitive heart. I am quite sure that it is against the intention of the Commanding Officer, and that he will not hesitate, an instant, to put a stop thereto.

    I have the honor to be respectfully,
     Sir,
      Your most obedient humble
        servant
    A. M. A. Blanchet,
      Bp of Nesqualy

FIGURE 28. Letter from A. M. A. Blanchet to Major Pinkney Lugenbeel, commanding officer, Fort Vancouver. (See letter 27.) University of Washington Libraries, accession no. 4614-001.

FIGURE 29. Father Aegidius Junger. Archives of the Archdiocese of Seattle, VR 610.1134.

FIGURE 30. Main Street, Walla Walla, in 1877. Walla Walla, a center of Catholic population, was Father Junger's first post in 1862; he was assigned the task of getting a church building erected. Photograph from *Lyman's Illustrated History of Walla Walla*. Oregon Historical Society, no. 99509.

FIGURE 31. Father Jean-Baptiste Abraham Brouillet, vicar-general of the Diocese of Nesqualy. Archives of the Archdiocese of Seattle, VR 820.254.

FIGURE 32. St. James Mission plan, painting by J. B. Blanchet, dated 1866. Buildings include the cathedral, orphanages, convent, rectory, hospital, and Academy of Holy Angels. The orchard and cemetery are also depicted. Archives of the Archdiocese of Seattle, VR 700.4299.

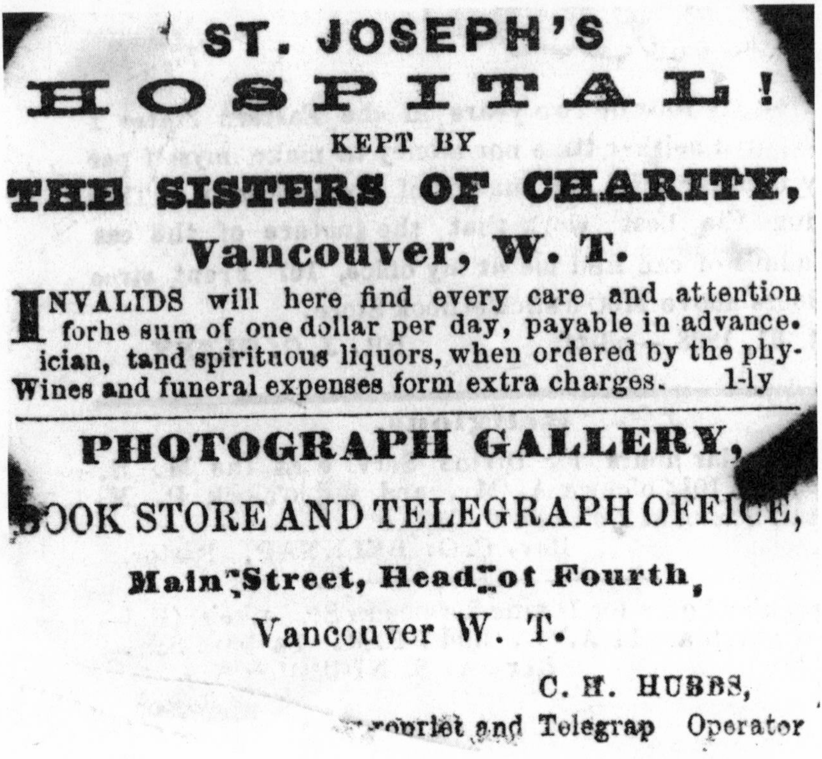

ST. JOSEPH'S HOSPITAL!

KEPT BY

THE SISTERS OF CHARITY,

Vancouver, W. T.

INVALIDS will here find every care and attention forhe sum of one dollar per day, payable in advance. ician, tand spirituous liquors, when ordered by the phy- Wines and funeral expenses form extra charges.   1-ly

---

PHOTOGRAPH GALLERY,

BOOK STORE AND TELEGRAPH OFFICE,

Main Street, Head of Fourth,

Vancouver W. T.

C. H. HUBBS,

~~~~brie and Telegrap   Operator

FIGURE 33. Advertisement for St. Joseph Hospital, Vancouver, Washington Territory, printed in the *Vancouver Register*, 1869. Photo copy. Courtesy of Providence Archives, Seattle, 23.D12.2.27.

FIGURE 34. Dr. David Wall, resident of Vancouver, assisted the Sisters of Providence in their medical work and was a major benefactor of the community. His sister, Anastasia Wall, entered the religious community in 1861, taking the professed name of Philomena of Jesus. Courtesy of Providence Archives, Seattle, 23.D111.8.

FIGURE 35. Sister Joseph (Esther Pariseau), 1850. The pair of scissors in this portrait of Mother Joseph, while a young sister at the motherhouse in Montreal, represents her well-known skills at handwork. Courtesy of Providence Archives, Seattle, SP13. B2.132.

FIGURE 36. Sister Marie Louise Robitaille, first tertiary Sister of Providence in the Northwest, arrived on July 11, 1864, with a group led by Mother Joseph. Also known as sisters of the third order, or externs, these religious women generally came from families of lesser means than those of fully professed sisters and did considerable manual labor. Photograph by O. M. Hofsteater, Vancouver, Washington, 1893. Courtesy Providence Archives, Seattle, SP 11c.1.

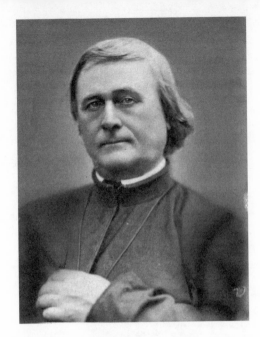

FIGURE 37. Father Peter John De Smet.
Archives of the Oregon Province of the
Society of Jesus, 802.09a.

FIGURE 38. St. Vincent de Paul Academy, Walla Walla. Courtesy Providence Archives,
Seattle, 32.A2.1.

FIGURE 39. Convent and school at Steilacoom mission, 1860s. Courtesy Providence Archives, Seattle, 31.C1.1.

FIGURE 40. Children and teachers (Sisters of Providence) at school, Cowlitz mission, St. Francis Xavier, 1880s. This was officially the earliest Catholic mission in the Pacific Northwest, established in 1838. Courtesy Providence Archives, Seattle, 55.A1.1.

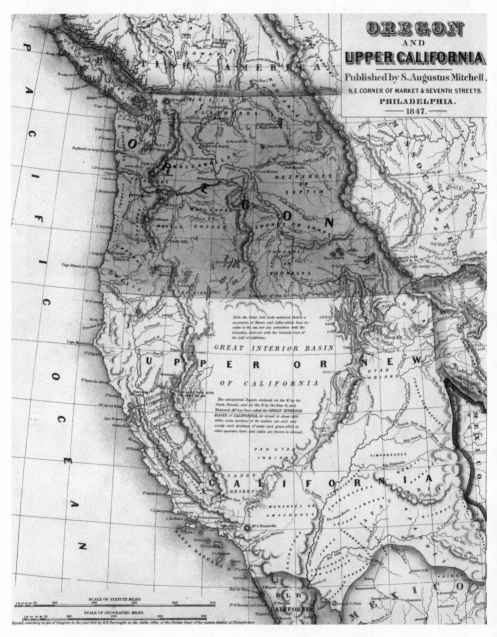

FIGURE 41. Oregon Territory, Upper California. Manuscripts, Archives and Special Collections, Washington State University Libraries, WSU 093.

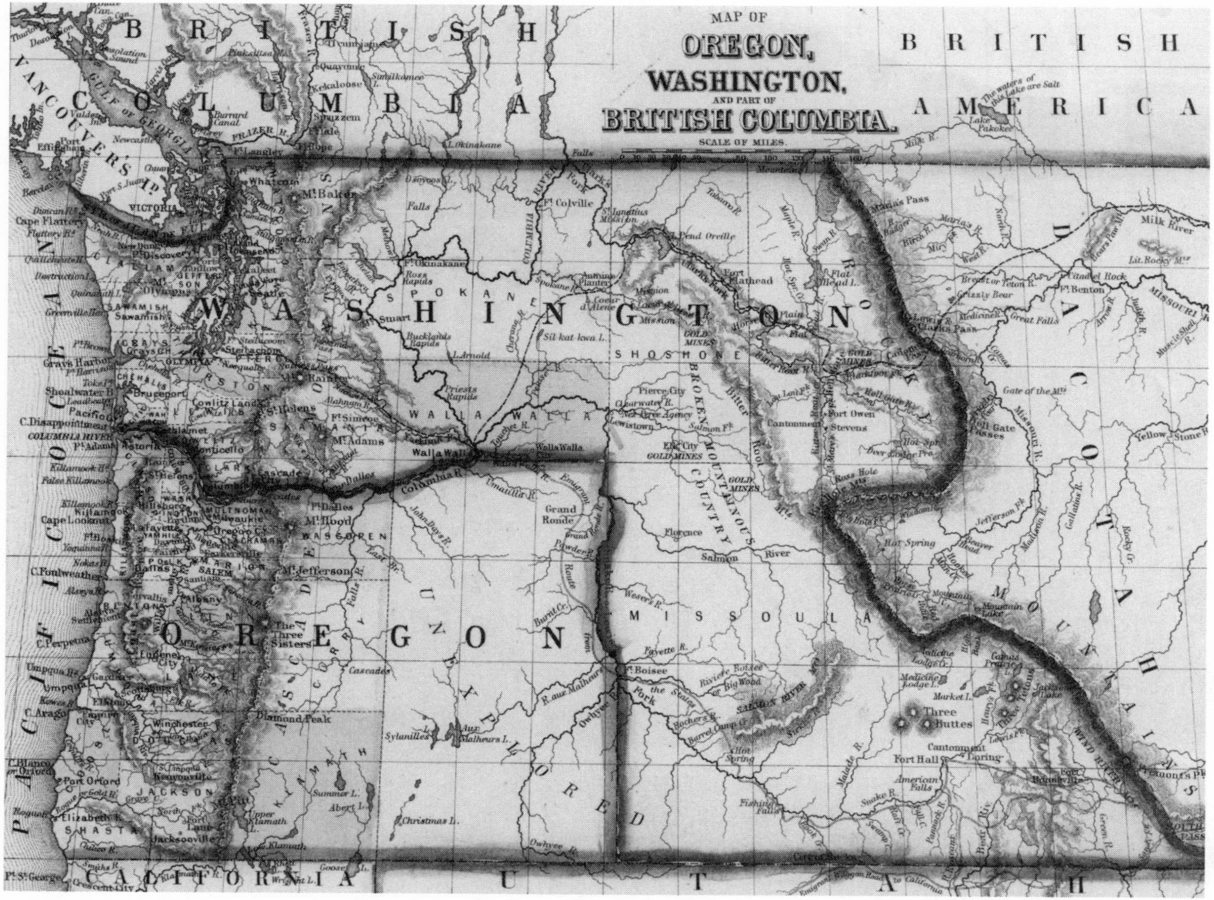

FIGURE 42.
Expanse of Washington
Territory when Oregon
first became a state.
Manuscripts, Archives
and Special Collec-
tions, Washington State
University Libraries,
WSU 017.

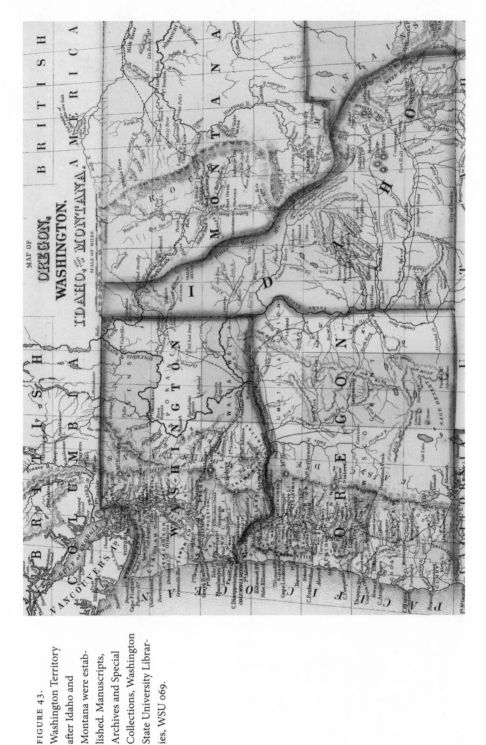

FIGURE 43.
Washington Territory
after Idaho and
Montana were estab-
lished. Manuscripts,
Archives and Special
Collections, Washington
State University Librar-
ies, WSU 069.

FIGURE 44. Seattle, Washington Territory. This panoramic view of Seattle in 1874 is taken from Elliott Bay. Manuscripts, Archives and Special Collections, Washington State University Libraries, WSU 548.

FIGURE 45. Father Francis Xavier Prefontaine. Father Prefontaine built the first church and served as the first Catholic priest of Seattle. Archives of the Archdiocese of Seattle, VR 820.1878.

FIGURE 46. Bishop A. M. A. Blanchet. Archives of the Archdiocese of Seattle, VR 820.253.

FIGURE 47. Providence Academy, Vancouver, Washington, 1880s. The academy was largely the work of Sister Joseph and J. B. Blanchet, nephew of the Blanchet bishops and a skilled artisan who helped construct numerous Catholic establishments in Oregon and Washington Territory. The well-preserved building is still standing in Vancouver. Courtesy Providence Archives, Seattle, 22.A2.33, no.314.

FIGURE 48. Chapel of Providence Academy, Vancouver, Washington. Courtesy Providence Archives, Seattle, ca. 1883, 22.C1.2.

FIGURE 49. Photograph of Holy Angels College for Boys, 1888. Courtesy Providence Archives, Seattle, 22.E22.2, no. 153.

FIGURE 50. St. James Cathedral (1880s), Vancouver, Washington, where A. M. A. Blanchet presided as the first bishop of Nesqualy. Courtesy Providence Archives, Seattle, 22.E14.5, no. 479.

To the Directors of the Leopoldine Society, January 25, 1864

The arrival of able young clergy and new settlers only increased Blanchet's need for resources, and he turned again to Europe, this time to Austria's Leopoldine Society, which had aided him during his 1856 tour. Established in Vienna in 1829 at the instigation of Vicar-General Frederick Rese of the heavily German-populated Diocese of Cincinnati, the Leopoldine Society— Leopoldinen Stiftung—was modeled on the Society for the Propagation of the Faith, for the purpose of aiding Catholic missions in North America.

In a cover letter to this report, Blanchet requests that any contributions be transferred directly to the American College of Louvain, to defray costs of travel for new priests. This report is of particular interest both for its overview of Catholic-sponsored activities in the diocese during the previous eight years and for its description of the cosmopolitan character and human geography of Washington Territory at the time—"composed of whites and Indians . . . a mix of Americans, French, Spanish, Chinese."

In the report Blanchet identified the three major "non-Indian" establishments of the diocese in terms of a right angle, with Vancouver, on the Columbia River, at the pivotal center; Walla Walla, near the junction of the Columbia and the Snake, at one end of an east-west arm; and, Steilacoom, on the southern Puget Sound, at one end of a north-south arm. In 1864, Vancouver, when considered as part of the urban conglomerate of Portland, was the economic and settler core of the region. As Robert E. Ficken explains, human transportation and shipment of cattle and wheat to and from the inland plateau had to go by way of the east-west arm of the Columbia, requiring reloading in this urban center. The same held true for the north-south corridor. Given the difficulty of reaching south Puget Sound by sea, most people and goods were funneled by river and land along the north-south Cowlitz corridor. Furthermore, from the perspective of its scattered and impermanent settlements and industries—lumbering and mining—the region north of Steilacoom was an extractive satellite of San Francisco and so largely outside the domain of territorial control.[1]

Given his request to fund diocesan priests in these three missionary establishments, it made sense in this letter for Blanchet to emphasize works in the predominantly white settlements where these missions were located. Among the priests' responsibilities at the "center" was teaching at the Academy of Holy Angels, where Latin was currently being taught by Father Mans of the American College of Louvain; at the two ends were resident priests, including Father Junger, also from Louvain, who served a scattered population over an extensive circuit at the end of the east-west arm.

Encouraged by the Leopoldine Society's having helped fund travel for the first group of sisters in 1856, Blanchet also addressed the phenomenal growth of the Providence establishment in Vancouver—school, hospital, orphanage, home for the developmentally disabled—and travel costs for the additional sisters that were needed.

Vancouver, January 25th 1864

STATISTICS OF THE DIOCESE OF NESQUALY, FOR THE LEOPOLDINE SOCIETY, VIENNA, AUSTRIA

The Diocese of Nesqualy was erected on May 31st 1850. On one side, it extends from the summit of the Rocky Mountains to the Pacific Ocean; & on the other, from the 46th to the 49th parallel; in other words, it is from 200 to 250 leagues by 60 to 70. The population is not yet dense, but people inhabit areas the farthest from the center, as well as those the closest. This population is composed of whites and Indians.[2]

There are three principal missionary stations for serving non-Indian Catholics, namely Vancouver, Steilacoom, and Walla Walla, from which others receive the missionaries' aid. The missionary of Steilacoom on Puget Sound is responsible for the entire northern part of the diocese. He has to travel from fifty to sixty leagues to visit the various settlements where there are a number of Catholics. The missionary of Walla Walla visits settlements in the east where there are no resident priests.

It was at Vancouver that the first missionaries arrived, on November 24th 1838, and settled, after a voyage of more than six months across the continent. The town of Vancouver, residence of the bishop of Nesqualy, is located on the right bank of the Columbia River, some thirty leagues from its mouth. The bishop's cathedral is made of timbers and measures 60 x 36 feet. The Academy of Holy Angels, near the church, is attended by a good number of children, mostly Catholics. Latin has been taught there for a year, and there is hope that in a few years, subjects will be formed for the clerical state.

Also near the cathedral and on the other side from the academy is a convent of Sisters of Charity. This establishment dates from 1856. Having been in Europe that same year, I collected contributions to provide for the pressing needs of the diocese, and in particular for the foundation of a religious community. I received generous gifts from the Leopoldine Society and from a large number of Catholics in Vienna, as well as in other cities that I visited, which allowed me to realize this project I had planned a number of years earlier. Upon my return from Europe, I passed through Canada, my homeland, where I obtained some Sisters of Charity from the House of Providence in Montreal. On December 8th I arrived in Vancouver with three professed sisters and two postulants. They were very few in number, but I was unable to procure more. The little core would grow with time. It was the mustard seed of the Gospel. It has in fact quintupled in seven years, either through reinforcements from the motherhouse, or through the addition of a few subjects from the region.[3] These good sisters are not without work to do. They have in their care a hospice for the retarded, a hospital for the ill, two orphanages, one for boys, the other for girls, housing more than fifty children. In addition, they have a boarding school and a day school for youngsters; finally they visit the sick in their homes.[4]

But they cannot satisfy all the needs, and their numbers must be increased. In several localities, they are being sought as teachers for young girls. Non-Catholic Americans appreciate the benefit that comes from entrusting their children to them. Two new establishments are already prepared, one in Steilacoom, the other in Walla Walla. It is to be understood that I encourage such establishments with all my strength. For, in addition to the good which results for the Catholics, there is well-founded hope that our schools will serve increasingly to dispel the prejudices of certain Protestants, or non-Catholics, and even that a number of students will enter the bosom of the Holy Church. Although we do not seek to influence non-Catholic children directly, the good examples that they have before their eyes, and the obligation that they conform in every way to the rules, can but leave an impression on many. We have already baptized several in Vancouver. To provide for all the present needs, to comply with all the requests, I would need about twenty additional sisters. What is holding us up are the costs of moving or travel. The voyage from Canada costs from 200 to 250 piastres (from 1,000 to 1,200 francs).

Religious orders have established four missions among various Indian nations. They are the Missions of St. Ignatius among the Pend-Oreilles, of the Sacred Heart among the Coeur d'Alenes, and of St. Paul at Colville in the Rocky Mountains. These are directed by the Reverend Fathers of the Society of Jesus. The other mission, established among the Snohomish on Puget Sound, is under the care of the Reverend Father Oblates of Mary Immaculate. All these missions are prospering and count several thousand Christian souls. If I had a greater number of missionaries at my disposal, I would establish several others. Sisters are also being requested for these missions. They would undoubtedly do much good. I am determined to satisfy such praiseworthy requests as soon as possible.

The secular clergy are few in number. Even now, I have but six priests, four of whom are from Canada, one from Germany, and one from Belgium. These latter two were formed at the American College of Louvain. I will depend on this college for missionaries when needed in the future. They are well trained there. Room and board during the three years of study are covered by the diocese, as are the costs of the voyage for each, which is rising to about 300 piastres (1,500 francs).

The regular missionaries are eight in number, six fathers of the Society of Jesus and two Oblate fathers of Mary Immaculate, whose motherhouse is in Marseilles. English is the language of the country, but as in California, the population is very diverse. There is a mix of Americans, French, Spanish, Chinese &c. Churches or chapels number fourteen. The number of Catholics is not known exactly. It is believed to be around ten thousand.

A. M. A. Bl. Bp. of Nesq.

AAS, A5: 270–74; APFP, F-99, FOL. 61, OPM.

1. Ficken, *Washington Territory*, 2.

2. According to the 1860 federal census, the largest counties in Washington Territory were Clark (2,384), Pierce (1,115), Thurston (1,507), and Walla Walla (1,318). By 1870, all four, especially Walla Walla, had grown: Clark (3,081), Pierce (1,409), Thurston (2,246), and Walla Walla (5,300); two other counties had reached over 1,000: Jefferson (1,268), King (2,120). Though inaccurate especially in counts of indigenous populations, these statistics reveal the wide scattering of population clusters to which Blanchet refers. *A Compendium of the Ninth Census*, June 1870 (Washington, D.C: Government Printing Office, 1872), 71.

3. In addition to the sisters who arrived in 1858 and 1859 (see letter 26, note 6), seven sisters (Catherine, Pre Baptiste, Olivier, Joseph d'Aramathie, Frédéric, Hyacinthe, and Paul Miki) arrived in July 1863, again in the company of Vicar-General Brouillet; subjects from the region who made their profession of vows in August 1864 were Maria Sullivan of Portland (Sister Mary Augustine), daughter of a benefactor; Anastasia Wall (Sister Philomena of Jesus), sister of good friend, advisor, and benefactor, Dr. David Wall; and Nancy Crate (Sister Mary John Baptiste), daughter of an HBC employee from London. Blanchet appears to have counted as well the five sisters and three novices who arrived on February 1, 1864. "Régistre de l'Institut des Soeurs de Charité Servantes des Pauvres et des Malades depuis la fondation le 16 mars 1843," Providence Archives, Mother Joseph Province, Seattle; "Notes sur le Diocèse de Nesqualy," AAS, B6; McCrosson, *The Bell and the River*, 151, 172; F. X. Blanchet, *Ten Years on the Pacific Coast; and Jacksonville, a National Historical Landmark City*, ed. and trans. Edward J. Kowrach (Fairfield, Wash.: Ye Galleon Press, 1982), 14.

4. The Sisters of Charity accepted care for their first mental patient on June 5, 1861, and held the Washington Territory's contract to care for the mentally ill (including the developmentally disabled) from 1861 to 1867, at which time they had twelve. A twenty-nine-member lay Society of Ladies of Charity, composed of Catholics, Methodists, Episcopalians, and Jews, each pledged to contribute twelve and a half cents a week in support of St. Joseph Hospital, opened on June 7, 1858, and paid the sisters a dollar a day for each sick person they sent to the hospital, some thirty-three by 1864. On April 15, 1857, Providence of the Holy Angels school opened; it had twenty-one boarders and nineteen day pupils in 1864; an even larger number of orphans were under the sisters' care. From 1863 to 1864, the sisters made 143 home visits to the sick and 60 home watches (vigils with the dying). In addition, the sisters, with the help of a few Canadien servants, also provided food, cooked, mended, washed, and often sewed clothing for the orphans, patients, boarders, clergy, and themselves and cared for the sacristy of the church. McCrosson, *The Bell and the River*, 121, 142-50, 175-6; "Chronicles, 1863-1864," in "Chronicles of the House of Providence, 1856-1875."

To Sister Joseph of the Sacred Heart, Superior, February 11, 1864

No sooner had Blanchet assigned newly arrived sisters and clerics than he faced calls for still more in his growing diocese. In terms of sisters, not only was the Providence establishment in Vancouver shorthanded, but settlers were requesting them in Steilacoom and Walla Walla, and priests were seeking "women black robes" for their Indian missions. As letters 30 and 31 attest, Blanchet persistently grasped at funding sources to meet the travel costs of yet another group of sisters: his own increasingly limited funds; Brouillet's collections in Washington, D.C.; a potential loan from Bishop Bourget; and contributions from the Society for the Propagation of the Faith, the Association of the Holy Infancy, and the Leopoldine Society. Still short of resources, he turned to Vancouver's sister superior herself.

Blanchet knew from his own experiences in Mexico, Europe, and eastern Canada that begging in person was effective. On September 23, 1863, he and the Providence community of Vancouver bade farewell to Sister Joseph, who would spend almost ten months traveling, soliciting funds in her home country, and convincing Mother Superior Philomène to allow an additional group of sisters to go west. She had been gone four months when news of her successes reached Vancouver. Leaving his characteristic state of worry, Blanchet wrote this joyful response, which he followed up with a telegram.[1]

The sister superior, often known as "Mother" Joseph, was the right choice for this task. She knew how to cajole and to plead, and, as much as anyone, she represented the Oregon mission. In 1847, when the community's former chaplain was consecrated bishop of Nesqualy, she had sewn his vestments. In 1852, she had asked to be among the first group of sisters who set out for the diocese, but serving then as general bursar of the Providence community, she was considered too valuable to let go. In 1856, her wish had been granted. Of robust constitution and unfettered energy, and a skilled carpenter and seamstress, she had propelled the rapid development of services in Vancouver, overseen building, and managed finances, often outpacing the physical endurance of her sisters. In her frequent letters to Mother Caron, Bishop

Bourget, and others, she expressed an inner longing for spiritual renewal in the charism of the community.[2] Sister Joseph's voyage proved to be of personal value and lasting benefit to the diocese. The specific requests that Blanchet writes of below were largely met.

Vancouver, February 11, 1864

Reverend Sr. & dearest Daughter in J.C.,

The letter you wrote me last November arrived in due time; it could but give me great joy. The caravan's arrival on the 1st instant simply overjoyed me, as did the accompanying letters that confirmed the good news that you had given me.[3] Monsignor of Montreal's letter is consoling and precise: "The Community, he says, is prepared to bleed from all four parts to supply you with subjects."[4] The letter from the Reverend Mother Superior also expresses the best intentions. May God be a thousand times blessed! We can now move forth from our near standstill. The new reinforcements you bring should enable us to provide for the most pressing needs. I would like, in fact, to see enough sisters come in the spring so that I will not be obliged to make further requests for several years to come. So how many should you bring? We must provide for Father Chirouse's mission (Tulalip), then the Pend d'Oreilles, a portion of Walla Walla, then the same for Steilacoom.[5] I presume that two would suffice for each of these locations. But isn't it appropriate to have a few for this station (of Vancouver) as well? I believe so. By my calculations, then, you should try to acquire fifteen sisters for the diocese, and not less than twelve. The greatest difficulty undoubtedly will be to come up with the needed funds. I trust, however, that in making the best of your talent, you will collect enough, especially if you have received the money from Paris. Father Truteau has not said a word, nor have you.[6]

I presume that you will not have a priest to accompany you. I am writing to Grand Vicar Truteau to request that he have the young Boulet go along; he offered his service last year for the academy. I would like him to take passage in 2nd class; that would not prevent him from helping you with the luggage.[7] Come back as soon as possible. Your voyage is blessed, glory be to God!

Father Brouillet departs for Washington next month. He is here at the moment, and he leaves next Monday for his station with Sister of the Nativity, as well as Sisters Colomban and Paul Miki; he will return after getting them settled.[8]

The sisters will be paid every three months for care of the retarded, in accordance with the second clause of the contract, from the initial funds that will be placed in the treasury. In his Report to the Legislature, Mr. Walker, the auditor, said that you are to be paid *on a cash basis*, that is to say, not in *greenbacks*, according to the legal value of the dollar.

This is good, . . . I think your sisters have already written to you about all of this. You will undoubtedly write to inform us once the date for the caravan's departure is set. Try not to disappoint us once again. May the Lord bless you and bring you, safe & sound, with your companions.

Aug. M. A., Bp. of Nesqualy

Items requested:
One cross of gold fabric, Parisian
One cross of green fabric, also Parisian[9]
An assortment of common liturgical vestments
Cruets

P.S. I am told that Reverend Father De Smet has asked for Sisters. He has been requested, I trust, to pay their passage. He has many resources.

MOTHER JOSEPH OF THE SACRED HEART PERSONAL PAPERS COLLECTION, PROVIDENCE ARCHIVES, SEATTLE; AAS, A5: 282 (SUMMARY).

———•———

1. Sent March 19, 1864, from Portland, the telegram stated, in English: "A chaplain desired; more Sisters; telegraph departure; Father Brouillet here; make haste." It arrived in Montreal on the twenty-first. This is the only telegram entered in the Blanchet registries (AAS, A5: 278).

2 McCrosson, *The Bell and the River*, 63, 79, 173.

3 Five professed sisters (La Nativité, M. Joseph, Colomban, M. du Mont Carmel, and M. Alexandre) and three novices (Augustin, Philomène, and J. Baptiste) arrived on February 1, 1864, with Father Francis Xavier Prefontaine (AAS, B6).

4 "I think that Providence is going to bleed from all four parts in order that a caravan as large as possible leave with Sr. Joseph, so that you can satisfy the requests you are receiving from all parts for your Sisters of Providence. Kindly keep in mind, though, dear *Seigneur*, that this

Community is still young; and that it needs to establish itself on a solid base before spreading out. Kindly obtain for them as well all the spiritual help they need, to fortify themselves more and more in the good spirit that St. Vincent de Paul bequeathed to them, and whose rules and constitutions they follow" (Bourget to Blanchet, December 18, 1863, ACAM, RLB-13, 327).

5. Father Chirouse, briefly serving as superintendent of instruction on the Tulalip Reservation, expected to see a school for girls completed in the fall of 1864. He thought that funds (including tuition charged to parents of métis pupils) would be sufficient to pay sisters $12 annually, and he requested the names of the two sisters to teach girls on the reservation (Chirouse to Sister Joseph, December 15, 1863, box 13, Correspondence, Priests, 1863–1905, Providence Archives, Seattle). Father Urban Grassi, S.J., requested sisters for the new site of St. Ignatius Mission, which in 1855 had been moved to Kalispel land just below Flathead Lake, where some two thousand Catholic Indians lived, primarily Flatheads, Kutenais, Pend d'Oreilles, and Kalispels (see letter 19, note 4; Burns, *Jesuits and the Indian Wars*, 86). Four sisters departed from Walla Walla on September 17, 1864, and arrived at St. Ignatius after thirty days of travel by horse. They were Sisters Marie de L'Enfant Jésus, Paul Miki, Marie Edouard, and Rémi, three of whom had just arrived from Montreal with Sister Superior Joseph, while Paul Miki had been in Walla Walla prior to her departure (Sisters of Charity of Providence, *The Institute of Providence: History of the Daughters of Charity Servants of the Poor known as the Sisters of Providence*, vol. 5, *The Sisters of Providence in Oregon, 1856* (Montreal: Providence Mother House, 1930), 187–88.

6. Abbé Alexis-Frédéric Truteau (1808–1872) was serving as vicar-general of the Diocese of Montreal and chaplain to the Sisters of Providence of Montreal at the time of this letter.

7. Jean Boulet, born 1834 in Rowell County, Quebec, worked for ten years in the cotton mills of Holyoke, Massachusetts, and was studying at St.-Hyacinthe Seminary in Quebec in 1863 when he departed with Mother Joseph and Father L. N. St. Onge for the Diocese of Nesqualy in June 1864. He taught at the boys' academy, College of Holy Angels (1864–66); served as missionary to the Yakamas (1866–70); studied theology at the bishop's house of Vancouver (1871–74), while also teaching boys; was ordained by A. M. A. Blanchet on July 19, 1874; and then served as secretary to the bishop until he replaced Father Chirouse at the Tulalip Reservation in 1878. Speaking the Chinook, Skagit, and Klickitat languages, among others, he served as priest to Indian reservations stretching from the Nisqually to the Lummi and built Assumption Church of Bellingham in 1869. Leona Laube, "Father Boulet, Pioneer Priest, Sage, and Educator," *Bellingham Sunday Herald*, July 31, 1910, typescript copy in Relander Collection, box 55, file 20, Yakima Regional Library, Yakima, Wash.

8. With the outside of the Walla Walla convent (St. Vincent Academy) sufficiently completed, Father Brouillet accompanied three sisters selected for the mission to Walla Walla: Sister Mary of the Nativity (Clemence Robert, 1819–1890); Sister Colomban (Isabelle McWilliams, 1838–1898), an American; and Sister Paul Miki (Mathilde Roby, 1842–1880). The founding date was February 18, 1864. McCrosson, *The Bell and the River*, 189; "Régistre de l'Institut des Soeurs de Charité Servantes des Pauvres et des Malades depuis la fondation le 16 mars 1843," Providence Archives, Mother Joseph Province, Seattle; "Notes sur le Diocèse de Nesqualy," AAS, B6.

9. Blanchet is referring to a large piece of cross-shaped fabric presumably interwoven with gold-colored thread. It is attached to the front and/or back of a chasuble (outer ecclesial vestment worn by a priest at Eucharistic services); the arms of the cross extend the entire length and

breadth of the chasuble; and the color of the fabric varies with the liturgical season or occasion. By "Parisian," Blanchet appears to be referring to a particular shape of the cross that had come into style at the time but that later was prohibited by the Church. This vestment ornamentation in the shape of a cross makes symbolically visible the analogy of a priest, while wearing the chasuble, representing Christ bearing the cross. L'abbé Boissonnet, *Dictionnaire Albabetico-Méthodique des Cérémonies et des Rites sacrées . . . le tout d'après la liturgie romaine*, 3 vols. (Paris: Migne, 1847), 1:806.

LETTER 33

Charles Vary, Missionary, July 23, 1864[1]

Steilacoom, the base for activity along the north-to-south corridor of Blanchet's missionary diocese, offered more promise as a Catholic center than it would realize. The gap between promise and realization frustrated the bishop, perhaps never more so than now. Settlers had promised, but failed, to adequately support sisters, a convent, and a school. This was particularly disappointing in light of the recently arrived reinforcements of sisters to Vancouver.[2]

With settlers' expression of desire for sisters to establish a school and their promises of support in 1862 and 1863, two sisters were sent from Vancouver in the fall of 1863, though a convent was not yet under construction. Sisters Catherine and Marie of the Precious Blood, along with two secular assistants, arrived in Steilacoom in November and opened a school in January 1864.[3] The number of students and hence tuition revenue, as well as contributions, were less than anticipated, and costs for constructing a convent and school higher. The sisters also found difficult the spiritual deprivation caused by Father Vary's frequent absences as he attended to his mission territory. In June 1864, the sisters left Steilacoom uncertain whether or not they would return.[4]

In this letter Blanchet urges the priest-in-charge, Father Vary, who had assumed duties at Steilacoom in 1860, to redouble his efforts to collect funds and provide for a convent and school on the city block that resident Mr. Hughes had donated for this purpose. Blanchet wanted a flourishing Catholic institutional presence in Steilacoom, a town he still viewed as the commercial and political capital of Puget Sound. He did not appreciate the difficulty of Father Vary's situation, functioning as resident priest for the town and as itinerant missionary from Olympia to what today is the Canada–United States border. Blanchet thought that Vary could do better, despite the fact that the priest's experience with fund-raising in Steilacoom echoed Sergeant Archbold's observations regarding settlers around Steilacoom (see letter 22).

Larger events conspired to slow the establishment of the religious institutions that both Blanchet and Vary desired. Land speculation around Steilacoom in the wake of the Fraser River gold strike of 1858 dampened development there. Ore strikes in Idaho in 1861 and the rotation of volunteer companies through Fort Steilacoom in lieu of regular U.S. Cavalry troops called east to fight in the Civil War, all led to population shifts and so affected support for the Church.[5]

Internal personnel challenges also existed. Blanchet's comments about money, loans, and proper deportment by clergy regarding these matters suggests that he was aware that his clergy were not exempt from the lure of wealth, so much a part of the western adventure.

Vancouver, July 23rd 1864

My Dear Father,

Your letter of the 18th instant arrived this morning. The letter from the Sisters of Saint Anne is certainly flattering of you, enough it seems to put you at ease. I suggest that you forget the past and think only about the present and the future. As for the interest, it is useless to take any further action. Your word was sufficient for me. Besides, had you drawn some interest from your own money, who would dare blame you?

What you must avoid with great care, however, is allowing anyone to think that we are more attached to our temporal interests than to the religion for which we are ministers. To deliberately give rise to such thoughts would be enough to prevent our ministry from bearing fruit. By showing our disinterest, we will convince the public that we are inspired above all by an ardent zeal for the glory of God & the salvation of souls. In doing so, we will inspire people to reach into their pockets to provide for our keep as well as for other works, such as a church, convent, school.[6]

As for the money collected last year, my dear Father, it was understood here that it was for building the convent; that is what you implied then in your letters, if I am not mistaken. You wanted to continue the collection and to buy the timber during the winter; you asked what the size of the house should be, &c. It is in light of these worthy inclinations on your part that I felt prompted to comply immediately with your urgent request, & consented to procuring some sisters for you before the convent was built. I was so convinced that you would not pull back that I wrote to Montreal, reporting your progress in establishing a convent in Steilacoom, so that I might inspire the community to send an adequate number of sisters to provide for you. I provided you with sisters rather than Walla Walla, which was pressing me as well & had begun its convent. Then winter went by, spring as well; no further steps were taken toward the convent. What a change!

The community has not yet pronounced the final word concerning the sisters' mission in Steilacoom.[7] I should make no secret to you that your letter is unlikely to encourage the continuation of efforts that had begun under such fortunate auspices, at least in appearance. According to what you say, the sisters of this mission would already be indebted for last year by 400 to 500 dollars, and would have no assurance or even moral certainty that during a second year they would be provided their keep or a means of paying what you claim. I leave you to judge, my dear Father, if this is a very encouraging outlook for them. If they had a house in Steilacoom that belonged to them, I have grounds to believe that they would not hesitate to come another year.

When I see a convent in Walla Walla, built for the most part by the generous contributions of our non-Catholic brothers; in The Dalles, another convent built by the same means; in Salem, Oregon, a church that is known to be the finest in the province, and built, so to speak, in the center of religious fanaticism; when I see that in Jacksonville, Oregon, pledges for a convent amount to more than 2,500 dollars and promise to exceed 3,000, I wonder why the same isn't being done on the Sound, given the assurance that it is desired by a good number of non-Catholic citizens as you wrote last year. Let us move forward, Gentlemen Missionaries, our hands to the plough, with courage, with perseverance! And you will succeed. At least do not give up on the work until you are convinced, after making an effort, that it is impossible. The work was supposed to have begun last year. Don't make our enemies laugh at our own expense: this is true for the honor of religion, as well as for your honor. Go, knock on all the doors until you have collected a sufficient amount to build a humble abode for the Sisters of Charity, who will be so useful to you for teaching the young & reforming behavior, at least among persons of their gender. May one of you get started right away, & cover all the localities. To follow in the steps of Oregon missionaries in this manner, is a glory that you cannot decline.

My dear Father, my call is addressed first to you, because you are the pastor in charge, and because you have already proven yourself in collecting for orphans. But if there are reasons why you cannot do the work, invite your assistant to do so. I believe he will succeed.[8]

As for the salary request, I will write later. I will only express my regret that Father Prefontaine already appears too anxious to fill his pockets.

.....I am &c......
A. M. A. B. N.

AAS, A5: 287–90.

———•———

1. Charles Vary (1835–1878) was born in Longueil, Quebec; studied at the College of St. Thomas de Blainville; was ordained on March 21, 1858, by Bishop Demers; and served for two years in the Diocese of Vancouver Island. In October 1860, he was loaned to the Diocese of Nesqualy, where he soon was assigned to Steilacoom, the residence for the priest responsible for all of Washington Territory west of the Cascade crest, from Olympia north to today's Canadian border. His circuit included Olympia, Steilacoom, Seattle, Port Madison, Port Gamble, Nook Harbor, Seabeck, Port Ludlow, Port Townsend, Whidbey Island, Camano Island, Utsaladdy, Bellingham Bay and the San Juan Islands, Chelais Point on Gray's Harbor, and Oysterville on Willapa Bay. Vary interrupted his work from Steilacoom briefly in 1862 when Bishop Blanchet sent him to Idaho to raise money for the orphanages at Vancouver. In 1864, an assistant arrived to share the ministry in the vast mission territory. Sisters of Charity of Providence, Institute, 5:387–88; Blanchet to Vary, October 12, 1860, AAS, A5: 137–39; Gimpl, "Immaculate Conception Mission," 53–54.

2. Mother Joseph left Montreal in June 1864, with eight professed, experienced sisters (Marie de l'Enfant Jésus, Amarine, Rose de Marie, Marie Etienne, Marie du Rosaire, Marie de la Foi, Marie Edouard, and Rémi) and three tertiaries. They arrived on July 11, 1864, in the company of ecclesiastics Louis-Napoléon St. Onge and Jean Boulet (AAS, B6).

3. "Chroniques de la Mission de St. Joseph de Steilacoom, 1863," 1, Providence Archives, Mother Joseph Province, Seattle; Gimpl, "Immaculate Conception Mission," 57–60.

4. "Chroniques de la Mission de St. Joseph de Steilacoom, 1863," 2; Gimpl, "Immaculate Conception Mission," 63.

5. Steilacoom's fortunes as a commercial center never recovered from the disruption caused by the movement of troops at Fort Steilacoom during the Civil War, the closing of the fort in 1868, and competition from newly established Commencement City (later Tacoma), which would be named the terminus of the Northern Pacific Railway in 1873.

6. Both preoccupation with wealth and skepticism regarding designated religious personnel pervaded the Pacific Northwest frontier. Clergy and religious institutions, while they provided the benefits associated with settled life, also represented the threat of social control to those who found the West more congenial than the longer-established cities and towns of the East or Midwest, where religious leaders and attitudes played a more dominant role in social life. The theme of resistance to the imposition of clerical influence, and the need for clergy to prove themselves equal to the challenges of the West, runs through denominational histories of the region. As well, as historians Laurie Maffly-Kipp and Ferenc Szasz have argued, the realities of economic life in the West undercut assumptions of steady habits and economic reward that supported religious influence in the Midwest and the East. Nor were diocesan clergy, who were not bound by vows of poverty, immune to the promise of wealth that clung to the myth of the West. Laurie Maffly-Kipp, *Religion and Society in Frontier California* (New Haven, Conn.: Yale University Press, 1994), 38–62, 110–47; Ferenc Szasz, "The Clergy and the Myth of the American West," *Church History* 59 (December 1990): 505–6; Ferenc Szasz and Margaret Connel Szasz, "Religion and Spirituality," in *The Oxford History of the American West* (New York: Oxford University Press, 1994), 359–60, 366; D. Michael Quinn, "Religion in the American West," in *Under an Open Sky: Rethinking America's Western Past*, ed. William Cronon, George Miles, and Jay Gitlin (New York: W. W. Norton, 1992), 164–66; Erle Howell, *Methodism in the Northwest* (Nashville: Parthenon Press, Printers, 1966), 68–114; Jeffrey Burns, "Building the Best: A History of Catholic Parish Life in the Pacific Northwest," in *The American Catholic Parish: A History from 1850 to the Present*, vol. 2, *Pacific States, Intermountain West, Midwest*, ed. Jay P. Dolan (New York: Paulist Press, 1987).

7. The sisters returned to Steilacoom in the late fall of 1864 and continued their work teaching, visiting prisoners and the sick, and caring for orphans until St. Joseph's closed in 1875. Gimpl, "Immaculate Conception Mission," 64–67, 73.

8. Blanchet was referring to Father Francis Xavier Prefontaine. See letter 34.

<hr>

LETTER 34

To Francis Xavier Prefontaine, Missionary, July 24, 1864[1]

Steilacoom's gap between promise and accomplishment carried over into internal ecclesial life as well. A day after writing Father Vary, Bishop Blanchet addressed the young Father Francis Xavier Prefontaine, whom four months earlier he had appointed assistant priest at Steilacoom. New to the priesthood, now experiencing missionary work in the West as it was and not as he had imagined it, Prefontaine was not happy. He complained to the bishop about Father Vary and about his pay. In response, he received both rebuke and counsel from his bishop.

Father,

I received your letter of the 17th instant. It is much to be regretted that you are having differences with Father Vary. Wherever the wrong may lie, there is simply no doubt that harm will come of it, scandal, should this continue. After the scandals of last year, you need be on your guard, & rather than give rise to new scandal, try to erase the damage their notoriety has already caused.[2] Questions of money, of personal interests between missionaries, are hardly a fitting way to edify the faithful, & they do not fail to provoke mirth among non-Catholics, at the least. To allow these divisions to break out in public shows a lack of prudence, to say nothing more. You understand what I mean. I am not deciding your dispute at the moment. I will tell you, however, that a priest coming from Canada or elsewhere cannot, should not, expect to receive more than an honest keep for at least some time. If the lesson of the great Apostle, *Habentes alimenta & quibus tegamur, his contenti sumus* ["Having food and something to clothe us, with these we have been satisfied," 1 Timothy 6:8], is applicable anywhere, it is in missions where everything remains to be done, and with minimum resources. For this reason, I find you have been stepping outside of the appropriate boundaries since the beginning of your apostolic career. Indeed, how do you know that 150 piastres will not suffice for your keep? Once the experience of a year has convinced you of this, you will have a plausible motive for complaining.

But what is more astonishing is the menace that accompanies your complaint: "Lacking 200 dollars, I will return to Canada!" That certainly is a bit hasty! One thing seems certain to me: in returning to Canada for the alleged reason, you would hardly be showing that it was *only* the desire to obtain the glory of God & salvation of souls that brought you here. On that subject, I want to speak to you frankly. Any priest who goes to a mission country without being sheathed in courage and the will to suffer privations of more than one sort, this priest deludes himself, mistakes his vocation; it would be a thousand times better for him to remain in his own country, in his diocese, where he would have all he wishes. That would be better *for him*, & I add for *the missions* as well; for he could cause great harm, & slow down the work of God.

These, Father, are the sober reflections that your letter has fostered. I have, I believe, expressed myself clearly, but with no intention other than to enlighten you, & to show you the path that a priest who believes or who thought that he had a vocation for the missions, must follow.

You say that "earnings, all expenses paid, amount to 600 dollars." Could you kindly inform me how you can assure me of this? For, until I received your letter, my impression had been otherwise. In conclusion, to use your own expression, I will say: "I have to inform you" that for the moment I can only assure you an honest keep, and I still lack proof that 150 dollars a year will not suffice. When you are charged with leading a mission, you will probably receive more.

Another question: tell me if a priest could live in Steilacoom while serving Olympia and some other locality as well. Tell me also by what authority the starting of the sisters' classes in Steilacoom was announced, after two months of vacation, given that nothing has yet been decided here on the future of this ill-fated mission.[3]

.....I am &c......
A. M. A. B. N.

AAS, A5: 290–92.

—————•—————

1. Francis Xavier Prefontaine (1838–1909) was born in Longueil, Quebec. After completing seminary studies in Montreal, he was ordained by Bishop Bourget in November 1863 and volunteered for the Diocese of Nesqualy. He arrived in February 1864, an eager, ambitious diocesan priest enchanted with adventure in the West. He never returned to Montreal, spending his entire ministry in western Washington. He is best known as the first resident priest in Seattle, which he visited initially in 1867. Schoenberg, *Catholic Church in the Pacific Northwest*, 192–193.

2. We were unable to discover the particular scandal to which Blanchet is referring. Inference from the text suggests that it had to do with the strained relationship and conflict between

Fathers Vary and Prefontaine spilling out into the community. Blanchet was especially sensitive to any behavior that would fuel anti-Catholic sentiment.

3. On June 27, 1864, the *Puget Sound Herald* announced that Father Prefontaine was taking applications for students at St. Joseph Academy for the new school year. The sisters did not agree to return until August 1864. In November 1864, Sisters Marie Joseph, Marie du Mont Carmel, and Jean de Dieu returned to Steilacoom. Gimpl, "Immaculate Conception Mission," 64–68.

LETTER 35

To the Secular and Regular Clergy of the Diocese, July 8, 1867

Bishop Blanchet sent this memorandum of instruction to all the clergy under his charge six months after returning from the Second Plenary Council of Baltimore.[1] In contrast to so many letters presenting shortages and needs in the diocese, the formal tone and content of this circular suggest a more stable situation. In Blanchet's view, institutional presence was the foundation for sustained, consistent piety and practice among clergy, religious, and the laity. Its very existence extended supernatural life to all.

The memorandum is an artifact of ecclesiastical bureaucratic routine and much more than that. Through it Blanchet not only discharged his episcopal responsibility to communicate the actions of the council, but he also encouraged his priests, religious, and laypeople to participate more actively in the wider Church.

Vancouver, July 8th 1867

CIRCULAR

Father or Reverend Father,

In conformity with the desires of the Fathers at the Second Plenary Council of Baltimore, the Sunday of the Feast of the Assumption of the Blessed

Virgin Mary[2] is designated in this diocese for the collection for Our Holy Father the Pope. You are to announce the collection immediately before the sermon on the preceding Sunday and to read the article of the Council's Pastoral Letter that urges the faithful to come to the aid of the Holy Father who, due to the malice of the Church's enemies, finds himself in a critical situation.[3] You will urge the faithful to contribute generously to the relief of our Father, of this I am certain. Missionaries who serve more than one station should make the collection during the visit immediately following reception of these letters. I would like the proceeds to be sent here as soon as possible.

I am taking this opportunity to suggest that you encourage the faithful under your jurisdiction to form local branches of the Society for the Propagation of the Faith,[4] and to subscribe to *The Ave Maria*, "a Catholic journal devoted to the honor of the Blessed Virgin." It is a weekly journal published in Notre Dame, Indiana.[5] I would like to see every Christian family in the diocese receive it, as it is a sure means for regenerating our flocks. This journal costs only three *dollars* a year in *greenbacks*. A lifetime subscription is twenty dollars.[4]

I am &c. . . .
Aug. M. A. Bp. of Nesqualy

AAS, B8: 6.

———•———

1. The Second Plenary Council of Baltimore convened on October 7 and closed on October 21, 1866. Gathered with the authorization of Pope Pius IX, the attending archbishops, bishops, and abbots clarified doctrinal teaching and set policy for Catholic practice and discipline to be followed in all ecclesiastical provinces in the United States and its territories. Major agenda items included the care of recently freed slaves, seminaries, gaining control of unattached priests, legal arrangements for holding church property, the relationship of bishops to religious orders, and fasts, feasts, and holy days of obligation (*The Catholic Encyclopedia*, s.v. "Plenary Councils of Baltimore"). A. M. A. Blanchet attended the council, leaving Vancouver in August 1866 and returning on December 8, 1866, with four more Sisters of Providence from Montreal.

2. The feast of the Assumption of the Blessed Virgin Mary celebrates the tradition that upon her death, Mary was taken into heaven; her body was spared the process of corruption in the grave. The feast is celebrated on August 15.

3. By the end of the Austro-Prussian War, also known as the Third Italian War of Indepen-

dence (June–August 1866), Pope Pius IX, protected by a garrison of French troops, retained control only of Rome. The Kingdom of Sardinia controlled the remaining territory that once was part of the Papal States. Loss of the Papal States and legislation enacted by the governing Kingdom of Sardinia reduced the pope's income and power. At the same time that the American bishops were convening in Baltimore, the Italian war hero and patriot Giuseppe Garibaldi was leading a political party that promoted the seizure of Rome and sought international support for the elimination of the papacy. What Blanchet instructs his clergy to read aloud at Mass is the relevant section from Martin John Spalding, *Pastoral letter of the Second Plenary Council of Baltimore: The archbishops and bishops of the United States in plenary council assembled, to the clergy and laity of their charges* (Baltimore: John Murphy and Company, 1866).

4. From the beginning, Blanchet's missionary venture had been supported with funds from the Society for the Propagation of the Faith collected in Montreal and in France. The Diocese of Nesqualy was now mature enough for the bishop to encourage laity to organize local branches of the society and in this way participate in the Church's worldwide missionary work. The Second Plenary Council of Baltimore also encouraged establishment of the society in dioceses, thus furthering the transition of the U.S. Catholic Church from a missionary institution financially dependent upon the French Society for the Propagation of the Faith to a self-sustaining national organization. For a history of this transition, see Michael Pasquier, *Fathers on the Frontier: French Missionaries and the Roman Catholic Priesthood in the United States, 1789–1870* (Oxford: Oxford University Press, 2010).

5. The journal's title and the clause in quotation marks are in English. Holy Cross Father and University of Notre Dame founder Edward Sorin began *Ave Maria* magazine in 1865. The magazine was intended to honor Mary and promote devotion to her, to support the spirituality of families, and to feature American Catholic writing. Marvin R. O'Connell, *Edward Sorin* (Notre Dame, Ind.: University of Notre Dame Press, 2001), 504–10.

LETTER 36

To Jean-Baptiste Auguste Brondel, Missionary, August 31, 1867

The list of Steilacoom-based missions on Puget Sound served by Fathers Vary and Prefontaine, ranging from the Cowlitz to Whatcom Rivers, speaks to the arduous nature of their far-flung circuits.[1] Their ability to carry out the requests in the bishop's circular of July 8 likely varied with the circumstances of each station. Having spent seven years in the Oregon Province, on loan from the Diocese of Montreal, Father Vary asked to return to Canada in 1867; there, he entered the Jesuit novitiate at Sault-au-Récollet, where he found religious life easy in comparison to his apostolate on Puget Sound.[2]

The next priest to serve at the Steilacoom-based mission, a Belgian, contributed to eleven years of Church growth on the Sound and spent an additional, intermittent year, 1877–78, in Walla Walla and Frenchtown, before assuming still more demanding responsibilities. As a child, Jean-Baptist Auguste Brondel (1842–1901) heard his father read the widely published missionary letters of Peter De Smet, S.J. Fired with zeal to follow in his countryman's path, he completed his classical course of studies at the college of St. Louis in Bruges. Brondel then attended the American College of Louvain, where he excelled, was incorporated into the Diocese of Nesqualy, and was ordained in 1862. At the suggestion of Rector Father John de Nève, he remained at the college for two additional years in part to perfect his English, a decision for which he later was grateful. Father Brondel arrived in Vancouver on All Saints' Day, 1866. He remained there for ten months, teaching at the Academy of Holy Angels and mastering the Chinook trade language, before he assumed his charge in Steilacoom. There, through submission to what he considered the will of God, he overcame disappointment in not serving more Indian missions.[3]

Having been raised to speak at least French and probably German, in addition to his native Flemish (and to read classical languages), Jean Brondel was well prepared for his apostolate. Hailing from a multilingual country, Belgium, he easily adapted to the multiethnic, multiracial, religious, and linguistic complex of the Pacific Northwest.[4]

Vancouver, August 31st 1867

Father,

Until revocation, you will exercise the holy ministry with the powers of missionary pastor on the Bay (Puget Sound). To the north, your jurisdiction will extend, on one side, to the town of Seattle and its surroundings inclusively, and on the other, to Port Madison; and to the south, it will extend to Olympia and its surroundings, also inclusively. Steilacoom will be your residence. You will serve as official spiritual director for the sisters of the convent. It will be your duty to guide them in the path of perfection, as revealed by the Holy Spirit through your fervent prayers.

I pray that the Lord shower abundant blessings on your apostolic works.[5]

..I am most cordially, Father, Your devoted servant
..Aug. M. A. Bp. of Nesqualy

AAS, B8: 7.

---

1. On November 18, 1864, Bishop Blanchet divided the Sound into two parts. Father Vary's charge began at Port Gamble and Seattle (see letter 38), inclusively, and extended to the south. Father Prefontaine's included all the parts of the diocese to the north of Port Gamble and Seattle. "Recueil sur l'histoire du diocèse de Nesqualy, pour servir à son histoire," box 610, folder 6, RG 660, AAS. (This undated document is a summary made by the bishop of personnel assignments and other official acts, from March 3, 1847, to November 18, 1864.)

2. After leaving Steilacoom and completing his Jesuit novitiate, Father Vary served as missionary first at Sault Ste. Marie in Michigan, then in Ontario until his death on April 12, 1878. Sisters of Charity of Providence, *Institute*, 5:388–89.

3. Anonymous, *The Right Reverend John B. Brondel, Bishop of Helena; A Memorial* (Helena, Mont.: State Publishing Company, 1904), 5–7.

4. A decade later, in a letter to his brother in Belgium describing Steilacoom's Easter solemnity of 1877, Brondel revealed both his success in drawing attendees and the range of their origins: the church was filled from early morning to evening with farmers coming from as far away as eighteen miles; "five young ladies sang a high mass with unction, four choir boys assisted the priest with incense; fifty candles illuminated the altar, decorated with the best ornaments, tapestries, the walls decorated with greens, of the eighty persons present, all but five were Catholic, and belonged to seven different nationalities." J. B. A. Brondel to Charles Brondel, April 2, 1877, Archives, Diocese of Helena, Helena, Mont.

5. Blanchet's wishes were granted. Twelve years later, on December 14, 1879, Father Brondel was consecrated bishop of Vancouver Island by his predecessor and Louvain college classmate, Charles John Seghers, who, having served as bishop of Vancouver Island following the death of Bishop Modeste Demers in July 1871, had been appointed coadjutor with the right of succession to Archbishop F. N. Blanchet in Oregon City. On March 5, 1883, Brondel was appointed apostolic administrator of Montana. On March 7, 1884, Pope Leo XIII appointed Brondel first bishop of the newly erected diocese of Helena, which included the territory of today's state of Montana. There, among other missions, he had within his jurisdiction the Jesuit priests and the Sisters of Providence at St. Ignatius. With considerable effort, he would enable the Northern Cheyenne, to whom he was particularly close, to retain their Tongue River home as a reservation. *The Right Reverend John B. Brondel*, 9–12; Schoenberg, *Catholic Church in the Pacific Northwest*, 289.

To Ignace Bourget, Bishop of Montreal, October 10, 1867

When Blanchet wrote this letter, Bishop Bourget was nearly sixty-eight years old and had served as bishop of Montreal for thirty years. Effective leader of the Canadian Catholic Church, he had launched the institutional revolution that made Quebec unique in North America for its church control of health, education, and social welfare. His priests were among the first bishops in several North American dioceses, and he had sent religious communities throughout the continent to provide spiritual and temporal care to Catholics and First Nations. Having spearheaded discussions in Rome to separate the Oregon Country from the Diocese of Quebec in 1843, at the request of his superior, Archbishop Signay, he had since maintained a sense of personal interest in the survival of the Oregon Province. This letter's tone of gratitude was in order.[1]

Writing with the warmth of a friend addressing a longtime supporter and colleague, Blanchet describes a recent tour of his diocese. In this romantic tableau, Blanchet, seventy years of age himself, has replaced the saddle of his first letters with a buggy. Rather than a neophyte in a largely Native American land, he has become a veteran frontier bishop making episcopal rounds on newly surveyed roads to the corners of his multiethnic diocese. In spite of advances in transportation, travel throughout much of the territory was still for the hardy. The emphasis on Canadien communities and the success of the Sisters of Providence establishments reflects the interests of the recipient.

Vancouver, October 10th 1867

Monsignor,

I am seizing this opportunity to give you some sign of life, and among other things, to report that Mother Philomène's visit had a decidedly good influence on the little community. Her maternal advice and slight modifications of the offices, by the grace of God, restored peace along with its inevitable fruits. We pray that they not be lost.[2]

Father Charles Vary has requested to return to his diocese, and I have consented. I place him back in your hands. Thank you most sincerely for having entrusted him to me during a time when I lacked a means to provide for the spiritual needs in some parts of the diocese. He rendered a great service. God will recompense him for his work.

If the Fathers' Petition of the Second Plenary Council of Baltimore succeeds, then Idaho and that portion of Montana lying to the west of the summit of the Rocky Mountains will soon be detached from the Diocese of Nesqualy, to form a separate apostolic vicariate. With this partition, the diocese will have no missions beyond Colville, which is to the east & about 400 miles from Vancouver; and it will extend no more than about eight degrees from the east to the Pacific, and three degrees from the north to the south, as described above.[3]

During the summer, I was able to visit the missions of what will be the eastern and western extremities of the diocese after the apostolic vicariate is erected. The Colville Valley is about 400 miles to the east of Vancouver, and can only be reached by a tortuous road. The journey from Walla Walla by "buggy," a carriage with four wheels, takes four and a half days. This journey is anything but pleasant. Long stretches of rugged, rocky roads traverse arid plains, and there are mountains to be scaled, sometimes by foot, to relieve the horses. Houses are as rare as stones are common, you see scarcely three or four in the space of 150 miles; but you do not stay there even when they are located where you need to camp for the night, it is preferable to sleep in a tent near a stream. There, the fire is lit in an instant, the pot is hung for tea or coffee, the meat is cooked or warmed again in the frying pan. Once it's ready, the table is set without ado, we sit on the grass if there is any, and eat heartily, after having been jolted about more than we would have wished for twelve to thirteen hours. Some time thereafter, we stretch out on a rustic bed that is set up in two or three minutes, and sleep more or less well, as in former times. In the morning, after having breakfast with the same ado as supper of the night before, we again take to the road at 5:30 or 6:00, only to experience the same bumps and jolts as the day before. In this manner we spend the four and a half days en route there as well as the return. This is what bishops' tours are like here when they want to visit flocks confided to their care in the most remote corners of their dioceses.

In the Colville region there are two missions. The one for whites is composed mostly of Canadiens and their descendants. Forty Catholic families are scattered across this valley almost thirty miles in length. A forty by twenty-foot chapel, built through the efforts of Father Menetrey, S.J., serves all the Catholics in the valley, the farthest living fifteen to twenty miles away. The soil here is very good; the settlers could be rich within a few years if they had a market for their products and were more industrious.[4]

The Indian mission is twelve to fifteen miles farther and completely separate from the whites'. Due to a misunderstanding, the missionary and the Indians were not there when I came.[5]

In Walla Walla, 200 and some odd miles from here, is a chapel for the English-speaking population. The convent of the Sisters of the House of Providence is a distance of a few arpents from it.[6] St. Rose chapel, built for the Canadiens settled along the Walla Walla River, is six or seven miles from the city. About twenty families live there. They have the best land of the region, yet they are no better off for that. For the most part, they are a degenerate brood, lacking in diligence and thrift, & weak in faith.

At the other extremity of my visit are the Lummis, at the far end of Bellingham Bay, a short distance from Mount Baker, 250 miles by road from here. The Lummis are reputed to be the best Indians of Puget Sound and the surrounding area. They are 269 in number, are all Christians, and live comfortably, in part because they cultivate their very fertile land. Father Chirouse, O.M.I., has instructed them. They are two days by canoe from Father's residence; several times a year during the major feast days, they visit him in large numbers. On my way there I encountered several canoes headed toward Father's residence in Tulalip for the Assumption of the Blessed Virgin Mary. They turned and followed me; by the time I arrived at their mission, no less than eight canoes were within a short distance of mine. I stayed there a few days and administered the sacrament of Confirmation to a fair number. Reverend Father Beaudre, O.M.I., accompanied me and prepared them. The ardent faith they showed in approaching the Tribunal of Penance and the Holy Table was truly enlightening.[7] This is the largest nucleus of Christian Indians in this part of the diocese. There is a plan to move several little camps of Indians, presently dispersed here and there, to this mission; if this happens, there will be no fewer than 600 souls living here. Before my departure, these good Lummis begged me to provide them a resident missionary and some sisters to teach their children. If the confederation I just mentioned takes place, I trust that the government will provide a means for responding to their wishes.[8]

On the road from Vancouver to the Lummi Mission is St. Francis Xavier Mission, on the Cowlitz River. This mission, about eighty miles from here, was established in 1839. It flourished for several years. But after the death of the first settlers, Canadiens and former engagés of the Hudson's Bay Company, it was reduced to a most sorry state. It is beginning to pick up again, thanks to some new settlers who are more industrious and less prodigal. At the request of Catholic and non-Catholic settlers, Reverend Father Richard,[9] who is in charge, began a convent school for girls, which he hopes to finish next year. The Sisters of Providence will occupy it, should the community be able to provide some sisters.[10]

About forty miles farther along the road from the Cowlitz mission is Olympia, the capital of the territory, situated on the shore and at the lower end of the Sound. There, few Catholics are to be found.

From there, one proceeds twenty-five miles to Steilacoom, a little town where the convent is located. The sisters have lovely property on a plateau that overlooks the town and offers a most stunning view. Steamers and sailing ships go by from time to time, and the islands that are strewn about provide a pleasant sojourn for the young. The convent is prosperous and respected by citizens of all religious denominations on the Sound. Obstacles that arose in establishing it seemed a guarantee that it would bring about much good; I was not mistaken. The mission chapel is on the same block as the convent, facing the Sound. It is forty by twenty feet in size. There are about twenty-five families in this mission, with as many living in the town as in the countryside.

Thirty miles to the north of Steilacoom is the town of Seattle, initially known as New York! Shortly thereafter it was called Alky, which means *in the future, after a while* in Chinouk. This town is at the end of a large sound and promises to become important. The territory's university is located there. Although few Catholic families live in the town, there are some in the surrounding countryside, as many whites as Indians on the White River. It has been proposed that a church be built in the near future. There is also a desire to see a convent there, but the time is not yet right for a foundation of this sort. It is about thirty miles from Seattle to Tulalip. This year I was able to make the trip on a little steamer that carries the mail for several localities between Seattle and Whatcom, eight miles from the Lummi Mission I just spoke of. The mission buildings are situated at the end of a little bay, on land that is difficult to clear and, worse yet, not very suitable for cultivation. However, by dint of work and patience, the missionaries, along with their Indian pupils, have cleared at least a dozen arpents, where they plant barley, oats, potatoes, &c, which lends to their keep. In past years they were obliged to make summer excursions on the Sound to obtain clothing. Until this year, the fathers received little from the government in support of the settlement, though they had at least thirty at the boarding school. This year they had close to sixty from different tribes, including the Lummis. The Oblate missionaries reside with the tribe called Snohomish. It is there that in 1864 I confirmed 134 Indians, young and old, at a gathering of 300. Since then, I have confirmed a fair number upon each visit. The house occupied by the missionaries, built with government funds, is thirty-two by eighteen, with two floors and a lean-to for the kitchen and refectory. The pupils' house is of the same dimensions, as well as the one built for the sisters. Between the latter and the priests' house, sufficient space was left for a chapel. Next to the house destined for the sisters, there will be another for their pupils.

As a result of mediation on the part of Reverend Grand Vicar Brouillet, the government promised 500 dollars annually for the support and instruction of the boys (by the priests), and of the girls (by the sisters). That is very little, given especially that the payment is to be made in paper (*legal tenders*). There is hope, however, that the government will give a supplement or will increase the allocation. Whatever happens, the sisters are prepared to take on their share of obligations and are only awaiting the signal to come to their station. Something worth noting: the government desires to have sisters teach not only the Indian girls of the Tulalip Mission; allocations are promised to the same effect for the Lapwai Mission among the Nez Percés of this diocese, and for the Umatillas in the archdiocese. So we have reason for rejoicing over this government policy for our missions and over the appreciation that has been shown for the services rendered by the sisters. The number of Indians continues to diminish. In 1864, however, an agent believed that there were still 10,000 in the Puget Sound area and along the Pacific shore; a greater number were counted in the mountains to the east of Washington Territory. The Oblate fathers alone have baptized more than 3,000 on the Sound. Other missionaries have baptized several thousand more. The majority of Indians die in their infancy before reaching the age of reason; whence it might be said that our missionaries have populated the celestial region with legions of blessed ones who, without doubt, will intercede for those who made it possible for them to enjoy the abundance of the house of the Lord and quench their thirst in the torrent of his paradise. May I partake one day of their happiness!

Your most devoted,
Aug. M. A. Bp. of Nesqualy

ACAM, FILE 195.133, 867–71.

———◆———

1. Roberto Perin, "French-Speaking Canada from 1840," in Murphy and Perin, *Christianity in Canada*, 211–12; Pouliot, *Monseigneur Bourget et son temps*, 2:67.

2. Mother Philomène, superior general of the Sisters of Providence, arrived for an official visit at Vancouver on December 8, 1866 (in the company of A. M. A. and F. N. Blanchet, returning from the Baltimore council and Montreal, and four new sisters—Jean de la Croix, Benoît-Joseph, Bernardin de Sienne, and Ambroise—and three tertiary sisters). She visited the sisters' establishments in Walla Walla from February 20 to March 27; Steilacoom and Tulalip from May 1 to July 5, 1867. It is likely that her visit to the Sound coincided with the episcopal visit that Blanchet describes in this letter. During the superior general's visit, Sister Praxedes was named superior (sister servant) and vicar over the Providence missions located throughout the Old Oregon Country, and Sister Joseph named bursar. Mother Philomène departed for Montreal on October 15, 1867, accompanied by Father Vary. This letter's date and opening line suggest that she was asked to deliver it. The original letter is preserved in the Providence Motherhouse Archives in Montreal.

3. On March 3, 1863, Congress set off that portion of Washington lying east of Oregon and the 117th meridian of west longitude, to form the Idaho Territory. On May 26, 1864, Congress set off the Montana Territory, from the northeastern part of the Idaho Territory. Blanchet had suggested that separate vicariates for Idaho and Montana be erected, for otherwise "a bishop sufficiently spry to visit its entire expanse" would be necessary (Blanchet to J. S. Alemany, Bishop of San Francisco, April 6, 1866, AAS, A5: 320). The Apostolic Vicariates of Idaho and Montana, originally split along the Continental Divide, were erected March 3, 1868. Louis Aloysius Lootens of the American College in Louvain served as first vicar apostolic of Idaho from 1868 to 1876. Other than Lootens's time in Idaho, and until Brondel's appointment to Montana in 1883, both vicariates were governed at a distance, Idaho by Oregon City and Montana by Nebraska. Right Reverend Cyprian Bradley, O.S.B., and Most Reverend Edward Kelly, D.D., Ph.D., *History of the Diocese of Boise, 1863–1952*, 2 vols. (Boise, Idaho: Roman Catholic Diocese of Boise, 1953), 1:36–39; Schoenberg, *A History of the Catholic Church*, 197.

4. Father Joseph Menetrey, S.J. (1812–1891), arrived in Oregon in 1848. Blanchet is describing the church of Immaculate Conception that Irish soldiers built in 1862 at military Fort Colville (1859–1882), located next to the unincorporated white and Canadien settlements of Colville. Schoenberg, *Catholic Church in the Pacific Northwest*, 190, 209.

5. See letter 19, note 4, for a description of the Jesuit mission of St. Paul.

6. The 200 miles refer to the distance from Vancouver to Walla Walla, traveled by steamers up the Columbia and overland from Wallulu (formerly Fort Walla Walla) on the Columbia to Walla Walla. The trip of four and a half days and 200-plus miles is from Walla Walla to Colville. A measure used on former seignorial domains in Quebec, an arpent was about 180 French feet, 191.835 British feet, or 58.47 meters.

7. "Tribunal of Penance" refers to the Roman Catholic sacrament of reconciliation, a ritual in which a person confesses sins to a priest and receives absolution, enacting forgiveness from God. The "Holy Table" refers to the altar. Those receiving Communion come forward toward the altar to receive it.

8. The Lummi mission was located on the northern shore of Bellingham Bay, north of Tulalip Mission St. Anne.

9. Father Charles-Louis Augustin Richard was ordained at Vancouver, February 14, 1864. He served at the Cowlitz mission from 1865 to 1873. Parishioners' concerns about his collecting money and materials under false pretext resulted in a threatened lawsuit against him. The bishop replaced him with a Belgian, Father Peter F. Hylebos of the American College of Louvain, who brought stability to the mission (AAS, A6).

10. The Sisters of Providence opened a convent and staffed a school at Cowlitz beginning in 1876.

LETTER 38

To Francis Xavier Prefontaine, Missionary, October 14, 1867

Just four days prior to writing this letter to Father Prefontaine, Blanchet, who had recently visited Seattle, wrote to Bourget of the town's promise to become important and of the proposal for a church and an establishment of sisters, the last of which he considered premature (see letter 37). Now he turned his attention to the young priest's request to relocate to Seattle. At the time he made his request, Father Prefontaine was still the associate for the Steilacoom mission. But for over two years he had been serving the mission from a northern base in Port Townsend.

While locating Prefontaine in Port Townsend may have provided a practical solution to a strained relationship with Father Vary (see letter 34), it also made strategic sense. In 1867, Port Townsend was the major commercial city on Puget Sound, its location congenial to large sailing vessels. It was easier to get to other points on the northern Sound from Port Townsend than from Steilacoom.[1] From this vantage point, Father Prefontaine watched post–Civil War development on Puget Sound, including growth along its northern portion and indications that Seattle would expand.

The ebb and flow of population in his diocese—and the always open question of whether the population would support a Catholic establishment—complicated Blanchet's decisions about where to place the personnel at his disposal. With the strong likelihood that the railroad terminus would be sited at Tacoma, and the impending departure of the army from Fort Steilacoom, he knew that the fate of Steilacoom as a major population, governmental, and commercial center was sealed. So, while insisting that Prefontaine continue to contribute to the Steilacoom mission, Blanchet was willing to allow him to attempt an establishment in Seattle.[2]

This letter shows Bishop Blanchet grappling not only with the placement of Catholic establishments but also with their timing. In addition, it reflects his ongoing concerns with mission finances and his desire to keep a firm hand on his subordinates.

Vancouver, October 14th 1867

Father,

I just received your letter of the 9th instant. I see that with Dr. O'Brien's departure, your position is hardly enviable.[3] Little remains for you to do, and there is not much source of revenue. But, according to all appearances, you will bring in more from the various ports than last year, since the logging business is better than it's been for several years. As for Seattle, I would have no objection to letting you go there if I knew that the Steilacoom Mission could survive on its own, or without Seattle. Last year, there was a request to have a priest in Seattle, and we were told that he would find his keep there. If people are of the same disposition, and if you are willing to give a portion of your collections from the stations to the north or to the west to the missionary at Steilacoom, should he be in need, I think that your plan could be of benefit to all parties. Let me know what you think of this proposal. Depending upon your response, I will see what remains to be done.

Turning to the present, I see that you are silent about the visit to the Indians of the Sound that I had asked you to make last summer. Have you failed to visit them? And if so, for what grave reasons? It is important that I know, and it is your duty to tell me.[4] Inform me about this matter at your earliest.

Aug. M. A. Bp. of Nesq.

AAS, B7: 6–7.

———•———

1. Rossi, *Six Years on the West Coast*, 169.

2. Prefontaine visited Seattle for the first time in October 1867. He rented a house near Third Avenue and Yesler Way, converted one room into a church, and said Mass on November 24, 1867. Schoenberg, *Catholic Church in the Pacific Northwest*, 206–8. Edward J. O'Dea (1856–1932), the first U.S.-born bishop of Nesqualy (1896–1906; Seattle 1907–32), would make Seattle his see city and receive Vatican approval to rename the diocese "Seattle."

3. Dr. Patrick O'Brien, director of the naval hospital, gave 500 francs to build the church in Port Townsend. He had provided room and board to Father Rossi at minimal cost. Rossi, *Six Years on the West Coast*, 169.

4. On February 4, 1867, Blanchet had written Prefontaine: "I made the resolution to have all Indians who are in your jurisdiction visited this year. And as it is appropriate, I charge you in this visit" (AAS, A5: 331). The tone of Blanchet's query about this visit conveys his concern about Prefontaine's submission to his authority. The injunction shows that priests were serving off-reservation, indigenous peoples on the Sound.

LETTER 39

To J. B. A. Brouillet, Vicar-General, January 20, 1868

On February 6, 1867, Bishop Blanchet charged Vicar-General Brouillet with jurisdiction over the Mission of St. Patrick of Walla Walla, to include all the Catholic population in the county of Walla Walla and surroundings, and the Mission of St. Rose during the absence of the missionary there. Brouillet cared for this vast mission until the end of November 1872, when he returned for a fourth time to Washington, D.C. Sacramental records of Walla Walla and St. Rose during these almost six years reveal multiple ethnicities among Catholics. Within the space of a typical three-week period, from July 14 to August 4, 1867, Father Brouillet baptized Louise, the child of Indian parents from California, adopted by Jesus Hunios; buried Juan Solis from the Republic of Mexico; baptized Charles, son of Canadiens Francis Lapierre and Madeleine Maloin, sponsored by William and Joanna Kolhoff; and buried Samuel O'Donnell.[1]

With this growing, multiethnic population, there appears to have come, as well, an expansion in church activities. Traditional devotion was not lost; for example, on November 1, 1867, Father Brouillet, with Bishop Blanchet's approval, erected the Way of the Cross in the chapel of the Sisters of Providence at Walla Walla, in the presence of the sisters and their pupils.[2] But, to the bishop's horror, Father Brouillet also apparently approved Walla Walla residents' holding a ball on Christmas Day, to benefit the sisters' establishments. In this prickly letter of admonishment, Blanchet reveals the limits of his ability to adapt to the mixing of religious and social activities that characterized much religious life on the frontier.[3]

Vancouver, January 20th 1868

Father,

News of the Christmas day ball in Walla Walla created a sensation here. As it was announced some weeks in advance, you undoubtedly gave appropriate warning to the Catholics, in church and elsewhere, but were not listened to. Those poor Catholics, who think only of the present! A ball on Christmas day is what we are told here! And for the benefit of the sisters!!! Will they accept the fruit of profaning such a significant day? If they do, how would a priest then dare raise his voice against similar entertainment on days consecrated to God?

We simply couldn't understand it. The general sentiment was, in fact, that the sisters should not accept the proceeds from the ball, and if they have, that they should return them, as a lesson to the Catholics, and to show the Protestants that the lure of profit is no excuse for tolerating what is reprehensible in the eyes of all good Catholics. As for me, I can only express regret should the slightest [*sign*] of approval have been given; and hope that this will not prove harmful in any way to our holy Religion.

......I am . . . .

Aug. M. A. Bp. of Nesq.

AAS, B7: 15.

———————•—•———————

1. Munnick and Munnick, "St. Patrick and St. Rose of Lima, in *Catholic Church Records of the Pacific Northwest*, vol. 7, 55–56–57 through 58–59–60.

2. Ibid.

3. See Maffly-Kipp, *Religion and Society in Frontier California*, 110–47.

LETTER 40

To Peter De Smet, Society of Jesus, February 15, 1871[1]

Blanchet penned this hopeful letter to the Jesuit, Father Peter De Smet, eleven years after his first formal complaint to Superintendent of Indian Affairs Edward Geary about a Methodist's appointment as superintendent of instruction on the Yakama Reservation (see letter 24). The situation at Simcoe had only worsened, since Reverend Wilbur's appointment as agent.[2] But, with Ulysses S. Grant's new "Indian Peace Policy," Blanchet saw hope for finally getting Catholics into official positions on the Yakama Reservation and on other reservations where Catholic missionaries had been most active.

The "Peace Policy" was intended to combat rampant corruption in the Indian service and to implement a more successful means of pacifying the western tribes and assimilating Indians into U.S., Euro-American culture than previous policies had provided. However, the revisions in the new federal Indian policy were never fully implemented. Despite high-minded intentions, the Indian service remained a pawn in battles of political patronage and power, riddled with widespread corruption and premised on racist assumptions about Native Americans.[3]

The key feature of the Peace Policy that prompted Blanchet to write De Smet was the allocation of reservations to different Christian denominations for the purposes of their recommending men of sound moral character to be agents; providing sub-personnel, including teachers; and contributing funds to the project of assimilating and "Christianizing" Indians. Blanchet had long supported having denominations involved in the Indian service, believing, as did his Protestant adversaries, that religious persons with strong moral principles would be more suited to doing this important and difficult work and resistant to corruption. He too believed that this new, "peaceful," and "enlightened" approach to Indian affairs would be an improvement over current practice. (As the subjects of assimilation, the Indians themselves had no self-representation in the process. The absence of their voices is striking.)

In a December 1870 message to the U.S. Congress, President Grant formally announced his Peace Policy. In it the president stated that agencies would be assigned to "such religious denominations as had hitherto established missionaries among the Indians and perhaps to some other denominations who would undertake the work on the same terms—that is, as missionary work."[4]

In Grant's words Blanchet read the promise of redress to his long-standing grievance regarding the Methodist Wilbur's presence among the Yakamas at Simcoe. Believing that Father De Smet, the already famous founder of the Jesuits' Rocky Mountain Mission whom he knew personally, had been appointed a member of the Board of Commissioners of Indian Affairs, the group that would recommend the allocation of reservations among denominations, Blanchet wasted no time in seeking his aid.

Vancouver, February 15th 1871

My Reverend Father,

I am pleased to hear that you are one of the commissioners of Indian Affairs.[5] If it is true that the administration is serious about appointing Catholic agents to our Indian missions, you assuredly will not fail to assist us with our valid requests. You are already acquainted with several of the missions in the diocese that were founded by regular as well as secular missionaries. These include Colville Mission founded by your fathers, Tulalip Mission on Puget Sound, founded by the Oblate Fathers, St. Joseph of Ahtanum in the Yakima Valley, founded by the same fathers. The Yakama Mission goes back to 1847.

According to the new system, these missions are entitled to have Catholic agents.[6] The Indians on Puget Sound were all evangelized by the Oblate Fathers (and earlier by the first missionaries who arrived in 1838). Among others are the missions of the Puyallups and the Nisqually, and the Scocomish. So the Puyallups and the Scocomish should also have Catholic agents. I think that the Puyallup agent also serves the Nisqually. Missionaries also evangelized the Chehelis before 1847. They should have a Catholic agent as well. I think they have been relocated at Quinault.

I have already submitted the name of J. B. Boulet[7] as agent for the Simcoe of Yakama. Reverend Father Grassi was to have put forward someone for Colville. Citizens of the Tulalip area sent a petition for the appointment of the reservation's Reverend Father Eugène-Casimir Chirouse. If this petition is not heeded, you can submit the name of Alexander Spithill,[8] whom the Reverend Father recommends as a person capable of carrying out the duties.

As for the other agencies that I am requesting, I will be ready to submit names to you as soon as I know if they have been given to Catholics. Our interests are within our grasp.

While awaiting a reply, I remain most fondly,
A. M. A. B. Bp. N.

AAS, B7: 75.

<hr />

1. Peter De Smet, S.J. (1801–1873), was born in Termonde, Belgium; emigrated to the United States in 1821; and entered the Jesuit novitiate at Whitemarsh, Maryland. In 1823, he helped found the Missouri Province of the Society of Jesus. In 1838, he began his work as a missionary to the Indians, facilitating peace negotiations between tribes and, later, between Indians and whites. In 1840, he led the foundation of the Rocky Mountain Mission of the Jesuits. He traveled to Europe in 1843 to solicit funds and personnel for work with the Indians, returning to Oregon in 1844. De Smet subsequently was called back to St. Louis for other assignments. He continued to speak, write, solicit funds, and in other ways advance the Jesuits' work with Indians. He also

served as a negotiator with the U.S. Army in treaty negotiations with Plains tribes. *The Catholic Encyclopedia*, s.v. "De Smet, Pierre-Jean."

2. The "Methodist" was Rev. James Wilbur, whom Abraham Lincoln appointed as agent on June 9, 1864 (Helland, *There Were Giants*, 90).

3. On the history of the Grant Peace Policy, see Prucha, *The Great Father*, 1:479–553; Keller, *American Protestantism and United States Indian Policy*; Rahill, *Catholic Indian Missions and Grant's Peace Policy*; and Elsie Mitchell Rushmore, *The Indian Policy during Grant's Administration* (Jamaica, N.Y.: Marion Press, 1914). On De Smet's involvement with it, see Killoren, *"Come, Blackrobe,"* 334–44; and Robert C. Carriker, *Father Peter John De Smet: Jesuit in the West*, Oklahoma Western Biographies Series (Norman: University of Oklahoma Press, 1998), 230–33.

4. Quoted in Rahill, *Catholic Indian Missions and Grant's Peace Policy*, 36.

5. Blanchet was mistaken about De Smet being a member of the Board of Indian Commissioners. In fact, he was not, but he had been invited to meet with the board when it gathered with representatives of denominations about the implementation of the new policy of dividing reservations among them. De Smet was invited by Secretary of the Interior Delano, who had consulted with only a few bishops, and he was the sole Catholic present at the joint meeting on January 3, 1871. De Smet also had been invited to the May 1870 meetings of the Executive Committee of the United States Indian Commission at which initial discussions of the apportionment of reservations among denominations took place, but he had not been able to attend. Most of the U.S. Catholic bishops were unavailable for meetings in 1870 because they were in Rome for the First Vatican Council. Rahill, *Catholic Indian Missions and Grant's Peace Policy*, 38, 46–47; Killoren, *"Come, Black Robe,"* 340.

6. Blanchet based his claim for Catholic entitlement on Grant's 1870 message to Congress.

7. On J. B. Boulet and his work among the Yakamas, see letter 32, note 7.

8 Alexander Spithill (1824–1920), of Scotland, came to California in 1849 and arrived in Puget Sound in October 1856. He was employed to carry U.S. mail between reservations and military posts, subsequently settling on Camano Island, where he worked at a spar camp. He established the first logging camp in the Marysville area and, in 1870, married his third wife, Anastasia Newman, a Tulalip of mixed heritage, with whom he had nine children. He taught farming and carpentry on the Tulalip Reservation from 1869 to 1872. Hunt and Kaylor, *Washington, West of the Cascades*, 1:404; William S. Prosser, *A History of the Puget Sound Country: Its Resources, Its Commerce, and Its People* (New York: Lewis Publishing Company, 1903), 410–11.

To James Roosevelt Bayley,
Archbishop of Baltimore,
June 15, 1873[1]

The hope with which Blanchet wrote De Smet in 1871 had been dashed. Of the thirty-eight reservations to which the Catholic Church considered itself entitled under Grant's Peace Policy because of its claims to early and ongoing missionary effort, it had been assigned only seven of the initial assignments of seventy-one. Those were the Flathead, Tulalip, Colville, Grand Ronde, Umatilla, Grand River, and Devil's Lake reservations.[2]

Neither formal requests from A. M. A. Blanchet, his brother, Archbishop François Norbert Blanchet, and other ecclesiastics nor lobbying of President Grant by sympathetic prominent Catholics in Washington, D.C., succeeded in securing the changes to the initial assignment of reservations that they sought. In response to President Grant's unwillingness to intervene on behalf of Catholic claims and to the clear Protestant bias of the Board of Indian Commissioners and the secretary of the Interior, Columbus Delano, Bishop Blanchet, Father Brouillet, and others worked to establish a permanent, nongovernmental presence in Washington, D.C., to represent Catholic Indian interests.[3]

In 1873, Archbishop Bayley appointed Washington attorney Charles Ewing as the first Catholic commissioner of Indian Affairs.[4] This appointment was the initial step in the creation of the Bureau of Catholic Indian Missions. The appointment formalized, Bishop Blanchet wanted his vicar-general, J. B. A. Brouillet, who had been in Washington helping with the effort, to return to the diocese.

Keenly aware of Brouillet's successful experience negotiating on behalf of Catholic missions for over a decade, Blanchet knew his value to the new Catholic office. He was not, however, willing to continue having the Diocese of Nesqualy bear the expense of Brouillet's contribution to the work of Catholic Indian affairs, a work that he believed was the responsibility of all bishops.

Monsignor,

I received your favor of [. . .] May. Here is my response. Grand Vicar Brouillet has secured a lawyer to defend the Vancouver section at the next session of Congress, and he has entrusted matters concerning our Indian missions to the agent approved by the bishops for all such issues. Monsignor of Oregon and I have therefore decided that he can return to his station, once he has conveyed essential information on our missions to the appointed agent.

I am not surprised that Mr. Ewing wishes to keep him to assist with the difficult task he has undertaken, nor can I blame him. I think that this could be very useful if not necessary in several instances. But I am concerned that Vicar General Brouillet's vast mission is suffering from an absence that has already been prolonged beyond expectations, and then there is the additional, important matter of finances.[5] The Diocese of Nesqualy, the poorest of all the dioceses in the U.S., cannot take on the expenses of an assistant alone.

If the important issue of the Indian missions is presently attracting the attention of bishops in the Republic, it is owing undeniably to the actions of the bishops of Oregon and Nesqualy, who have unceasingly pleaded this cause for the last several years to the Indian Department, and in newspapers. Through such actions, they have succeeded in arousing public opinion. In referring to this achievement I am not seeking recognition for them. Far from it. I simply want to make it understood that, having incurred costs in getting to this point, which now, by the grace of God, is to the benefit of all, any new sacrifices should be shared by all interested parties. In other words, if Mr. Ewing needs an assistant, all the bishops involved should contribute to the costs, not just the poorest.

I believe that this, Monsignor, needs be borne in mind with regard to Mr. Ewing's request.

If conditions allow, I would be happy to see Father Brouillet remain in Washington, or to send him back there to work for the good of all Indian missions in the various dioceses. I think that he is well qualified to handle such matters, given his experience of twenty-five years.

Respectfully and most faithfully yours, Monsignor,
A. M. A. Blanchet, Bp. of Nesqualy

AAS, B7: 126–27.

———•———

1. James Roosevelt Bayley (1814–1877) was born at Rye, New York. From an elite family, he became an Episcopal priest and then, in 1842, converted to Roman Catholicism. He was ordained as a Catholic priest in 1844 and served as a professor and vice-president of the seminary at Fordham. In 1853, he became the first bishop of Newark, New Jersey. He was named archbishop of Baltimore on July 30, 1872, taking over the primary see in the U.S. Church in the midst of the Catholic conflicts with the Grant administration over reservations and Indian missions. Lack of familiarity with the issues and ill health impeded the pace and energy with which he addressed the project. *The Catholic Encyclopedia*, s.v. "Bayley, James Roosevelt."

2. The initial allocation of reservations was based on the list drawn up in 1870 by Vincent Coyler, secretary of the Board of Indian Commissioners that Congress had created in 1869. Few changes were made to the list that he submitted to then secretary of the Interior Jacob D. Cox. In the original 1871 allocations of seventy-one reservations, "Hicksite and Orthodox Friends already controlled a total of sixteen; Methodists received fourteen; Presbyterians, nine; Episcopalians, eight; Roman Catholics, seven; Baptists, five; Dutch Reformed, five; Congregationalists (American Missionary Association), three; the American Board, one; Unitarians, two; and Lutherans one" (Keller, *American Protestantism and United States Indian Policy*, 35–36; also 219–22). Keller's treatment of confusion about the definition of what should have been counted as "missionary work" and dispute among denominations over it contributes to an understanding of the complexity of the contest in which Blanchet was engaged (see Keller, 33–36). Modeled on the successful Freedman's Commission, itself an example of a tradition of evangelical Protestant reform movements, the Board of Indian Commissioners was to be composed of successful, religiously minded businessmen and reformers. At the time of the board's allocation to denominations, no Catholic sat on the Board of Indian Commissioners, and no clear principles for assigning denominations to reservations had been specified. With Indian assimilation and Americanism associated with evangelical Protestantism, the exclusion of Catholic representation is not surprising. For other sources on the history of the Peace Policy, see letter 40, note 3.

3. Some reassignments were made, and in 1873 the Catholics gained Standing Rock and Papago, but lost Grant River (Keller, *American Protestantism and United States Indian Policy*, 219). On the efforts of A. M. A. Blanchet, F. N. Blanchet, and others to create a permanent Catholic presence in Washington, D.C., one that could speak for the entire Catholic Church in the United States on Indian issues, see Rahill, *Catholic Indian Missions and Grant's Peace Policy*, 76–119. Among the sympathetic Washington, D.C. Catholics was Father George Deshon (1823–1903), Grant's roommate at West Point, who graduated second in his class in 1843, after which he taught mathematics and ethics there. He resigned his commission as captain in the U.S. Army and was received into the Roman Catholic Church in 1851. Deshon entered the Redemptorists and was

ordained a priest in 1855; in 1858, with Isaac Hecker and two others he founded the Paulist Institute. (*The Catholic Encyclopedia*, s.v. "Deshon, George"). Also sympathetic was Eleanor [Ellen] Boyle Ewing Sherman (1824–1888), wife of General William T. Sherman, who was the daughter of Senator Thomas Ewing of Ohio. Katherine Burton, *Three Generations: Maria Boyle Ewing (1801–1864), Ellen Ewing Sherman (1824–1888), Minnie Sherman Fitch (1851–1913)* (New York: Longmans, Green, 1947); Patrick W. Carey, *Catholics in America: A History* (Westport, Conn.: Praeger, 2004), 51. While she had some influence on General Grant in the 1860s, by the 1870s she claimed to have none because her father's family did not belong to the Republican Party. Ellen Ewing Sherman to Martin John Spalding, Washington, July 13, 1869, quoted in Rahill, *Catholic Indian Missions and Grant's Peace Policy*, 64n11.

4. General Charles Ewing (1835–1893) was named first Catholic commissioner of Indian Affairs by Archbishop Bayley in March 1873. Son of Ohio Senator Thomas Ewing, Charles Ewing was educated in Catholic schools, studied law at the University of Virginia, and attained the rank of brigadier general during the Civil War. After the war, he resumed the practice of law. Rahill, *Catholic Indian Missions and Grant's Peace Policy*, 72–85; *The Twentieth Century Biographical Dictionary of Notable Americans*, s.v. "Ewing, Charles."

5. Brouillet was responsible for Walla Walla, anchor of diocesan missionary work east of the Cascades.

LETTER 42

To Charles Seghers, Bishop of Vancouver Island, December 30, 1873[1]

A. M. A. Blanchet had been a missionary bishop for twenty-seven years when he responded to Charles Seghers, the newly appointed bishop of Vancouver Island. Bishop Seghers's appointment marked a turning in the history of the Ecclesiastical Province of Oregon, for he succeeded Modeste Demers, one of the original two missionaries from Quebec who arrived in the Oregon Country in 1838. With the Province straddling an international border, questions of discipline and practice arose.

In his response to Segher's letter, Blanchet states candidly his preference for the discipline and practice of the Catholic Church in Quebec. It was, he believed, more in conformity with Rome, his template of the "universal church," than was the Catholic Church in either the United States or France.

Monsignor,

I received your letter of the 23rd instant. Still a word concerning discipline. A peculiar thing! Although I came to this country nine years after the first missionaries, even more than they, I valued our preservation of the discipline they had brought from Quebec. In adopting and publishing the decrees of the Councils of Baltimore, I said that "they should be followed in all that is not contrary to the practices that the first missionaries brought from Quebec." In this way I hoped to preserve some vestiges of discipline from the old Church of Canada, whose glory it is to have founded the Church of Oregon.

In 1848, the United States was without full uniformity of discipline. It was not until the first Plenary Council of Baltimore that the decrees of the Councils of Baltimore were extended to all the provinces.[2] But even then they did not establish complete uniformity. I presume that such uniformity will never exist in the Church of the United States, just as it does not exist in the Church of France, &c.

As a whole, the discipline of Quebec conformed more closely to the laws of the universal Church. Now, the Holy See stresses that the general laws be followed unless there is a need to do otherwise. This is why the Holy See did not give in to the request one council made to abolish certain feasts. On the contrary, it insisted that an effort be made to establish uniformity by adhering as closely as possible to the discipline of the universal Church. For this reason, the Immaculate Conception and the Circumcision[3] were proclaimed feasts of obligation for all provinces.

As the discipline brought from Quebec was more in conformity with the discipline of the universal Church, I am taking the liberty to say that it is unlikely that Rome would have wished for us to embrace the discipline of the United States.

As for the days of fasting indicated by the Council of Oregon, I am not aware of any indult that authorizes them. The adage, *Qui tacet consentire videtur* ["He who keeps silent is assumed to consent"], could apply here.

I do not anticipate any success with "a request aiming to place us in conformity with the Province of San Francisco &c."

As you wrote that you intend to send S. Victor's body[4] by way of the

Sound, I did not think it necessary to say anything. You would do well to address it to Father Brondel in Steilacoom.

In a circular dated September 24th 1869, I made it known that all priests officially belonging to the dioceses of Oregon and Vancouver were authorized to preach and confess in this diocese. It would be well to inform Father Mandart of this; and to tell him that I convey all the ordinary powers of pastor, for safety's sake, to him.[5] If you were to do the same for the priests on the Sound, including the Reverend Fathers of Tulalip, that would be good.

As for the boundaries of our dioceses, in 1854 I was of the opinion that they should conform to the civil divisions, and this is still my thought. My request still being in force, it suffices that you submit your desire concerning this matter to Rome, after you reach an understanding with Monsignor the Archbishop.

I will use this opportunity to join many others in offering my best wishes to Your Lordship for the New Year, for the greater glory of God and the good of the faithful confided to your care.

I am &c. . . .
Aug. M. A. Bp. of Nesqualy

AAS, B7: 147–49.

—————•—————

1. Charles John Seghers (1839–1886) was born in Ghent, Belgium; studied for the priesthood at the American College in Louvain; and arrived as missionary priest for the Diocese of Vancouver Island beginning in 1863. He was consecrated bishop of Vancouver Island on June 29, 1873. Seghers succeeded F. N. Blanchet as archbishop of Oregon City in 1880, but returned to be bishop of Vancouver Island again in 1885. He was murdered on November 28, 1886, while on an episcopal visit in Alaska. Gerard G. Steckler, S.J., *Charles John Seghers, Priest and Bishop in the Pacific Northwest, 1839–1886: A Biography* (Fairfield, Wash.: Ye Galleon Press, 1986); James M. Hill, "Archbishop Seghers Pacific Coast Missionary," *Canadian Catholic Historical Association Report* 18 (1951): 15–23.

2. The First Plenary Council of Baltimore convened on May 9–20, 1852. Six archbishops and thirty-five bishops attended. The Canadian bishop of Toronto also attended. The council made the enactments of the seven provincial councils of Baltimore binding on all dioceses in the United States. *The Catholic Encyclopedia*, s.v. "Plenary Councils of Baltimore."

3. Feast of the Circumcision, celebrated at the end of the Octave of Christmas, is the liturgical

celebration of the circumcision of Jesus of Nazareth, in fulfillment of the Jewish law.

4. "S. Victor's body" refers to a wax representation of the saint used as a container to hold a relic. Altars in Catholic churches required the presence of a first-class relic, that is, a fragment from the body of a saint.

5. Father J.-M. Mandart [Mandard], a French priest, had been in Sitka for six years beginning in 1868. Emilien Lamirande, S.R.C., "Le diocèse de l'île de Vancouver (1846) et le vicariat apostolique de la Colombie-Britannique (1863): Limites et situation jurisdique," *Studia canonica* 21 no. 2 (1987): 374.

LETTER 43

To J. B. A. Brouillet, Vicar-General, November 24, 1874

By mid-October 1874, at the urging of his bishop, Vicar-General Brouillet had returned to his mission, which included the Walla Walla establishments of St. Patrick Church, St. Vincent Academy for girls under the care of the Sisters of Providence, St. Joseph Academy for boys, and St. Rose of Lima Chapel in Frenchtown. Father Brouillet's stay in Walla Walla was short, just long enough to put the mission's finances and personnel in order. On February 8, with the blessing of his bishop, he again returned to Washington, D.C.[1]

Striking in this letter is Blanchet's insistence that one of the two priests serving the mission in Brouillet's stead be able to speak French and, if possible, that he be Canadien. His immediate rationale was pragmatic: two-fifths of the mission's Catholics were Canadiens; this ethnic group would be more likely to support one of their own. Up to this time, in trying to establish the Catholic Church among Anglophones in his diocese, Blanchet had insisted that his priests, largely native French speakers, learn English. Ironically, Father Thomas Duffy, an Anglophone from Ireland, who had been serving the mission of Walla Walla since 1870 in Father Brouillet's absence, had not learned French, despite his bishop's promptings.[2]

Evacuated as a consequence of the settlement ban and the Battle of Walla Walla in 1855, many Canadien residents, including William McBean and Marcel Raymond, had returned to the Walla Walla valley by 1859, when the country was officially opened to settlement and claim taking. Other French Canadians had come west with the gold rushes, settled in the Walla Walla valley, and brought along their native language and, it appears, Quebec's tradition of church support. Among these was J. B. Abadie, who turned his Frenchtown home over to Mother Joseph and Sister Catherine when they first traveled to Walla Walla in 1863. Local residents had flocked to the home and donated to the anticipated Walla Walla convent.[3] In addition to helping support Catholic institutions, this reinforcement may have helped slow the cultural erasure already under way at other Canadien settlements in the Washington Territory, such as Colville and Cowlitz.

This ethnicity helps explain Blanchet's desire, expressed in this letter, for the French-speaking priest to be French Canadian. Recent events north of the border provided further rationale. Following the Canadian Confederation of 1867, métis residents of the former HBC-owned Red River region rallied around Catholic métis leader Louis Riel in a successful struggle for the right to self-determination. Anti-Catholic politics in Canada's capital of Ottawa led French Canadians of the newly created province of Quebec to identify with the resisters, calling them "nos amis." Memories of New France's unsuccessful resistance to Great Britain in 1760, and of the Patriote rebellions of 1837–38, surfaced in newspaper reports. Contrary to its tradition of respect for political authority, the Catholic Church hierarchy of Quebec joined in support of Riel. The métis, with growing pride in their uniqueness as a people, formed a provisional government, and, following protracted negotiations, the original minuscule province of Manitoba was created, 140 miles in width and 120 miles deep, from south of Lake Winnipeg to the American border. A dual denominational public school system and recognition of both French and English as official languages were among the rights granted, on the model of diversity that Quebec had been granted in becoming a British province separate from Ontario in 1867.[4]

In writing this letter, the bishop—Canadien at core—may well have hoped to see these triumphs for the French language and state-supported Catholic schools in the Canadian provinces of Manitoba and Quebec instill in Walla Walla residents a new sense of pride in their language and religion.

Father,

I received your letter of the 17th instant, giving the total revenue from December 6th 1872 to the first of the present. How much remains owing? You do not say. Whatever this may be, if it is true that Father Duffy has paid 2,000 piastres in debts over his ordinary expenses, he must have collected more than 1,000 piastres a year. Moreover, Father Duffy believes that the annual revenue is sufficient to support two priests; while pastor during your absence, he managed to do this, so I do not see your reason for concern.

According to the last census, two-fifths of the Catholics in Walla Walla are Canadien. A priest who speaks their language is a must. Once they have one, I am confident that they will once again provide a portion of his keep, particularly if he is *Canadien*.[5] Try to procure one for them as soon as possible.[6]

I am . . .
Aug. M. A. Bp. of Nesqualy

AAS, B7: 165.

———•———

1. Once in the capital, Brouillet continued his work on behalf of education and (Christian) religious self-determination for reservation Indians. In 1876, he was appointed treasurer of the Catholic Bureau of Indian Affairs (also known as the Office of the Catholic Commissioner), which he had helped to create, and he formed the Ladies' Catholic Indian Missionary Association. In 1879, he became director of the then titled Bureau of Catholic Indian Missions, visited Vancouver, W.T., in 1881, and by 1883 had helped expand the number of Catholic contract schools on U.S. reservations to eighteen, including the Umatilla Reservation school, location of his 1847 Cayuse Mission St. Anne. Suffering from semi-paralysis and snow blindness after exposure to a blizzard during a visit to the Boys' Industrial School on the Devil's Lake Agency of the Dakota Territory, Abbé Brouillet died in Providence Hospital in Washington, D.C., on February 5, 1884. Among the many eulogists, one found him to be "the closest likeness to a true apostle that he had ever known." Blanchet to Brouillet, August 20, 1874; December 23, 1874; AAS, B7: 161, 167–68; Rahill, *Catholic Indian Missions and Grant's Peace Policy*, 176, 285, 311, 329, 334.

2. Blanchet made arrangements to have Father Thomas Duffy (1843–1885), following completion of studies at All Hallows College of Dublin in 1868, study French at the American College of Louvain, but then decided to have him come directly from Ireland, with the expectation that he would learn French in the diocese, which Duffy failed to do: "I regret also that you have not followed my advices [sic] often repeated concerning the study of french [sic]. . . . In to what part soever of the diocese you may be sent, you will find french people; it would be certainly a great consolation to you to be able to hear their confessions, reconcile them to God, and give opportune advices." Blanchet to Superior V. A. Fortune, April 15, 1868; May 6, 1868; AAS, B7: 24, 28. Quote in Blanchet to Duffy, March 18, 1873, AAS, B7: 119–20.

3. It was during that preliminary visit that Mr. Joseph Barron also provided land in the town of Walla Walla, where the convent was built, to Mother Joseph for $1 (outright donations at the time being illegal) (see letter 29, note 4). McCrosson, *The Bell and the River*, 189; Clem Bergevin, "The Frenchtown Story: Community, Not a Town," *Union Bulletin* (Walla Walla), August 27, 1967.

4. *The Encyclopedia of Canada*, s.v. "North West Rebellions"; Peter Waite, "Between Three Oceans: Challenges of a Continental Destiny," in *The Illustrated History of Canada*, edited by Craig Brown (Toronto: Key Porter Books, 2000), 324–30; Arthur Silver, "French Quebec and the Métis Question, 1869–1885," in *The West and the Nation: Essays in Honor of W. L. Morton*, ed. Carl Berger and Ramsay Cook (Toronto: McClelland and Stewart, 1976), 95–103. Faced with political subordination since 1840, French Canada increasingly sought transnational cultural survival through the Catholic Church and the French language, condensed into the motto *La langue, gardienne de la foi* ("language, guardian of faith"). Sylvie Lacombe, "French Canada: The Rise and Decline of a 'Church Nation,'" *Québec Studies* 48 (Fall 2009 / Winter 2010): 138–40.

5. The census to which Blanchet refers may have been the 1873 diocesan census, based upon reports from mission priests, of which only a summary remains with no mention of ethnicity. It reports five hundred Catholics at Walla Walla and two hundred at St. Rose. It is unlikely that he was referring to the most recent U.S. federal census of 1870, which did not identify individuals by religion and did not recognize persons of mixed racial heredity. In discussing the question of "persons with any perceptible trace of Indian blood, whether mixed with white or negro stock" and whether they be classified with the father or the mother, the "superior" or the "inferior" blood, it was resolved that "the habits, tastes, and associations" determine census classification. By recognizing Walla Walla's still largely métis ethnic community as part of the French Canadian (Canadien) population, as was the practice in Canada, Blanchet was countering the erasure of cultures and, indirectly, Victorian assumptions about racial purity and attendant sexism found in U.S. census reports (AAS, A4; *Compendium of the Ninth Census*, 18–21).

6. According to an announcement in the *Walla Walla Statesman* of September 2, 1876, as cited by Harriet D. Munnick and Adrian R. Munnick, Father Richard "labored faithfully to gather up the faithful" for the purpose of constructing the new St. Rose of Lima Church of Frenchtown, where he offered the first Mass on October 8, 1876. Charles-Louis Augustin Richard, French Canadian, served at Lewiston and Cowlitz prior to this time (see letter 37, note 9). AAS, A4; Munnick and Munnick, "Walla Walla Registry III," in *Catholic Church Records of the Pacific Northwest*, vol. 7.

To Ignace Bourget, Bishop of Montreal, June 17, 1875

With a sense of accomplishment, thanks in no small part to French Canadian collaboration, Blanchet wrote again to his mentor and friend to report on the completion of the new Providence convent. Recognizing the need for more space and the advantage of gathering the Providence services of Vancouver into a single house, Mother Caron, then superior general of the Institute, with the support of Bishop Blanchet, had authorized construction of the building during her visit from Montreal in 1873. Though the United States was in the grip of a depression, building proceeded on the four city blocks bordering Tenth and Reserve Streets that the Providence Corporation had gradually acquired over the years. Multitalented Jean-Baptiste Blanchet, architect, carpenter, and woodworker, had accompanied his two Blanchet uncles west in 1866. A friend and confidant of Sister Joseph, Jean-Baptiste collaborated with her on this project, as well as on the building of institutions, chapels, and altars throughout the Northwest. The new multipurpose building opened on September 7, 1874.[1]

The building was also a monument to the accomplishments of the Sisters of Providence, who by 1875 had founded schools, hospitals, and other social services throughout the diocese and beyond—Vancouver, Steilacoom, Walla Walla, Missoula, Tulalip, St. Ignatius of Montana, and Colville—and who by 1876 would add Portland (Saint Vincent Hospital), North Yakima, and Cowlitz to their locations.[2] Now at age seventy-seven, Blanchet, who had been as generous with his start-up funds as with his litany of criticisms and concerns, was ready to offer his unqualified admiration.

With the constant and justifiable fear of the diocese's collapse behind him, with the number of Catholics increasing, and with a successful Providence establishment at his doorstep, Blanchet could savor some measure of success. Regarding his response to the chapel in the new building, Sister Joseph wrote to Bishop Bourget: "Although our chapel is still unfinished, it was blessed yesterday, the feast of St. Joseph, by Bishop Blanchet. . . . Our good Bishop wept while reciting the liturgical prayers."[3]

Dearest *Seigneur,*

Time is nigh for me to offer a sign of life, not that my health leaves anything to be desired. For some time now, it is as good as one could hope for at the age of nearly 78, though I am becoming weary. This is not so for Your Lordship, who for some time now has had little respite from his sufferings. As nature suffers, so the crown of glory is enriched.

I would like to tell you a word or two about your beloved daughters. As in former times, they are not lacking in devotion. As far as I can tell, they are working earnestly toward their spiritual advancement. The orphans, both boys and girls, as well as the other young pupils, are being raised in the fear of God and sin, and are walking in the path that will lead them to light, if they persevere. Thus it is that a new generation is being formed that one day will be of influence. Their virtues will serve to regenerate the present population whose faith is lacking in fervor, as is so often the case in newly settled lands.

Our Academy of Holy Angels here is attended by all Catholic children, and contributes its part to rekindling piety and love of God.[4]

I said that the sisters are working earnestly toward their spiritual advancement. And what are they doing with regard to the temporal? Great things, as you shall see. Since September 8th last, the sisters and others under their charge have been in their new convent that passes for the marvel of all Washington Territory, or the diocese of Nesqualy. For the last two years, their total expenditures amount to a jolly sum of 68,000 piastres, of which 44,000 were for the new building. The summary of their accounts, which I examined yesterday, shows that their debts amount to no more than 16,000 piastres. Due to their hard work, their collections, revenues from the hospital and student pensions, they were able to pay 52,000 piastres in two years, including several thousand they had incurred before construction began. Extraordinary, isn't it?

Assuredly, *Digitus Dei est hic* ["The finger of God is here"]. So far, their trust in divine Providence has not been in vain. May it be the same in the years to come.

To reduce the remaining debt, they will continue to make collections in the United States in locations where they receive permission from the bishops. Sister Joseph of the Sacred Heart departed this morning to join Sister Pierre d'Alcantara, who has stopped in San Francisco on her way back from South America. They will then head for destinations where they hope to accomplish more, after having of course consulted with the Archbishop of San Francisco, who they trust will support them. I am pleased that Sister Joseph was chosen for this work, for if there is any chance of success, it is she who has the qualities to make it happen.[5]

In truth, the community has been happy to have her lead the task since its inception. Her plan and the way she has carried it out have drawn the admiration of many people qualified to judge such things. *Sit nomen Domini benedictum!* ["Blessed be the name of the Lord!"]. I thought that you would be pleased to hear about your daughters' activities and good works.

I conclude in wishing you better health. And in your fervent prayers, please think about him who, like Your Lordship, cannot expect to live much longer: *Ut moriatur anima mea morte justorum, et fiant novissima mea horum similia* ["May my soul die the death of the just, and my last end be like to theirs"].

As always, I very sincerely remain your Lordship's most devoted servant, Aug. M. A. Bp. of Nesqualy

P.S. I would like to know how many priests in the Society of Masses for the Deceased are still living. The Secretary could tell me this.

ACAM, FILE 195.133, 875–7.

————•————

1. Sisters of Charity of Providence, *Institute*, 5:230–32, 249; McCrosson, *The Bell and the River*, 170, 196; Paul-Etienne Blanchet, ed., *Livre-souvenir de la Famille Blanchet, publié à l'occasion de la célébration du Troisième Centenaire de Naissance de Pierre Blanchet* (Quebec: E. Trembly, 1946), 90–91.

2. Recent scholarship has questioned historical assumptions that religious life was an impediment to the development of women's consciousness, hypothesizing instead that it was a latent form of feminism. Though subject to the bishop and local chaplain, these multilingual pioneer women of the Northwest embraced a career outside of marriage and motherhood and traveled widely—some managed large budgets, others served as teachers, musicians, nurses, backup doctors, carpenters, needlework artisans, and seamstresses—all, in one way or another, enjoying considerable job security, if for motives of charity more than pay. Sisters of Charity

of Providence, *Institute*, 5:336; Micheline Dumont, "Une perspective féministe dans l'histoire des congrégations des femmes," *Etudes d'histoire religieuse* 57 (1990): 30–31; Perin, "French-Speaking Canada from 1840," in Murphy and Perin, *Christianity in Canada*, 212–13.

3. Sister Joseph to Bishop Bourget, April 12, 1875, cited in Sisters of Charity of Providence, *Institute*, 5:268.

4. In 1862, Mother Joseph wrote that due to their influence, the Methodists benefited from the school tax, so were able to construct schools and teach children free of charge, and in 1863, she wrote that in order to attract paying pupils (funds that were needed to support poor Catholic pupils and other services), the Providence schools needed to be superior to the "public" schools. Although Blanchet's hope in 1850 to muster these "public" school taxes was dashed (see letter 14), the sisters' continual efforts to improve their teaching and their addition of music as an offering helped to attract growing numbers of paying pupils to both the boys' and the girls' schools. Sister Joseph to Bishop Larocque, March 1862; Sister Joseph to Mother Philomène, August 10, 1863; both found in Sisters of Charity of Providence, *Institute*, 5:134–35, 155.

5. Sisters Olivier and Peter of Alcantara undertook an alms collecting tour from 1874 to 1875, collecting, among smaller sums elsewhere, $4,000 in Chile and $2,800 in Peru; Sister Joseph then joined Sister Peter of Alcantara, collecting $600 in Victoria, $400 in New Westminster (where Father D'Herbomez, O.M.I., was bishop), $1,300 in the Fraser River mining district of Caribou, and $600 with the help of Father Chirouse on Puget Sound. Sister Joseph made further collections in Quebec from November 28, 1876, to February 13, 1878, amounting to $5,000. Sisters of Charity of Providence, *Institute*, 5:242–49, 284–85, 329.

LETTER 45

To His Eminence Cardinal Alessandro Franchi, Prefect of the Sacred Congregation of the Propagation of the Faith, July 9, 1876

With the assistance of his secretary, Father Aegidius Junger, Blanchet composed this report to the Vatican on the Diocese of Nesqualy just three years before his retirement. In the previous letter, he had shared a sense of accomplishment with his friend Ignace Bourget, who understood intimately the difficulties of building the Church in a frontier diocese. In this response to a questionnaire premised on the ideal of a fully mature diocese, he conveys a more measured tone. While acknowledging modest growth in the number of nonindigenous Catholics and steady growth among Indians, and detailing the increase in the number of establishments and personnel, the bishop cannot but make clear that he remains a missionary bishop to a scattered people in need of encouragement, discipline, and care.

Blanchet's report conveys two themes that characterized his entire episcopacy: his intent to keep his diocese conformed to Rome in liturgy and governance to the fullest extent possible, and his willingness to adapt pastorally to the realities of frontier life, for example, when he discusses in response 53 those "smitten with love."

Vancouver, W.T., July 9th 1876

REPORT ON THE STATE OF THE DIOCESE OF NESQUALY IN 1876

1. Augustin Magloire Alexandre Blanchet, Canadian of birth, born August 22nd 1797, elected Bishop of Walla Walla July 24th 1846, transferred May 31st 1850 to the seat of Nesqualy, which he occupies today.

2. The diocese of Nesqualy is bordered to the north by the 49th parallel and Vancouver Island; to the south by the Columbia River and the 46th parallel; to the west by the Pacific Ocean; and to the east by the Territory of Idaho. It is the poorest diocese on the Pacific Coast and in the United States. Whites number from 30,000 to 32,000 souls; indigenous peoples (Indians or *Sauvages*), about 12,000 souls.

3–4. The diocese of Nesqualy is in the Province of Oregon; the bishop is suffragan of the Archbishop of Oregon City.

5. The cathedral in Vancouver measures 60 by 36 feet and is constructed of wood; the bishop's residence is immediately adjacent.

6. The bishop received special faculties from the Holy See, contained in the Indults, articles 29, 13, 8, and 4, and several Indults for Indulgences, the Way of the Cross, &c., which were acknowledged several years ago by the Sacred Congregation.

7. The bishop has no revenue of his own; since his consecration, he has received his keep from the Society for the Propagation of the Faith. Proceeds from renting pews at the cathedral and other churches, from administering sacraments, &c. in the missions, provide for the missionaries' keep and for maintaining the churches and chapels.

8. The main localities of the diocese are: Vancouver, on the banks of the Columbia, about 110 miles from its mouth; Olympia, capital of the

territory, about 100 miles to the north of Vancouver; Steilacoom, twenty-five or thirty miles from Olympia; Seattle, thirty miles from Steilacoom; Port Townsend, twenty-five or thirty miles from Seattle; Walla Walla, more than 200 miles from Vancouver; and Colville in the Rocky Mountains, more than 200 miles from Walla Walla.

9.   A pastoral visitation was made to the Colville Mission in 1874; to the Yakama and Kittitas Missions last May; visitations to localities closer to the center take place almost every year. Canonical directives are followed as closely as possible.

10.   There has been no Provincial Council since 1848, nor any Diocesan Synod. Due to their distance from the center, it is difficult to gather the missionaries together. The bishop has compensated by issuing diocesan legislation on discipline and liturgy, in conformity, to the extent possible, with canon law, the decrees of the Councils of Baltimore, and the discipline that the first missionaries brought from Quebec. It has recently been resolved that a council will be held as soon as possible, and measures are being taken to this end.

11.   The bishop faces no physical threats of any sort in the exercise of his authority.

12., 13, 14, 15, 16.
There are neither chapters nor prebends.[1]

17 & 18. There is no seminary. Everything is lacking, funds and personnel.

19, 20, 21.

There are but simple missionaries, who are not obligated to offer the Holy Sacrament of Mass for the faithful, according to the decision of Rome.

22.   Where there are resident missionaries, the Holy Sacrament is preserved in the mission church, and with propriety.

23.   The borders of each mission are designated in the missionaries' letters of mission.

24 & 25. There are no canonically erected parishes, and as a consequence, there are no parish priests. The regular clergy is charged with missions of the indigenous peoples (Indians or *Sauvages*). These are the Reverend Fathers of the Society of Jesus and the Oblates of Mary Immaculate. With the exception of Vancouver and Seattle, there is only one secular priest at each respective mission.

26.   According to the census of 1873, there were more than 600 Catholics in Vancouver and its surroundings; 291 in Seattle; more than 400 in Olympia and Steilacoom; about 400 in Cowlitz, Kalama, Cathlamet, &c.; 700 in Walla Walla; 3,383 in Tulalip, &c.; 1,155 in Colville and its

surroundings; more than 500 in Yakima and its surroundings. The number of Catholics has increased since then. Counting whites and Indians, there are very likely more than 10,000 Catholics. In some localities, a good number of the Catholics are fervent in their devotion; in others, faith is not strong.

27.   There are two academies and five Catholic schools, with twenty to sixty pupils.

28.   Catholic doctrine, purged of error, is taught in the vernacular.

29.   It is difficult to know the exact number of non-Catholic schools. There are several in each county. Catholic children attend these schools in localities where there are no Catholic schools. We anxiously await the decision of Rome on that matter.

30–31. The secular priests are all from foreign countries. There are four Canadiens, four Belgians, one German, and one Irishman. One of them is in Washington [D.C.], working for the benefit of Indian missions; one teaches at the academy, and the others serve in the holy ministry. They have high ethical standards. All the missionaries must travel to visit Catholics living in distant localities.

32.   The bishop does not know of any secular priest who has received faculties from the Holy See. Secular priests are supported by the missions that they serve. They are allocated 1,000 francs annually in addition to their room and board. This allocation does not include remuneration for Masses said.

33.   None of the secular priests studied under the Sacred Congregation of the Propagation of the Faith.

34–35. There are no indigenous clerics or priests.

36.   There are five Religious of the Society of Jesus, mostly Italian, and two French Oblates of Mary Immaculate.[2]

37.   The bishop has assigned specific districts to each order.[3]

38.   Reverend Father J. Giorda is superior of the Reverend Fathers of the Society of Jesus. Monsignor D'Herbomez, Apostolic Vicar, is superior of the Oblates of Mary Immaculate. The superiors place and move their missionaries independently.

39 & 40. They live in community in residences of their order, among the Indians, observing their own rules, it is assumed, as much as possible.

41.   While in residence they generally wear the habit of the order; not during voyages.

42.   They have no novitiate.

43. The bishop presumes that they have special faculties, but he is not aware of their being used in the interest of his diocesans.

44. They depend on the bishop for the functions of the holy ministry.

45. Some of them receive a given sum of money annually for maintaining Indian schools; others receive allocations from the Society for the Propagation of the Faith. Like the secular priests, they undoubtedly receive something for administering the sacraments. The bishop does not know, however, if they do. Their reputation is without blemish, their works invaluable, they are esteemed by all.

46. They work for the salvation of souls among Indians, and for the growth of religion wherever there is an opportunity, their success is not to be doubted.

47–48. There are no women religious other than the Sisters of Charity of the House of Providence, three of whom came from Montreal, Canada, in 1856. Today, forty are professed and five are novices or postulants. The convent is in Vancouver, where they have a boarding school and a day school for teaching the young, an orphanage for boys and another for girls, and a hospital. They maintain two schools among indigenous groups, one in Colville, the other in Tulalip.[4] They have some establishments in other localities for teaching the young. They take simple vows of poverty, chastity, and obedience. Wherever they go, they accomplish their works with admirable zeal and constancy; and they bring about much good.

49–50. There are neither foundations nor charitable bequests.

51–52. In some localities there are a good number of fervent Catholics; in others, they are indifferent. Some Catholics do not even dare be known as such. Others belong to secret societies. The bishop knows of no abuse in the preaching of the divine Word or the ministration of sacraments. There are societies that some bishops have condemned, e.g., "The Sons of Temperance" (*les Fils de la Tempérance*) and the "Grangers" which appear ostensibly to exist only for the welfare of their members. Both sexes meet together in these societies. Some Catholics have joined. The bishop has not yet been able to ascertain if there are any secrets that would place them among those the Church has condemned. For this reason, he thought absolution could be given at the Tribunal of Penitence if members promised to abandon the societies immediately, should they become prohibited.[5] There is fear nevertheless that these gatherings of Catholics with Protestants or non-Catholics pose a threat to the faith. The bishop asks that the Sacred Congregation instruct him on this matter for the peace of his conscience and the spiritual welfare of his flock.

53. Marriages are conducted according to rule. But the publication of

the three bans is not adhered to rigidly for fear that the parties might otherwise be wed before a magistrate. Still, there has been significant progress on this point, and it is hoped that in due time all marriages will be conducted according to rule. The Sacred Congregation insists that dispensations for mixed marriages not be granted readily, the Church understandably condemning them, because the Catholic party and children often end up being lost, even though the Protestant or non-Catholic party promises to grant complete freedom to practice the religion and to raise their children in the Catholic faith.[6] But in this country, where faith generally is not fervent, if a dispensation is denied, the parties very frequently, if not always, are wed before a magistrate. Once this happens, there is absolutely no protection for the woman and her children wishing to practice her religion, and after the marriage, such protection is difficult to obtain. In addition, the parties generally make preparations for marriage before they seek a priest. And when the parties, especially the young, are smitten with love for one another, it is virtually impossible to convince them to go their own ways, however powerful the reasons may be. Is the reasonable fear of having these marriages conducted without the protection mentioned above sufficient or not for granting the dispensation? I request that the Sacred Congregation inform me on this matter.

54. For the last twenty years, the number of non-indigenous Catholics has not increased rapidly. In 1854, there were six hundred Catholics, in a diocese significantly larger than the present one. Now there may be four to five thousand. There has been a significant increase among indigenous populations. They may also number between four and five thousand. It is not known how many were baptized and died, undoubtedly thousands.

55. Due to its vast expanse, a lack of financial support, and the small number of priests, it is impossible to provide for the spiritual needs of many Catholics who are scattered here and there in every part of the diocese. When circumstances allow, there will be traveling missionaries who will visit them several times a year. In this way we will rekindle faith among a good number, bring them back to the practice of their religious duties, and instruct their children in Christian doctrine, for which most have a great need.

Humbly submitted in its entirety
A. M. A. Bp. of Nesqualy

AAS, B8: 120–25.

1. *Chapter* refers to a group of clergy attached to a cathedral, while *prebends* refers to revenue from a cathedral and the clergy who have a claim to it.

2. The large number of Italian Jesuits was the consequence of the Rocky Mountain Mission being placed under the Jesuits' Turin Province in 1854. Burns, *Jesuits and the Indian Wars*, 54–55; Schoenberg, *Catholic Church in the Pacific Northwest*, 146.

3. The Oblates worked west of the Cascade Mountains on the Tulalip Reservation and the Jesuits on reservations east of the Cascade Mountains.

4. The schools were Providence of Our Lady of Seven Sorrows at Tulalip (1868) and Providence of the Sacred Heart at Colville (1873).

5. The Second Plenary Council of Baltimore forbade Catholics to enter any secret society that required an oath (Title XII), for example, the Masonic Order. Blanchet's response in items 51 and 52 regarding secret societies exemplifies his pastoral pragmatism.

6. Early sacramental records for Immaculate Conception Church at Steilacoom contain the sworn statement of non-Catholic spouses when they marry a Catholic: "I the undersigned do promise solemnly before God that I will give to my wife a perfect liberty of practicing her religion, and of raising our children of both sexes in the Catholic religion. The testimony whereof I have signed these presents in the presence of . . ." The statement is signed and witnessed. RG 1000, Early Missionary Records for Puget Sound, vol. 6, Steilacoom and Puget Sound, 1860–1890, AAS.

General Chronology

1846

May 12   US Congress declares war against Republic of Mexico

June 15   United States and Great Britain sign the Oregon Treaty, terminating joint occupancy of the Oregon Country

July 24   Pope Pius IX names A M A Blanchet bishop of Walla Walla and administrator of the ecclesial districts of Fort Hall and Colville

September 27   Ignace Bourget, bishop of Montreal, consecrates A. M. A. Blanchet bishop of Walla Walla

1847

March 23   Blanchet party departs from Montreal

September 5   Bishop Blanchet arrives at Fort Walla Walla

November 29   Killings of Marcus and Narcissa Whitman with twelve others at Waiilatpu

1848

January 2   Blanchet departs from Fort Walla Walla for the Willamette Valley, with the ransomed hostages from the Whitman Mission and Hudson Bay Company (HBC) personnel

February 2   Treaty of Guadelupe Hidalgo: Mexico cedes California and New Mexico to the United States for $15 million; Texas boundary at the Rio Grande recognized (ratified by US Senate, March 10; Mexican legislature, May 19)

February 28–March 1   First Provincial Council of Oregon, St. Paul

February–March   Volunteer forces skirmish with Cayuse Indians

May 26   Blanchet departs St. Paul for The Dalles; his original see, Walla Walla, is now inaccessible

| August 14 | President Polk signs bill establishing Oregon Territory, including modern-day Oregon, Washington, Idaho, and portions of western Montana and Wyoming |
| September 10 | First pack train leaves Oregon City for the California goldfields |

1849

| May 17 | Chief Factor James Douglas moves HBC administrative headquarters from Fort Vancouver to Fort Victoria |
| October 31 | United States establishes military reservation, Columbia Barracks, on HBC lands adjacent to HBC Fort Vancouver |

1850

May 31	Pope Pius IX names A. M. A. Blanchet bishop of Nesqualy, including, at the time, lands north of the Columbia and west of the Cascades; the brief arrives at The Dalles on September 29
September 27	Congress passes the Donation Land Claim Act
October 27	Blanchet establishes his episcopal see on HBC lands adjacent to Fort Vancouver, Columbia Barracks, and Columbia City (Vancouver)

1851

| March 21 | Blanchet departs for Mexico, the United States, and Canada |

1852

| May 9–20 | First Plenary Council of Baltimore; Blanchet attends |
| December 18 | Blanchet returns from his voyage, resides at Columbia City |

1853

| March 17 | Congress establishes Washington Territory, which includes today's Washington State as well as Idaho and western Montana north of the forty-sixth parallel; Isaac Stevens appointed governor, superintendent of Indian Affairs, and surveyor for a possible northern railway route |

July 29	Pope Pius IX issues brief, *Per Similes Nostras*, suppressing the Diocese of Walla Walla and transferring authority for the area to the Diocese of Nesqualy

1854

August	US Congress authorizes the making of treaties with Indians in Washington Territory
December 25	Treaty councils west of the Cascades begun, and last through early January

1855

May 29–June 11	Treaty council held at Walla Walla
July	Gold discoveries in the Colville Valley reported
August 28	Blanchet embarks on voyage to Europe and Montreal, Vicar-General Brouillet appointed diocesan administrator
September 23	Andrew Bolon, Indian subagent, killed
November 13	Yakama Catholic mission at Ahtanum sacked and burned by a military force
December 7–10	Battle of Walla Walla, mutilation of Walla Walla chief Peopeomoxmox's body by Oregon militia
December 28	Blanchet received by Pope Pius IX, in Rome

1856

April 3	Stevens declares martial law on Puget Sound, arrests settlers on Muck Creek, near home of Nisqually chief, Leschi
May 27	Blanchet meets with the Society for the Propagation of the Faith in France
September 11	Stevens holds second treaty council at Walla Walla, with no resolution to Indian-settler conflicts
October	US Army builds Fort Walla Walla, closes the ColumbiaPlateau (east of the Cascades) to white settlement
November 3	Blanchet departs from Montreal with Mother Joseph and four other Sisters of Providence; arrives in diocese on December 8

1857

March   Oblates of Mary Immaculate establish Mission St. Anne among the Snohomish

April 15   Sisters of Providence open day school, boarding school, and orphanage in Columbia City (Vancouver)

1858

February 19   Chief Leschi hanged, having been falsely accused of "murdering" a volunteer militiaman

March   Reports of gold on the Fraser River reach US west coast

April 6   Sisters of Providence open St. Joseph Hospital in Columbia City (Vancouver)

August 2   Crown Colony of British Columbia organized (former HBC district of New Caledonia)

September   Colonel George Wright and Major Robert Garnett of the US Army defeat major Indian forces east of the Cascades, in Washington Territory

October 29   Ban on white settlement in eastern Washington lifted

1859

February 14   President Buchanan signs legislation making Oregon a state

March 8   Senate ratifies Governor Stevens's 1855 treaties with tribes

March   Vicar-General Brouillet departs on first trip to Washington, D.C., to begin work in the interest of Indians and on the diocese's land claims

June 15   Opening of the Pig War

1860

Spring   First reports of gold on Nez Percé lands (Idaho)

June 14   Last employees of HBC leave Vancouver for Fort Victoria

1861

April 12   Opening of the US Civil War

1862

May 20   Homestead Act signed, promoting settlement of the West

1863

March 4   President Lincoln signs legislation creating Idaho Territory, reducing the size of Washington Territory to the state's current boundaries

Dreamer religious movement gains momentum among Indians on Columbia Plateau

1865

April 9   US Civil War ends

1866

October 7–21   Bishop Blanchet attends Second Plenary Council of Baltimore

1867

March 29   Queen Victoria signs the British North America Act, creating Canada as a federal dominion, effective July 1

September   Diocesan Fathers St. Onge and Boulet restore Yakama Catholic mission at Ahtanum

1868

March 3   Apostolic vicariates of Idaho and Montana erected, reducing the boundaries of the Diocese of Nesqualy to those of today's Washington State

1869

March 4   Ulysses S Grant inaugurated president (in office through 1877)

May 10   Union and Central Pacific Railroads join at Promontory Point, Utah—first transcontinental rail line

1870

Grant's peace policy implemented (in effect to 1882)

May 12   Province of Manitoba established, with special rights for Métis peoples

1873

June 16   In response to petition from Nez Percé Chief Joseph, President Grant issues executive order preserving half of Wallowa Valley for Nez Percés (reopens to whites in 1875)

1874

January 2   Bureau of Catholic Indian Missions founded, as the Office of the Commissioner of Catholic Indian Missions; General Ewing appointed commissioner and Vicar-General Brouillet, assistant

1876

June 25–26   Battle of the Little Big Horn—Lakotas, Cheyennes, and Arapaho defeat General George Custer and Seventh US Calvary

1877

October 5   Nez Percé Chief Joseph surrenders with 418 of his people to General Oliver O. Howard, in Bear Paw Mountains of Montana

1878

July 25   Bishop Blanchet sends Pope Leo XIII his request to retire

1879

August 6   Pope Leo XIII appoints Aegidius Junger second bishop of Nesqualy

October 28   F.N. Blanchet, archbishop of Oregon City, consecrates Aegidius Junger bishop of Nesqualy

1883

Northern Pacific Railway links Chicago with Seattle

1887

February 8   Congress approves Dawes Severalty Act

February 25   A. M. A. Blanchet dies, St. Joseph Hospital, Vancouver

Indian Shaker Church, begun by Squaxin Island tribal members John and Mary Slocum, draws increasing numbers of Native Americans

1889

November 11   Washington admitted to the Union as the forty-second state

Selected Bibliography

MANUSCRIPT COLLECTIONS
AND UNPUBLISHED MANUSCRIPTS

ARCHIVES, ARCHDIOCESE OF SEATTLE, SEATTLE (AAS):

Blanchet, A. M. A. "Journal de l'Evêque de Walla Walla, depuis Montréal, capitale du Canada, jusqu'à Walla Walla"; "Seconde Partie, Voyage au Mexique"; "Voyage en Europe, octobre 28, 1855–décembre 5, 1856." (AAS, A1.)

———. "Régistre des lettres écrites par Monseigneur l'Evêque de Walla Walla depuis le vingt-neuf septembre mil huit-cent quarante six, jusqu'au vingt-cinq septembre 1850." (AAS, A2.)

———. "Recueil de lettres faisant connaître ce qui s'est passé depuis la consécration de l'Evêque de Walla Walla, 1846, à Montréal, jusqu'à 1850, époque de sa translation au Siège de Nesqualy, pour servir à l'histoire de l'église de la Province ecclésiastique d'Orégon." (AAS, A3.)

———. "Notes sur les diocèses de Walla-Walla et de Nesqualy." (AAS, A4.)

———. "Régistre authentique des Pièces et Actes concernant le diocèse de Walla Walla et le diocèse de Nesqualy." (AAS, A5.)

———. "Journal de l'Evêque de Nesqualy; Statistiques du diocèse de Nesqualy depuis son érection jusqu'en 1873." (AAS, B6.)

———. "Régistre de la correspondance de l'Evêque de Nesqualy du 29 août jusqu'au 15 juin 1879." (AAS, B7.)

———. "2nd volume. Régistre contenant les actes authentiques de l'Evêque; Les correspondances de Rome du 19 février 1867." (AAS, B8.)

Brouillet, J. B. A. "Cahier des lettres et correspondance de J. B. A. Brouillet, prêtre, pendant son administration du diocèse de Nesqualy, Mars 1851." Diocesan Priests, RG 820.

Diocesan Correspondence (Blanchet, A. M. A.), 1850–1887, RG 610,

Records of Parishes and Missions, 1857–1937, RG 700.

Correspondence, Diocesan Priests, RG 820.

Correspondence, Religious Priests, RG 840.

Correspondence, Women Religious, 1857–1937, RG 900.

Early Missionary Records for Puget Sound, RG 1000.

ARCHIVES OF THE CHANCELLERY OF THE ARCHDIOCESE OF MONTREAL, MONTREAL (ACAM):

Correspondance, Seattle (Nesqualy), (Walla Walla) file 195.133.

Lettres de Mgr l'Evêque de Montréal (Bourget) à Mgr A.-M. Blanchet, évêque de Walla Walla (46–50) ou de Nesqualy (50–79) file 905.055 and Régistre des Lettres (RL).

ARCHIVES OF THE OEUVRES PONTIFICALES MISSIONNAIRES, LYONS, FRANCE (OPM):
Régistres des procès verbaux: Conseil central de Lyon (Registries of Minutes: Central Council of Lyons).
Correspondance de A. M. A. Blanchet, Evêque de Walla Walla et Nesqualy.

BIBLIOTHÈQUE NATIONALE DE QUÉBEC, MONTREAL:
"Correspondance de A. M. A. Blanchet, 1797–1887," recueillie, transcrite et annotée par Georges Aubin (Transcriptions of collection of correspondence of A. M. A. Blanchet, by Georges Aubin).
"Correspondance de A. M. A. Blanchet, Lettres reçues," recueillie, transcrite et annotée par Georges Aubin (Transcription of letters received by Bishop A. M. A. Blanchet, made by Georges Aubin).

OREGON HISTORICAL SOCIETY RESEARCH LIBRARY, PORTLAND:
George Abernethy Papers.
Joseph Lane Papers.

PROVIDENCE ARCHIVES, MOTHER JOSEPH PROVINCE, SEATTLE:
"Chronicles of the House of Providence, July 1, 1856 to July 1, 1876." Vancouver, Washington Collection.
"Chroniques de la Mission de St. Joseph de Steilacoom, 1863."
"Chroniques de l'Académie St. Vincent depuis sa fondation le 18 février 1864."
Mother Joseph of the Sacred Heart Personal Papers Collection [Correspondence, 1856–1901].
Personnel-Student Records, Providence Academy, Vancouver, Washington, Registries of the Schools and Academies of Vancouver.

BOOKS AND ARTICLES

Allaire, L'abbé J.-B.-A., *Dictionnaire Biographique du clergé canadien-français*. Vol. 1, *Les Anciens*; vol. 2, *Les Contemporains*. St.-Hyacinthe, Quebec: Imprimerie de "La Tribune," 1908.
Annales, Oeuvre de la Propagation de la Foi, Lyons, France.
Archer, John H. "The Anglican Church and the Indian in the Northwest." *Journal of the Canadian Church Historical Society* 28, no. 1 (April 1986): 19–30.
Asher, Brad. *Beyond the Reservation: Indians, Settlers, and the Law in Washington Territory, 1853–1889*. Norman: University of Oklahoma Press, 1999.
Axtell, James. *The Invasion Within: The Contest of Cultures in Colonial North America*. New York: Oxford University Press, 1985.
———. "Some Thoughts on the Ethnohistory of Missions." *Ethnohistory* 29, no. 1 (1982): 35–41.
Bagley, Clarence, ed. *Early Catholic Missions in Old Oregon*. 2 vols. Seattle: Lowman and Hanford, 1932.
Bancroft, Hubert Howe. *History of Oregon*. Vol. 1, *1834–1848*. San Francisco: History Company, 1886.

——. *History of Oregon.* Vol. 2, *1848–1888.* San Francisco: History Company, 1888.

——. *History of Washington, Idaho, and Montana, 1845–1889.* San Francisco: History Company, 1890.

Beckham, Stephen Dow, ed. *Oregon Indians: Voices from Two Centuries.* Corvallis: Oregon State University Press, 2006.

Berkhofer, Robert F., Jr. *Salvation and the Savage: An Analysis of Protestant Missions and American Indian Response, 1787–1862.* Lexington: University of Kentucky Press, 1965.

Bischoff, William, S.J. "The Yakima Indian Wars, 1855–1856." Ph.D. diss., University of Chicago, 1950.

Blanchet, Augustin Magloire Alexandre. *Journal of a Catholic Bishop on the Oregon Trail: The Overland Crossing of the Rt. Rev. A. M. A. Blanchet, Bishop of Walla Walla, from Montreal to Oregon Territory, March 23, 1847 to January 23, 1851.* Edition includes *Blackrobe Buries Whitmans*, by Jean-Baptiste Abraham Brouillet. Translated and edited by Edward J. Kowrach. Fairfield, Wash.: Ye Galleon Press, 1978.

Blanchet, Augustin Magloire Alexandre, and François Xavier Blanchet. *Les Débuts de l'Eglise catholique en Orégon: Scènes de l'histoire de l'Eglise catholique en Orégon, 1838–1850* (Beginnings of the Catholic Church in Oregon: Scenes from the History of the Catholic Church in Oregon, 1838–1850). Edited by Jérome Blanchet and Georges Aubin. Rimouski, Quebec: Association des Familles Blanchet, 1996.

Blanchet, François Norbert. *Historical Sketches of the Catholic Church in Oregon and the Northwest.* Ferndale, Wash.: Ye Galleon Press, 1910. Republished as *Historical Sketches of the Catholic Church in Oregon by Most Rev. Francis Norbert Blanchet.* Edited and introduced by Edward J. Kowrach. Fairfield, Wash.: Ye Galleon Press, 1983.

Blanchet, François Xavier. *Ten Years on the Pacific Coast; and Jacksonville, a National Historical Landmark City.* Edited and translated by Edward J. Kowrach. Fairfield, Wash.: Ye Galleon Press, 1982.

Blanchet, Paul-Etienne, ed. *Livre-souvenir de la Famille Blanchet, publié à l'occasion de la célébration du Troisième Centenaire de Naissance de Pierre Blanchet.* Quebec: E. Trembly, 1946.

Boyd, Robert. *The Coming of the Spirit of Pestilence: Introduced and Infectious Diseases and Population Decline among Northwest Coast Indians, 1774–1874.* Vancouver: University of British Columbia Press; Seattle: University of Washington Press, 1999.

——. *People of The Dalles: The Indians of the Wascopam Mission.* Lincoln: University of Nebraska Press, 1996.

Bradley, Right Reverend Cyprian, O.S.B., and Most Reverend Edward Kelly, D.D., Ph.D. *History of the Diocese of Boise, 1863–1952.* 2 vols. Boise, Idaho: Roman Catholic Diocese of Boise, 1953.

Brandt, Patricia, and Lillian A. Pereyra. *Adapting in Eden: Oregon's Catholic Minority, 1838–1986.* Pullman: Washington State University Press, 2002.

Brouillet, Jean-Baptiste Abraham. *The Authentic Account of the Murder of Dr. Whitman and other missionaries, by the Cayuse Indians of Oregon in 1847 and the causes which led to the horrible catastrophe.* 2nd ed. Portland, Ore.: S. J. McCormick, 1869.

——. *Blackrobe Buries Whitmans.* Published together with *Journal of a Catholic Bishop on the Oregon Trail: The Overland Crossing of the Rt. Rev. A. M. A. Blanchet, Bishop of Walla*

Walla, from Montreal to Oregon Territory, March 23, 1847 to January 23, 1851, by Augustin Magloire Alexandre Blanchet. Translated and edited by Edward J. Kowrach. Fairfield, Wash.: Ye Galleon Press, 1978

Brown, Craig, ed. *The Illustrated History of Canada*. Toronto: Key Porter Books, 2000.

Brown, Jennifer S. H., and Elizabeth Vibert, eds. *Reading beyond Words: Contexts for Native History*. Peterborough, Ontario; Orchard Park, N.Y.: Broadview Press, 2003.

Brown, Roberta Stringham. "A *Canadien* Bishop in the Ecclesiastical Province of Oregon." Canadian Catholic Historical Association (CCHA), *Historical Studies* 66 (2000): 34–55.

Burnett, Peter. *Recollections and Opinions of an Old Pioneer*. New York: D. Appleton and Company, 1880.

Burns, Robert Ignatius, S.J. *The Jesuits and the Indian Wars of the Northwest*. Moscow: University of Idaho Press, 1966.

Carriker, Robert C. *Father Peter John De Smet: Jesuit in the West*. The Oklahoma Western Biographies Series, vol. 9. Norman: University of Oklahoma Press, 1998.

Cebula, Larry. *Plateau Indians and the Quest for Spiritual Power, 1700–1850*. Lincoln: University of Nebraska Press, 2003.

Chadwick, Owen. *A History of the Popes, 1830–1914*. Oxford: Clarendon Press, 1998.

Chittenden, Hiram M. *The American Fur Trade of the Far West*. Vol. 1. New York: Press of the Pioneers, 1935. Reprinted, with a foreword by James P. Ronda. Lincoln: University of Nebraska Press, 1986. Page citations are to the reprint edition.

Chittenden, Hiram M., and Alfred T. Richardson, eds. *Life, Letters, and Travels of Father De Smet, S.J., 1801–1873*. 4 vols. New York: Francis P. Harper, 1905; New York: Arno Press and the New York Times, 1969. Citations and page numbers are to the 1969 edition.

Cholvy, Gérard. *Christianisme et société en France au XIXe siècle, 1790–1914*. Paris: Editions du Seuil, 2001.

Coan, C. F. "The Adoption of the Reservation Policy in the Pacific Northwest, 1853–1855." *Oregon Historical Quarterly* 23, no. 1 (1922): 1–38.

———. "The First Stage of the Federal Indian Policy in the Pacific Northwest, 1849–1852." *Oregon Historical Quarterly* 22, no. 1. (1921): 46–89.

Codd, Kevin A. "The American College of Louvain and the Catholic Church in the North Pacific Coast of North America, 1857–1907." Master's thesis, Catholic University of Louvain, 2002.

———. "A Favored Part of the Vineyard: A Study of the American College Missionaries on the North Pacific Coast, 1857–1907." Ph.D. diss., Katholieke Universiteit Leuven, 2007.

Codd, Kevin A., and Brian G. Dick. *The American College of Louvain: America's Seminary in the Heart of Europe*. Louvain, Belgium: American College, 2007.

Codignola, Luca. "Roman Catholic Conservatism in a New North Atlantic World, 1760–1829." *William and Mary Quarterly* 64, no. 4 (October 2007): 717–56.

Cronin, Kay. *Cross in the Wilderness*. Toronto: Mission Press, 1960.

Danylewycz, Marta. *Taking the Veil: An Alternative to Marriage, Motherhood, and Spinsterhood in Quebec, 1840–1920*. Ontario: McClelland and Stewart, 1987.

Davis, William Lyle. "Mission of St. Anne of the Cayuse Indians, 1847–1848." Ph.D. diss., University of California, 1943.

Deutsch, Herman J. "The Evolution of Territorial and State Boundaries in the Inland Empire of the Pacific Northwest." *Pacific Northwest Quarterly* 51, no. 3 (July 1960): 115–31.

Dickey, George. "The Founding of the 11th Military District, Oregon Territory." In *Military Influences on Washington History: Proceedings of a Conference, March 29–31, 1984, Camp Murray, Tacoma*, edited by William Woodward and David Hansen, 39–45. Tacoma: Washington Army National Guard, 1984.

Dickinson, John, and Brian Young. *A Short History of Quebec*. 4th ed. Montreal: McGill-Queen's University Press, 2008.

Dodds, Gordon B. *The American Northwest: A History of Oregon and Washington*. Arlington Heights, Ill.: Forum Press, 1986.

Drouin, Paul, O.M.I., ed. *Les Oblats de Marie Immaculée en Orégon, 1847–1860: Documents d'archives*. 3 vols. Ottawa: Archives Deschâtelets, 1992.

Duggar, Anne Clare, S.P. "Institutions of the Walla Walla Valley, 1847–1950." Master's thesis, Seattle University, 1953.

Dumont, Micheline. "Une perspective féministe dans l'histoire des congrégations des femmes." *Etudes d'histoire religieuse* 57 (1990): 29–35.

Ewing, Charles, eḍ. *Circular of the Catholic Commissioner for Indian Missions to the Catholics of the United States*. 1874. Ayer Collection 6470, Newberry Library, Chicago.

Fay, Terence J. *A History of Canadian Catholics: Gallicanism, Romanism, and Canadianism*. Montreal: McGill-Queens University Press, 2002.

Ficken, Robert E. "After the Treaties: Administering Pacific Northwest Indian Reservations." In "The Isaac I. Stevens and Joel Palmer Treaties, 1855–2005," special issue, *Oregon Historical Quarterly* 106, no. 3 (Fall 2005): 442–61.

———. "The Three Party Conflict: The Army and the Indian on the Pacific Northwest Frontier." In *Military Influences on Washington History: Proceedings of a Conference; March 29–31, 1984, Camp Murray, Tacoma*, edited by William Woodward and David Hansen, 59–78. Tacoma: Washington Army National Guard, 1984.

———. *Washington Territory*. Pullman: Washington State University Press, 2002.

Fisher, Andrew H. *Shadow Tribe: The Making of Columbia River Indian Identity*. Seattle: University of Washington Press and Center for the Study of the Pacific Northwest, 2010.

Fuller, George W. *History of the Pacific Northwest*. New York: Alfred A. Knopf, 1947.

Furtwangler, Albert. *Bringing Indians to the Book*. Seattle: University of Washington Press, 2005.

Galbraith, John S. *The Hudson's Bay Company as an Imperial Factor, 1821–1869*. Berkeley: University of California Press, 1957.

Gibson, James R. *The Lifeline of the Oregon Country: The Fraser-Columbia Brigade System, 1811–47*. Vancouver: University of British Columbia Press, 1997. .

Geary, Edward R. *Report of Edward R. Geary, Superintendent of Indian Affairs for Oregon and Washington, A. B. Greenwood, Commissioner of Indian Affairs*. Washington, D.C.: Office of the Commissioner of Indian Affairs, 1859. Online at University of Washington Libraries, American Indians of the Pacific Northwest Collection, http://content.lib.washington.edu/u?/lctext,2045 (accessed December 1, 2009); http://content.lib.washington.edu/cdm4/document.php?CISOROOT=/lctext&CISOPTR=113&REC=2 (accessed May 22, 2012).

Gimpl, Sister M. Caroline Ann, S.H.N. "Immaculate Conception Mission, Steilacoom, Washington." Master's thesis, Seattle University, 1951

Gjerde, Jon S. *Catholicism and the Shaping of Nineteenth-Century America*. Edited by S. Deborah Kang. Cambridge: Cambridge University Press, 2012.

Haeberlin, Hermann, and Erna Gunther. *The Indians of Puget Sound*. Seattle: University of Washington Press, 1973. Reprint of the 1952 reprint of the 1930 edition.

Hardy, René. *Contrôle social et Mutation de la culture religieuse au Québec*. Quebec: Editions du Boréal, 1999.

Harmon, Alexandra. *Indians in the Making: Ethnic Relations and Indian Identities around Puget Sound*. Berkeley: University of California Press, 1998.

Helland, Maurice. *There Were Giants: The Life of James H. Wilbur*. Yakima, Wash.: M. Helland, 1980.

Hoopes, Alban W. *Indian Affairs and Their Administration, with Special Reference to the Far West, 1849-1860*. Philadelphia: University of Pennsylvania Press, 1932.

Huel, Raymond J. A. *Proclaiming the Gospel to the Indians and the Métis: The Missionary Oblates of Mary Immaculate in Western Canada, 1845-1945*. Edmonton: University of Alberta Press and Western Canadian Publishers, 1996.

Hunt, Herbert, and Floyd C. Kaylor. *Washington, West of the Cascades; Historical and Descriptive; The Explorers, the Indians, the Pioneers, the Modern*. 3 vols. Chicago: S. J. Clarke Publishing Company, 1917.

Hussey, John A. *The History of Fort Vancouver and Its Physical Structure*. [Tacoma]: Washington State Historical Society, 1957.

Jackson, John C. *Children of the Fur Trade: Forgotten Métis of the Pacific Northwest*. Missoula, Mont.: Mountain Press Publishing Company, 1996.

Jeffrey, Julie R. *Converting the West: A Biography of Narcissa Whitman*. The Oklahoma Western Biographies Series, vol. 3. Norman: University of Oklahoma Press, 1991.

Josephy, Alvin M., Jr. *The Nez Perce Indians and the Opening of the Northwest*. New Haven, Conn.: Yale University Press, 1965.

Karson, Jennifer, ed. *Wiyáxayxt / Wiyáakaáawn / As Days Go By: Our History, Our Land, and Our People—the Cayuse, Umatilla, and Walla Walla*. Pendleton, Ore.: Tamástslikt Cultural Institute; Portland: Oregon Historical Society Press; Seattle: University of Washington Press, 2006.

Keller, Robert H., Jr. *American Protestantism and United States Indian Policy, 1869-82*. Lincoln: University of Nebraska Press, 1983.

Killen, Patricia O'Connell. "Writing the Pacific Northwest into Canadian and U.S. Catholic History: Geography, Demographics, and Regional Religion." *Canadian Catholic Historical Association (CCHA), Historical Studies* 66 (2000): 74–91.

Killoren, John J., S.J. *"Come, Blackrobe": De Smet and the Indian Tragedy*. Norman: University of Oklahoma Press, 1994; St. Louis, Mo.: Institute of Jesuit Sources, 2003. Citations are to the 2003 edition.

Kowrach, Edward J. *Mie. Charles Pandosy, O.M.I, a Missionary of the Northwest*. Fairfield, Wash.: Ye Galleon Press, 1992.

Lacombe, Sylvie. "French Canada: The Rise and Decline of a 'Church-Nation.'" *Québec Studies* 48 (Fall 2009 / Winter 2010): 135–58.

Landerholm, Carl, ed. and trans. *Notices & Voyages of the Famed Quebec Mission to the Pacific Northwest, Being the Correspondence, notices, etc., of Fathers Blanchet and Demers, together* with those of Fathers Bolduc and Langlois. Containing much remarkable information on the areas and inhabitants of the Columbia, Walamette, Cowlitz and Fraser Rivers, Nesqually Bay, Puget Sound, Whidby and Vancouver Islands.., 1838 to 1847. Portland: Oregon Historical Society, 1956.

Lang, William L. Confederacy of Ambition: William Winlock Miller and the Making of Washington Territory. Seattle: University of Washington Press, 1996.

Lavasseur, Donat, O.M.I. Les Oblats de Marie Immaculée dans l'Ouest et le Nord du Canada, 1845–1967. Edmonton: University of Alberta Press, 1995.

Limerick, Patricia Nelson. "Disorientation and Reorientation: The American Landscape Discovered from the West." Journal of American History 79, no. 3 (December 1992): 1021–49.

Maffly-Kipp, Laurie. Religion and Society in Frontier California. New Haven, Conn.: Yale University Press, 1994.

McCrosson, Sister Mary of the Blessed Sacrament, S.P. The Bell and the River. In collaboration with Sisters Mary Leopoldine and Maria Theresa. Palo Alto, Calif.: Pacific Books, 2006. Reprint of 1956 edition.

McKevitt, Gerald. Brokers of Culture: Italian Jesuits in the West, 1849–1919. Stanford, Calif.: Stanford University Press, 2010.

Meinig, D. W. The Great Columbia Plain: A Historical Geography, 1805–1910. Seattle: University of Washington Press, 1968.

Miller, Christopher L. Prophetic Worlds: Indians and Whites on the Columbia Plateau. 1985. Reprint, with a foreword by Chris Friday. Seattle: University of Washington Press, 2003.

Morgan, Murray. Puget's Sound: A Narrative of Early Tacoma and the Southern Sound. Seattle: University of Washington Press, 1979.

Morice, A. G., O.M.I. Dictionnaire historique des Canadiens et des Métis française de l'Ouest. Quebec: J. P. Garneau, 1908.

Munnick, Harriet D., and Adrian R. Munnick, eds. Catholic Church Records of the Pacific Northwest. Vol. 7, Missions of St. Ann and St. Rose of the Cayouse, 1847–1888; Walla Walla and Frenchtown (1859–1872), Frenchtown (1872–1888). Portland, Ore.: Binford and Mort Publishing, ca. 1989.

Murphy, Terrence, ed., and Roberto Perin, associate ed. A Concise History of Christianity in Canada. New York: Oxford University Press, 1996.

Nisbet, Jack. Mapmaker's Eye: David Thompson on the Columbia Plateau. Pullman: Washington State University Press, 2005.

Notices sur les Missions du Diocèse de Québec, qui sont secourues par l'Association de la Propagation de la Foi (Notices on the Missions of the Diocese of Quebec, which are assisted by the Association of the Propagation of the Faith). Published beginning in 1851 as Rapport sur Les Missions du Diocèse de Québec et autres qui ont ci-devant fait partie (Report on the Missions of the Diocese of Quebec and others that have hitherto been a part).

O'Connell, Marvin R. Edward Sorin. Notre Dame, Ind.: University of Notre Dame Press, 2001.

O'Donnell, Terence. An Arrow in the Earth: General Joel Palmer and the Indians of Oregon. Portland: Oregon Historical Society Press, 1991.

The Office of Indian Affairs, 1824–1880: Historical Sketches. New York: Clearwater Publishing Company, 1974.

Pasquier, Michael. *Fathers on the Frontier: French Missionaries and the Roman Catholic Priesthood in the United States, 1789–1870.* Oxford: Oxford University Press, 2010.

Payment, Diane P. *The Free People, Li Gens Libres: A History of the Métis Community of Batoche, Saskatchewan.* Calgary: University of Calgary Press, 2009.

Peterson, Jacqueline, and Jennifer S. H. Brown, eds. *The New Peoples: Being and Becoming Métis in North America.* Winnipeg: University of Manitoba Press, 1985.

Philips, Charles, and Alan Axelrod, eds. *Encyclopedia of the American West.* 4 vols. New York: Macmillan Reference, 1996.

Pollard, Juliet Thelma. "The Making of the Métis in the Pacific Northwest Fur Trade: Race, Class, and Gender." Ph.D. diss., University of British Columbia, 1990.

Pollard, Lancaster. *A History of the State of Washington.* Vol. 1. New York: American Historical Society, 1937.

Pouliot, Léon. *Monseigneur Bourget et son temps.* Vol. 1, *Les Années de préparation (1799–1840).* Montreal: Editions Beauchemin, 1955–56.

———. *Monseigneur Bourget et son temps.* Vol. 2, *L'Evêque de Montréal.* Montreal: Editions Beauchemin, 1955–56.

Priest, Loring Benson. *Uncle Sam's Stepchildren: The Reformation of United States Indian Policy, 1865–1887.* Lincoln: University of Nebraska Press, 1975.

Prosser, William S. *A History of the Puget Sound Country: Its Resources, Its Commerce, and Its People.* New York: Lewis Publishing Company, 1903.

Prucha, Francis Paul. *The Great Father: The United States Government and the American Indians.* 2 vols. Lincoln: University of Nebraska Press, 1984.

———. *Indian Policy in the United States: Historical Essays.* Lincoln: University of Nebraska Press, 1981.

Rahill, Peter J., M.A. *The Catholic Indian Missions and Grant's Peace Policy, 1870–1884.* Washington, D.C.: Catholic University of America Press, 1953.

Richards, Kent D. *Isaac I. Stevens, Young Man in a Hurry.* 1979. Reprint, Pullman: Washington State University Press, 1993.

———. "The Stevens Treaties of 1854–1855: An Introduction." *Oregon Historical Quarterly* 106, no. 3 (2005): 342–57.

Rossi, Louis. *Six Years on the West Coast of America, 1856–1862.* Translated and annotated by W. Victor Wortley. Fairfield, Wash.: Ye Galleon Press, 1983.

Rostkowski, Joëlle. *La Conversion inachevée: Les Indiens et le christianisme.* Paris: Editions Albin Michel, 1998.

Rousseau, Jacques, M.S.R.C. "Caravane vers l'Orégon." *Les cahiers des dix* (Montreal) 30 (1965): 207–71.

Rousseau, Louis, and Frank W. Remiggi. *Atlas historique des pratiques religieuses: Le sud-ouest du Québec au XIXe siècle.* Ottawa: Presses de l'Université d'Ottawa, 1998.

Ruby, Robert H., and John A. Brown. *The Cayuse Indians: Imperial Tribesmen of Old Oregon.* Norman: University of Oklahoma Press, 1972.

Rushmore, Elsie Mitchell. *The Indian Policy during Grant's Administration.* Jamaica, N.Y.: Marion Press, 1914.

Scheuerman, Richard D., and Michael O. Finley. *Finding Chief Kamiakin: The Life and Legacy of a Northwest Patriot.* Pullman: Washington State University Press, 2008.

Schoenberg, Wilfred P., S.J. *A History of the Catholic Church in the Pacific Northwest, 1743–1983.* Washington, D.C.: Pastoral Press, 1987.

Silver, Arthur. "French Quebec and the Métis Question, 1869–1885." In *The West and the Nation: Essays in Honor of W. L. Morton,* edited by Carl Berger and Ramsay Cook. Toronto: McClelland and Stewart, 1976.

Sisters of Charity of Providence. *The Institute of Providence: History of the Daughters of Charity, Servants of the Poor Known as the Sisters of Providence.* Vol. 2, *Heroic Years, 1845–1852.* Montreal: Providence Mother House, 1930.

———. *The Institute of Providence: History of the Daughters of Charity, Servants of the Poor Known as the Sisters of Providence.* Vol. 5, *The Sisters of Providence in Oregon, 1856.* Montreal: Providence Mother House, 1949.

Snowden, Clinton A. *History of Washington; The Rise and Progress of an American State.* 6 vols. New York: Century History Company, 1909.

Steckler, Gerard G., S.J. *Charles John Seghers, Priest and Bishop in the Pacific Northwest, 1839–1886: A Biography.* Fairfield, Wash.: Ye Galleon Press, 1986.

Stewart, Edward I. *Washington: Northwest Frontier.* 4 vols. New York: Lewis Historical Publishing, 1957.

Tassé, Joseph, *Les Canadiens de l'Ouest.* 2 vols. Montreal, 1891.

Taylor, Mary John Francis, S.N.J.M. "St. Francis Xavier Mission, 1838–1880: Cowlitz Prairie, Washington." Master's thesis, Seattle College, 1948.

Thomas, David C. "To Seek, Suffer, and Trust: Ascetic Devotion in a Modern Church on the Frontier." *Oregon Historical Quarterly* 102, no. 1 (Spring 2001): 48–71.

Thomas, Marian Josephine, S.N.J.M., "Abbé Jean-Baptiste Abraham Brouillet: First Vicar General of the Diocese of Seattle." Master's thesis, Seattle University, 1950.

Trafzer, Clifford E. "The Legacy of the Walla Walla Council, 1855." *Oregon Historical Quarterly* 106, no. 3 (2005): 398–411.

Trafzer, Clifford E., and Richard D. Scheuerman. *Renegade Tribe: The Palouse Indians and the Invasion of the Inland Pacific Northwest.* Pullman: Washington State University Press, 1986.

Trennert, Robert A., Jr. *Alternative to Extinction: Federal Indian Policy and the Beginnings of the Reservation System, 1846–1851.* Philadelphia: Temple University Press, 1975.

U.S. Bureau of the Census. *Historical Statistics of the United States: Colonial Times to 1970.* Pt. 1. Washington, D.C.: Government Printing Office, 1975.

Utley, Robert M. *The Indian Frontier of the American West, 1846–1890.* Albuquerque: University of New Mexico Press, 1984.

Van Kirk, Sylvia. *Many Tender Ties: Women in Fur-Trade Society, 1670–1870.* Norman: University of Oklahoma Press, 1980.

Victor, Frances Fuller. *The River of the West.* Hartford, Conn.: R. W. Bliss and Company, 1870.

Walsh, Henry L., S.J. *Hallowed Were the Gold Dust Trails: The Story of the Pioneer Priests of Northern California.* Santa Clara, Calif.: University of Santa Clara Press, 1947.

Warner, Mikell Delores Wormell, trans. *Catholic Church Records of the Pacific Northwest: Vancouver and Stellamaris Mission.* Annotated by Harriet D. Munnick. St. Paul, Ore.: French Prairie Press, 1972.

Watson, Bruce McIntyre. *Lives Lived West of the Divide: A Biographical Dictionary of Fur Traders Working West of the Rockies, 1793–1858*. 3 vols. Kelowna: Centre for Social, Spatial, and Economic Justice, University of British Columbia, Okanagan, 2010.

Whitner, Robert L. "Grant's Indian Peace Policy on the Yakima Reservation, 1870–1882." *Pacific Northwest Quarterly* 50, no. 4 (1959): 135–42.

———. "The Methodist Episcopal Church and Grant's Peace Policy: A Study of the Methodist Agencies, 1870–1882." Ph.D. diss., University of Minnesota, 1959.

Wilson, Douglas C., and Theresa E. Langford, eds. *Exploring Fort Vancouver*. Vancouver, Wash.: Fort Vancouver National Trust; Seattle: University of Washington Press, 2011.

Young, Ronald Wayne, O.M.I. "The Mission of the Missionary Oblates of Mary Immaculate to the Oregon Territory (1847–1860)." Ph.D. diss., Pontificia Universitas Gregoriana, 2000.

Patrons

The authors wish to acknowledge the following individuals and institutions whose generous financial support helped to make this book possible:

ANONYMOUS

IN MEMORY OF CHARLES AND FERN BROWN

GONZAGA UNIVERSITY

ESTELLE REID

MIKE REPASS

ST. JAMES CATHEDRAL, SEATTLE

ST. LEO PARISH, TACOMA

SISTERS OF PROVIDENCE, MOTHER JOSEPH PROVINCE

Index

Sahaptin-speaking tribes, 22nn7–8, 23n15, 30n8, 60n25

salmon, 77–78, 79n13

schools: French language in, 227; on Indian reservations, 118, 138–41, 141n2, 152, 228n1; Jesuit, 118; Protestant bias in, 84, 127, 129n10, 187; public school taxes, 84, 86n4, 233n4. *See also* Academy of Holy Angels; Providence Academy

Seattle, 200n1, 214n2; Catholic families in, 209; Catholic population, 235; illustration of, 181 fig. 44; missionary establishments in, 212–13

secret societies, 237, 239n5

sectarianism, 59n20, 60, 152

secular clergy, 188, 235–36; titles for, xi

Sede Vacante, 80, 82n1

Seghers, Charles John, 205n5; A. M. A. Blanchet's letter to, 223–25; biographical sketch, 225n1

settlers: American identity of, 17; anti-Catholic prejudice, 59n19; border-state, 41n7; Catholic, 16, 48; conflict between Indians and, 31–32, 139; at Cowlitz landing, 110–12, 113n4, 114–15; and displacement of Indians, 44n3; intermarriage, 6; poaching on HBC lands, 124, 150; request for federal adoption of Oregon, 37; settlement laws, 37, 45; squatting, 107n8; at Steilacoom, 190, 194–95; suspicions of HBC-Catholic collusion, 58n16; in the Willamette Valley, 8, 16, 34, 58n16, 116n5. *See also* Canadiens; emigrants; immigrants

Shale Stick, 23n13

Sherman, Eleanor Boyle Ewing, 223n3

Simmons, Michael, 115, 134, 138

Simms, John A., 158, 160n3

Simpson, George, 112n3, 116n4

Sisters of Charity of Providence [Sisters of Providence]: A. M. A. Blanchet's requests for, 84, 120, 125–27, 163, 186–88, 189n3, 190–91; accomplishments, 7, 206,

230–32; agency and autonomy of, 125; care for mentally ill and developmentally disabled, 186–87, 189n4, 192; care for orphans, 145, 147, 237; Christmas Day ball at Walla Walla, 215–16; collections, 148n4, 231, 233n5; feminism and, 232n2; food supply 149–50; founder (Emilie Gamelin), 102 fig. 20, 128n3; founders of Northwest mission, 102 fig. 21, 129n7; hogs belonging to, 150–51; living quarters, 126, 129n5, 129n9; Motherhouse in Montreal (illustration), 101 fig. 19; names on Sacred Heart, 167 fig. 23; orphanage in Vancouver, 143–44, 145n1; responsibilities at Diocese of Nesqualy, 125–27, 128n4, 129n6, 187, 189n4, 237; of the third order (externs), 175 fig. 26; St. Ignatius Mission, 193n5, 101 fig. 18; travel expenses, 84–85, 123, 163, 164n4, 188; voyage west, 120–21, 123, 147–48, 149n6, 165n7. *See also* Providence Academy; St. Francis Xavier Mission (Cowlitz); St. Vincent de Paul Academy; Steilacoom; Walla Walla; *and names of individual sisters*

Sisters of Saint Anne, Congregation of, 86n5

Sisters of the Congregation of Notre Dame, 62, 66n7

Sisters of the Holy Names of Jesus and Mary, 84, 86n5

Smith, Caleb Blood, 155n1, 156n5; A. M. A. Blanchet's letter to, 151–55

Snohomish (Sénéomus) Mission, 134, 137n7, 188; missionary housing, 210

Society for the Propagation of the Faith (Lyons and Paris), 33n1, 234; A. M. A. Blanchet's letters to, 31–33, 60–64, 66n9, 67n11, 146–48; A. M. A. Blanchet's report to the Directors of, 103 fig. 22, 120–23; formation of local societies, 202, 203n4; funding for missions, 66n10, 67n13, 77, 124n5, 147, 164n4, 203n4

Society for the Propagation of the Faith (Quebec), 73, 78